W9-BQZ-172

GENERAL EDUCATION: EXPLORATIONS IN EVALUATION

COMMITTEE ON MEASUREMENT AND EVALUATION

Appointed by the American Council on Education

PAUL R. ANDERSON, *Chairman*
President, Pennsylvania College for Women

SIDNEY FRENCH
Dean of the Faculty, Colgate University

EDWIN A. LEE
Dean, School of Education, University of California

E. F. LINDQUIST
Professor of Education, State University of Iowa

T. R. McCONNELL
Chancellor, University of Buffalo

DAVID OWEN
Chairman, Department of History, Harvard University

C. ROBERT PACE
Chairman, Department of Psychology, Syracuse University

JAMES W. REYNOLDS
Professor, Junior College Education, University of Texas

W. HUGH STICKLER
Director, Educational Research and Service
Florida State University

W. W. TURNBULL
Vice-President, Educational Testing Service

RALPH W. TYLER
Director, Center for Advanced Study in the Behavioral
Sciences, Chicago

General Education

Explorations in Evaluation

*The Final Report of the Cooperative Study
of Evaluation in General Education of the
American Council on Education*

PAUL L. DRESSEL, Director
LEWIS B. MAYHEW, Assistant Director

378.73
D773

AMERICAN COUNCIL ON EDUCATION
WASHINGTON, D.C.

LC
1011
.A6

COPYRIGHT 1954 BY AMERICAN COUNCIL ON EDUCATION
WASHINGTON, D.C.

LIBRARY OF CONGRESS CATALOG CARD NUMBER 54-11007

25478

PRINTED IN THE UNITED STATES OF AMERICA

PARTICIPATING SCHOOLS AND LIAISON OFFICERS

Antioch College, Yellow Springs, Ohio
OTTO F. MATHIASEN, Chairman, Examination Committee

Boston University, Boston, Massachusetts
JUDSON R. BUTLER, Dean, College of General Education

Colgate University, Hamilton, New York
CLEMENT L. HENSHAW, Professor of Physics

Colorado State College of Education, Greeley, Colorado
W. D. ARMENTROUT, Vice-President

Drake University, Des Moines, Iowa
DOYLE MIKESELL, Chairman of Basic Studies

Florida State University, Tallahassee, Florida
W. HUGH STICKLER, Director, Educational Research and Service

University of Florida, Gainesville, Florida
WINSTON W. LITTLE, Dean of the University College

Harvard University, Cambridge, Massachusetts
DAVID OWEN, Chairman, Department of History

Kansas State College of Agriculture and Applied Science,
Manhattan, Kansas
EARL E. EDGAR, Associate Director, Institute of Citizenship

Kansas State Teachers College, Pittsburg, Kansas
ERNEST MAHAN, Dean of Instruction

Michigan State College, East Lansing, Michigan
PAUL D. BAGWELL, Head, Communications Skills

University of Minnesota, Minneapolis, Minnesota
HORACE T. MORSE, Dean of the General College

Muskingum College, New Concord, Ohio
BERNARD MURDOCH, Dean

Oklahoma Agricultural and Mechanical College, Stillwater, Oklahoma
GEORGE WHITE, Director of General Education

Pennsylvania College for Women, Pittsburgh, Pennsylvania
LILY DETCHEN, Director, Evaluation Services

Stephens College, Columbia, Missouri
JAMES RICE, Dean

Syracuse University, Syracuse, New York
C. ROBERT PACE, Chairman, Department of Psychology

Western Washington College of Education, Bellingham, Washington
LUCY KANGLEY, Chairman, Committee on Research and Evaluation

Wright Junior College, Chicago, Illinois
MEYER WEINBERG, Department of Social Science

FOREWORD

EVALUATION of educational achievement is so complex a field that even test experts are humble in the presence of the many complications and constantly seek to improve their understanding as well as their techniques. The need to measure as surely as we can the effects of our educational programs is a compulsion felt by all educators and administrators. Any new light on this problem is therefore a stimulus and a challenge. The Cooperative Study of Evaluation in General Education was sponsored by the American Council on Education with the objective of discovery, and with the hope that the results would be useful to teachers, especially those in general education.

This volume is a report of the Director of the Cooperative Study to the Committee on Measurement and Evaluation, the committee appointed by the Council to give continuing study to evaluation and testing needs and problems in higher education. The Cooperative Study of Evaluation in General Education has been the major work of this committee up to the present. The very title of the report, with its emphasis upon the exploratory nature of the work which was done, suggests that we have far to go in finding ways of appraising more surely what needs to be done in the classroom. One of the appealing aspects of this study is that a large number of classroom teachers from nineteen colleges and universities of many kinds provided the working forces which carried out the major planning and research.

The Cooperative Study was made possible by the generous assistance of the Carnegie Corporation of New York and by annual contributions from the participating institutions. The Council has also participated in the financing. All of the participating institutions continued without interruption their support of the

Study. This is testimony to the significant objectives of the Study, the leadership of the Director and his staff, and the high caliber of the representatives of the nineteen colleges.

"Exploration" is a word which suggests the future. By their own testimony, those who had a part in the Cooperative Study are giving more attention in their teaching to objectives and to appraisal of progress toward objectives, and we may hope that this concern will continue in these many centers of initiative. It is the hope of the Director of the Cooperative Study and of the Committee on Measurement and Evaluation that this report will have similar effects in many institutions that did not enjoy the advantages of active participation.

ARTHUR S. ADAMS, *President*
AMERICAN COUNCIL ON EDUCATION

PREFACE

THIS VOLUME, the final report of the Cooperative Study of Evaluation in General Education, is a composite product undertaking several different tasks. It presents a brief description of the way the Study has operated. It reports on some of the research conducted by the several committees of the Study. It deals with some of the technical problems of educational testing and indicates some of the contributions which the project may have made toward their solution. Being a report written entirely by the Director and Assistant Director of the Study, it also involves a distinguishable, although not necessarily distinctive, point of view regarding general education and the role of evaluation in education. Although we have attempted to discuss the activities and the research results objectively, our own philosophies are implicit in our approach to the problems.

It was originally hoped that the Study, initiated in the spring of 1950, would cover a five-year period embracing (1) two years to study objectives, to develop evaluation procedures, and to plan a research design, (2) two years to follow groups of freshmen from the beginning of their first year to the beginning of their third year, (3) a final year to make statistical analyses of results, to investigate implications, and to prepare the final report. Circumstances enforced a modification of this whereby stages 1 and 2 were assigned to a three-year period of active endeavor and a final six months was employed for stage 3. Although this reduced length resulted in inability to carry out the two-year follow-through of freshmen, the actual nature of the project as it developed made this omission relatively unimportant.

A great deal was accomplished in regard to instructional problems, much more, in fact, than it has been possible or appropriate to report in this volume. The various committees found that all too little is being done in most general education courses to promote the progress of students toward the objectives inherent in general education. Indeed, it may be that the contributions to instructional problems will be more significant than the tests and the statistical data obtained through their use. Considered from this point of view, the reduced length of the project was less significant than it would otherwise appear to be. After all, long-term studies of student development cannot be of great value until more serious attention is given to relating classroom practice to the avowed educational objectives.

The participating institutions were assured that no comparisons among institutions would be reported in identifiable form. Hence, the authors have identified colleges and universities only in a few cases where the schools themselves have previously distributed reports containing the data. The anonymous quality of the data may detract from the interest of the report for some readers, but it also makes possible comparisons of attributes of courses and programs which could not be made otherwise.

If it is true that general education courses and programs frequently do not live up to expectations, as this report brings out in places, there is also much to inspire optimism. The mere fact that so many individuals would attend so assiduously to a study of evaluation in general education is one proof of the strength of the movement. Few general education teachers are satisfied with what they are presently doing and they are constantly seeking for new and better ways. We have hopes for significant developments in the future and we would like to believe that this report, by its realistic summary of present practice, may serve in some slight measure to expedite such developments.

PAUL L. DRESSEL, *Director*
LEWIS B. MAYHEW, *Assistant Director*

ACKNOWLEDGMENTS

T HE LIST of individuals who have contributed to this project would be a volume in itself. Numerous individuals in many colleges have provided assistance through letters, materials, and consultation. Many publishers have cooperated most heartily by giving permission to use copyrighted materials. This willingness to assist such a project is a heartwarming experience.

The names of the cooperating colleges and their liaison officers are given on page v. To these individuals is due much of whatever success the Study has achieved. Their names do not appear elsewhere in this report because the nature of the project emphasized the role of the teacher. To the liaison officer fell the many tasks of local planning for budget and committee meetings, for checking on individual commitments, for arranging for testing, statistical work, and the like, without seeking or expecting much overt appreciation. To all of them we express our appreciation and admiration.

The names of the members of the six intercollege committees are given on the first page of the appropriate chapter. It has not seemed desirable to list every individual who attended any committee meeting. Since some substitution was inevitable over a three-year period, we have attempted, with a few exceptions, to list the committees as they existed in the final year of the project. The Study was indeed a cooperative enterprise and this was exemplified at its best in the work of the committees. Without question, the bonds established among the committee members by their close work over the period of the Study will produce enduring cooperation and exchange of ideas. Each committee member also may take some satisfaction in having contributed to the general education of the Director and his assistant. For the enthusiasm and hard work of these individuals and for the association with them, we shall ever be grateful.

The Committee on Measurement and Evaluation of the American Council on Education is listed on page ii. The willingness of this group of busy men to give freely of their time and their wisdom was certainly a reservoir of strength for the Study and for the Director. Dean Schiller Scroggs, Oklahoma Agricultural and Mechanical College, was an active member of the committee for two years but found it necessary to resign prior to the close of the project. To Dr. Earl J. McGrath, the first chairman of the committee; to Dr. T. R. McConnell, his successor; and to Dr. Paul R. Anderson, the present chairman, the Director is particularly grateful for counsel and for readiness to contribute time and thought to the project.

The Cooperative Evaluation Study was largely due to the late Dr. George F. Zook, former president of the American Council on Education. The association with him during the early stages of discussion and of initiation of the project was a stimulating experience and one which resulted in the formulation of the broad outline to which the Study adhered, even though much alteration of its original plan was required as the project developed.

The interest and support of Dr. Arthur S. Adams, president of the American Council on Education, has been a major factor both in bringing the project to a successful conclusion and in providing for the appearance of this volume. The sympathetic interest of Dr. Oliver C. Carmichael, then president of the Carnegie Foundation for the Advancement of Teaching, in the project was a continuing source of inspiration. To them we once again express our thanks.

The warm support of the Educational Testing Service, particularly of its president, Dr. Henry Chauncey, has been deeply appreciated. Consultants were regularly provided to the committees, and tests and advice were freely given on request. By prior agreement the American Council on Education had resigned test production and administration services to the Educational Testing Service, but this particular project was seen more as a research and evaluation project having direct implications for the modification of general education curricula, with test development as an incidental but necessary step. The relationship established for this Study might well become a model for future cooperation on projects of this nature. Supplies of tests developed in the Study (see Appendix I) have been turned over to E.T.S. and that organization will take responsibility for deciding which, if any, of these instruments should be accepted as prototypes for further development.

Dr. Benjamin Bloom, college examiner, University of Chicago, and Dr. Robert J. Keller, director, Bureau of Institutional Research, University of Minnesota, although not directly connected with the project, advised on research design and carried out some related investigations. Dr. James McMenamin was associated with the central office of the Study in the year 1950–51, during which time he contributed much to the work of the Committee on the Evaluation of General Education Objectives in the Humanities.

Dr. Harold Dahnke undertook the difficult task of ordering and analyzing the extensive data sent in by the various colleges. His analyses should be productive of numerous other papers involving material not quite germane to the purposes of this volume.

In addition to the consultative service provided by the Educational Testing Service, the Study was fortunate in obtaining the participation of several other individuals possessing wide experience in general education and in evaluation. Dean H. T. Morse served as consultant for the Social Science Committee, where his humane skepticism served to keep the committee oriented to its predetermined goal. Dr. Louis M. Heil of Brooklyn College inspired the Science Committee to break away from established concepts and to bring evaluation practices actively into the classroom. Dr. Harold B. Dunkel of the University of Chicago and Dr. Milosh Muntyan of Michigan State College served as consultants for the Humanities Committee and the Critical Thinking Committee respectively, bringing to those groups important experiences and insights.

The Study owes much to the cooperation of Dr. John A. Hannah, president of Michigan State College. His interest was exemplified by his assignment of office space to the project and by his willingness to arrange for release of time from college duties for the Director and Assistant Director.

The Study was fortunate in having in succession three very efficient secretaries: Miss Wanlyn Oliver, Mrs. Jean Fisch, and Mrs. Ruth Schwahn, who were as much dedicated to the project as the directors themselves. To Mrs. Schwahn fell the arduous task of interpreting the poor writing or equally poor typing of many committee members and of the central staff. For her distinguished service on four fields of battle—dictation, typing, dittoing and mimeographing—our sincere thanks.

PAUL L. DRESSEL, *Director*

LEWIS B. MAYHEW, *Assistant Director*

CONTENTS

LIST OF TABLES

LIST OF FIGURES

WHY AN EVALUATION STUDY?

T. R. McCONNELL has observed that general education "is a movement which began as a re-examination of the nature and purposes of liberal education and which is leading toward a revitalization of the liberal arts, and perhaps to a complete reconsideration of the nature of the learning process."[1] The word "movement" is well chosen, for the major common element of various approaches to general education is to be found in the reaction against the compartmentalization and overspecialization permitted and even encouraged by the free elective system and the equally serious narrowness of training currently required in many fields of technical or professional perparation. This common element of reaction is scarcely sufficient to provide any clear or generally acceptable indication of the direction of development. General education is not, therefore, a single, easily recognizable phenomenon but, rather, it has a diversity of forms. This diversification is demonstrated in the courses, in the combinations of courses, in the subject matter, in the methods of instruction, in the types of administrative organization, and even, though to a lesser extent, in the objectives accepted.

In *Higher Education for American Democracy* we find that " 'General education' is the term that has come to be accepted for those phases of nonspecialized and nonvocational learning which should be the *common experience* of all educated men and women."[2] Yet on another page of the same report, italicized for emphasis, is found: "In the future as in the past, American higher

[1] T. R. McConnell, "General Education: An Analysis," in *The Fifty-First Yearbook of the National Society for the Study of Education, 1952, Part I—General Education* (Chicago: University of Chicago Press, 1952), p. 1.

[2] *Higher Education for American Democracy: The Report of the President's Commission on Higher Education, Vol. I—Establishing the Goals* (Washington: Government Printing Office; and New York: Harper & Bros., 1947), p. 49.

education will embody the principle of diversity in unity: each institution, State or other agency, will continue to make its own contribution in its own way. But educational leaders should try to agree on certain *common objectives* that can serve as a stimulus and guide to individual decision and action."[3] The italicizing of the phases "common experience" and "common objectives" is ours, and serves to focus attention on these two elements of general education which receive various interpretations and emphases which in turn result in quite different programs of general education. Experiences and objectives are by no means equivalent; it is undoubtedly possible to attain the same objectives by various experiences, but the experiences as the immediate and obvious elements of the educational program may easily supplant the objectives and become ends in themselves. Accordingly, general education programs may differ by virtue of difference in objectives; they may also differ, despite acceptance of common objectives, in the range of experiences which are provided as a means for the facilitation of the achievement of these objectives by the students. Appreciation of the difficulties of evaluation in general education requires some examination of the nature of these differences, for ultimately they reflect basic, though often implicit, philosophical differences as to the nature of education.

THE OBJECTIVES OF GENERAL EDUCATION

We have previously noted that, superficially at least, there is less disagreement about general education objectives than about the means of achieving them. The objectives found in *A Design for General Education*,[4] *General Education in Action*,[5] and the Report of the President's Commission are illustrative of the better and most commonly accepted statements. Most of the eleven objectives stated in *Higher Education for American Democracy*[6] are palatable in some degree to most general education faculties. Nevertheless, a survey of some twenty colleges during the formative stages of the Cooperative Study of Evaluation in General Education

[3] *Ibid.*, p. 6.

[4] *A Design for General Education* (Washington: American Council on Education, 1944), pp. 31–50.

[5] B. Lamar Johnson, *General Education in Action* (Washington: American Council on Education, 1952), pp. 19–32.

[6] *Higher Education for American Democracy*, pp. 50–58.

showed that in only five or six of these were objectives receiving anywhere near unanimous endorsement. Maintenance and improvement of health, acquiring the knowledge and attitudes basic to a satisfying family life, and the choice of a vocation, were three of the objectives that were frequently rejected as of major concern. While some general education programs professed no concern at all with these objectives, others accepted them as secondary or possibly ultimate goals which might be possible and indirect results of the attainment of other and more immediate objectives. There was also evidence of considerable disagreement among members of a given general education staff as to the range of objectives accepted for the program and a tendency to associate only one or two of the objectives with the particular course taught.

Thus, a set of general eduction objectives may not describe the foci of attention of all of a general education staff, but rather may be an accumulated listing of individual course objectives with perhaps a few others added to make a better-rounded description of the generally educated person. The list may represent administrative or faculty committee thinking rather than the consensus of a total staff.

The range of objectives accepted by a program or by an individual has some implications as to nature of the educational experiences provided. Rejection of objectives involving mental and physical health, vocational choice, and personal, social, and family adjustment, usually characterizes a program in which the courses are devoted to cultivation of the intellect and to the provision of an overview of the more significant aspects of the cultural heritage as embraced in science, social science, and the humanities. Acceptance of objectives in the affective domain or of the life adjustment type does not, on the other hand, necessarily involve any direct counterpart in courses or in extracourse educational experience. As Sidney Hook has noted, there is a tendency "to rest content with the formulation of goals, to overlook the difficulties in implementing them in concrete curriculums, and the still greater difficulties of evaluating to what extent we make good what our college catalogs promise."[7] Agreement on objectives, even when it is

[7] Sidney Hook, "Perennial and Temporal Goals in Education," *Journal of Higher Education,* January 1952, p. 12.

achieved, means little, for the stating of objectives is really inseparable from the decision as to the means by which these are to be achieved.

VARIATIONS IN EDUCATIONAL EXPERIENCE

College faculty members have a high degree of autonomy in the handling of their classes. Thus, it becomes impossible to characterize the instruction in a general education program or even in a single course unless only one instructor is involved. Even in this situation, the interaction of the instructor with individual students may result in differences in the educational experiences of individuals within the same class. Therefore, any characterization of types of educational experience must be an oversimplification. Yet, for convenience here and for later reference, we shall strive to describe three fairly distinctive types of educational experiences afforded to students.

In the attempt to provide a common experience to students, one or more each from science, social science, and humanities teachers chosen from several related traditional departments of specialization are frequently asked to organize a broad interdepartmental course. With or without formally stated objectives, the result may be simply a course inclusive of what is construed to be the essential knowledge in the broad area which should be in the possession of every generally educated person. Such courses, both by reason of the importance attached to the material thus selected and by reason of the extensiveness of the material to be covered, may and often do become entirely content-oriented. The function of the educational program, then, is to expose the student to this accumulated wisdom which he is expected to master. There is likely to be little concern and no adaptation to individual differences. Relevancy to current and future individual and societal needs is assumed, but the detection of the relevancy and the consequent application of the knowledge may be left to the student. The materials of the course become the ends, and the achievement of students is judged solely by their mastery of these materials. Content-oriented instruction frequently recognizes that other objectives and needs exist, but is inclined to assign responsibilities for them to other social agencies or to the personnel staff and the extracurricular aspects of higher education. Another assumption is that knowledge in itself is both the prerequisite to and the promoter of broader personal development. The phrase "content-oriented" is a reasonably adequate description of such an approach.

A somewhat different approach to course organization accepts more direct responsibility for the development of a number of intellectual skills which involve application of what is being learned to current and probable future problems. Ability to think critically about current social problems and ability to read current popular or semipopular scientific articles are typical of objectives which may be regarded as sufficiently important to provide criteria for the selection of materials to be included in the course. Relevancy of the material to the interests of students and to issues of the day may become a consideration in deciding what to teach just as much as the intrinsic worth of a particular segment of knowledge. Coverage of particular topics may even be sacrificed to provide for a number of exploratory experiences for the students that are designed to provide each individual with actual practice in attacking and thinking through problems for himself. Teachers accepting this point of view argue that retention, integration, and utilization of knowledge will result only as the student is given opportunity to discuss, to analyze, and to reach his own conclusions in regard to ideas or problems not previously digested by the instructor or the textbook. There is more concern about the exposure of the student to a number of points of view rather than to one accepted by the instructor or textbook author. Hence, field trips, discussions, and other group or individual projects become equal in importance to lectures and textbook assignments. Attitudes, values, personal adjustment, and similar objectives implied by these may, however, be ignored or become matters of concern only when they interfere with the intellectual development of the individual. Responsibility for such matters is delegated to extracurricular agencies, and the major educational experiences are still viewed as supplied within the framework of the formally organized courses. Greater emphasis on relevance and the explicit attention to intellectual objectives differentiates such an approach from the content-oriented one and justifies its designation as "intellectually oriented."

The third approach to general education has already been implied in the foregoing remarks. It may be characterized as student-oriented in that cognitive objectives are given no priority over affective ones. The tendency is to give priority to the total development of each individual and to consider all aspects of experience which are or can be provided by a college as of equal value insofar as they have significance in promoting the development of individuals in reference to a wide range of objectives. Ideally, the needs, interests, and desires of each person are taken into consideration in planning the particular set of experiences of most value to him. Relevancy of materials and experiences to the needs of the individual and to the total development of that individual becomes the prime consideration. Knowledge of content and intellectual development are not ignored, but the former is seen as a means to an end and the latter is no more important than other aspects of individual development. Whereas both of the previous two orientations may place great emphasis on the provision of common classroom experiences, the tendency in the student-centered orientation is to feel that no experience can mean quite the same thing to two different individuals. Emphasis is accordingly placed on the availability of a number of different courses or at least on the inclusion in each course of a number of means for individual adaptation such as acceleration, individual projects, special sections, and the like. The contrast between this viewpoint and the content-oriented one entitles the latter to the description "student-oriented."

No general education staff is in complete unanimity on any one of these three approaches nor, for that matter, are individuals consistent in their adherence to one of them. The consequence is that almost every general education program exhibits in microcosm the same inconsistencies, discrepancies, or disagreements that are found among general education programs in different schools. The differences are less profound than might be expected, however, because the instructional staff, faced with the necessity of offering a definite program to students and of exhibiting at least superficial harmony to the public, tends to regress to the grounds provided by its common concerns and by the similarity in training of its members. Thus, the selection and organization of content materials based presumably on the intrinsic worth of these as judged by staff consensus is the typical basis for most general education programs. "Content-oriented" is probably not unfair as a characterization of most general education instruction, although the actual intent of an increasing number of teachers and courses is an intellectual orientation. Relatively few programs, courses, or teachers are to be classified as student-oriented if they are to be judged by actual practice, although a significant proportion of general education instructors are strongly sympathetic to this point of view.

NEED FOR EXPERIMENTATION AND EVALUATION

The varying interpretations of a given objective, the varying roles that objectives play in a program, and the very real difficulty faced in the implementation of certain objectives, all conspire to make general education programs and the statements of general education objectives less interrelated than might be expected. Yet similarity in objectives does exist and constitutes, on the one hand, one of the strongest bonds relating otherwise virtually dissimilar programs and, on the other hand, perhaps the clearest basis for distinction between a general education course or program and the specialized departmental courses for which the major aim is preparation for further work in the same field. Indeed, the existence of, and the challenge presented by, this commonality of objectives was the major reason for the development of the Cooperative Study of Evaluation in General Education.

The nature of the challenge is twofold. First of all there is the question as to whether general education ventures achieve their accepted objectives to any greater extent than do the courses which they seek to replace. Even the most specialized course may and probably does make some contribution to general education, and the instructors of such courses frequently believe that they make as much contribution to the general education of the student as does the course developed for this specific purpose. There is not and there cannot be any single answer as to whether general education courses are superior to departmental courses. The variations in programs, courses, and instruction suggest that an answer can be approximated only for a particular program or type of program and that, even then, the nature of the answer may vary considerably for individual instructors in the program. The difference between a content-oriented general education course and a traditional departmental course must be primarily in terms of the difference in the content or materials studied. A judgment as to the relative efficacy of two such approaches must be based primarily on a judgment of the intrinsic worth and relevancy of the content. Such judgments are certain to differ widely.

Comparison of educational programs which differ in objectives requires that any consideration of their respective merits include not only evidence on the achievement of objectives but a judgment as to the worth and the appropriateness of these objectives. Such judgments involve philosophical differences about which no objective evaluation can be made. The evaluation of all of general education in comparison with specialized courses is, practically speaking, an impossible task and certainly an unprofitable one.

The second aspect of the challenge presented by the commonality of some objectives in general education rests in the diversity of means used to accomplish the same ends. The nature of this challenge was clearly underscored by the remarks of Dr. Earl McGrath: "To a very large degree these developments known as general education have proceeded on the basis of *a priori* reasoning with little more than opinion to back up the assumptions on which they rest. With a few striking exceptions little attempt has been made to determine experimentally whether one arrangement of subject matter, or one method of teaching, is better than another, or better than the more conventional forms and practices."[8]

The challenge of McGrath, coupled with similar thinking on the part of T. R. McConnell, Ralph Tyler, and others, was a second important factor leading to the development of an evaluation study. It seems improbable that all of the varied emphases in general education, whether in content, courses, organization, or mode

[8] Earl J. McGrath, "The Need for Experimentation and Research," *General Education in Transition*, ed. H. T. Morse (Minneapolis: University of Minnesota Press, 1951), p. 17.

of instruction, can be equally efficacious in producing student development with regard to even those objectives commonly accepted in the various programs. Yet differences in teachers and in students make it doubtful that a simple answer regarding such issues is possible.

It may be unwise, and it is certainly unnecessary, to imply that general education should be placed on trial. If the major aims of general education are accepted as desirable, it is really the means to these ends that are to be studied and evaluated. With the term general education applied to a wide variety of educational experiences from rechristened but still inviolate liberal arts programs, through vocational and homemaking courses in junior colleges, to a "hitch" in the service, it is manifestly impossible either to commend or condemn general education. Since general education arose out of a desire to change and thereby improve the educational experience of students, it might be expected that evaluation and research would be the tools for indicating the significance of these changes and the need and direction of further changes. McGrath's remarks are entirely consistent with this point of view, and McConnell's suggestion that general education may be leading "to a complete reconsideration of the nature of the learning process" likewise suggests that the role of experimentation and evaluation may be less that of passing judgment on general education and more that of providing direction based on scientific evidence.

CONCERN ABOUT EVALUATION

There have been numerous projects and programs of evaluation carried on in reference to general education. The volume *Evaluation in General Education*[9] includes reports of the evaluation practices at a representative group of colleges concerned with general education. Probably the General College of the University of Minnesota leads the field in the number of evaluation studies made. The College of the University of Chicago, Michigan State College, Stephens College, Antioch College, and many others, also have a lengthy and extensive history of concern about evaluation

---

[9] *Evaluation in General Education*, ed. Paul L. Dressel (Dubuque, Iowa: Wm. C. Brown Co., 1954).

and provide evidence that general education has not been lacking
in self-study. Most such studies have had only limited impact on
colleges other than those engaging in them; many of them, in fact,
have not been generally available.

On a national scale several projects which have dealt with general education problems have made contributions to evaluation.
The Cooperative Study in General Education,[10] directed by Dr.
Ralph Tyler and under the sponsorship of the American Council
on Education, developed numerous instruments useful in assessing
growth in regard to general education objectives. The Evaluation
Staff of the Eight-Year Study of the Progressive Education Association,[11] although at the high school level, attempted to evaluate
objectives identical with many of those accepted as general education objectives.

In 1948 Dr. George Angell conducted for the American Council
on Education a survey of evaluation practices and related these to
general objectives. Among the colleges surveyed it was apparent
that most evaluation was strictly content-oriented, but that objectives involving more than knowledge were commonly accepted
even though student achievement relative to them was not being
evaluated.

The American Council on Education has been mentioned
several times as a sponsor of various projects connected with general education. Having displayed such interest in the problems in
the past, it was natural that the Council, through its late president,
Dr. George Zook, should sense the need for evaluation activity.
The way was prepared, in part, by the fact that in connection with
the organization of the Educational Testing Service, the Council
had given up its production and administration services in testing
and had received a financial grant to assist in the exploration of the
new directions its work in measurement and evaluation might best
take. The challenge of McGrath, then United States Commissioner
of Education, and others was directly responsible for focusing at-

[10] *Cooperation in General Education: A Final Report of the Executive Committee
of the Cooperative Study in General Education* (Washington: American Council on
Education, 1947).

[11] Eugene R. Smith and Ralph W. Tyler, *et al., Adventure in American Education,
Vol. III—Appraising and Recording Student Progress* (New York: Harper & Bros.,
1942).

tention on general education as an area where such evaluation activity was highly desirable. The previously noted survey by Dr. George Angell confirmed that need. It was indeed fitting that the American Council on Education, through its Committee on Measurement and Evaluation, be the means of instituting a project concerned with evaluation in reference to general education.

First Steps

In October 1949 the Director of the Study was asked to initiate steps which might lead to an evaluation project involving cooperative activity by a number of colleges. A mail survey of forty-four colleges was conducted to determine interest in a cooperative evaluation venture. The survey involved three questions—the need for such a project, willingness to participate in it, and willingness to contribute to it. Twenty-seven of the administrators responding indicated a readiness for evaluation activity, but some were indifferent and a few were politely antagonistic. Reasons for the lack of interest were in themselves informative. One institution, with some reason, felt that it was so far ahead of others in evaluation that it would derive no benefit from a cooperative project. One or two others felt that evaluation must be a purely local activity. Several who indicated a desire for evaluative activity felt that their own programs were too new to be ready for evaluation. From the favorable responses a group of eighteen colleges was selected and invited to send two representatives each to an initial meeting held at Pittsburgh in December 1949. Those in attendance were administrative and evaluation officers. From a two-day discussion agreement emerged that a cooperative project was desirable, that it should be planned and executed by intercollege faculty committees, and that six committees should be formed dealing with six objectives found to be accepted by most, although not all, of the colleges present.

As the major argument for the cooperation of teaching faculty, the group insisted that too much of what had already been done and said about general education had failed to reach or affect teaching faculty. Similarly, evaluation activity would be very unlikely to affect faculty members unless they were directly involved. It was also recognized that a project involving cooperative effort might be slower moving and perhaps less prolific in the development of instruments and accumulation of evidence than a full-time central research staff, but the majority of those present were willing to sacrifice such accomplishment to the end of rapport with and involvement of teaching faculty. Finally, there was the conviction that teachers have a unique and vital contribution to make to any evaluation of instructional programs.

The six committees specified were to be related to the following six objectives:[12]

1. "To participate actively as an informed and responsible citizen in solving the social, economic, and political problems of one's community, State, and nation" (Committee on Social Science Objectives)
2. "To understand the common phenomena in one's physical environment, to apply habits of scientific thought to both personal and civic problems, and to appreciate the implications of scientific discoveries for human welfare" (Committee on Science Objectives)
3. "To understand the ideas of others and to express one's own effectively" (Committee on Communications Objectives)
4. "To attain a satisfactory emotional and social adjustment" (Committee on Attitudes, Values, and Personal Adjustment)
5. "To understand and enjoy literature, art, music, and other cultural activities as expressions of personal and social experience, and to participate to some extent in some form of creative activity" (Committee on Humanities Objectives)
6. "To acquire and use the skills and habits involved in critical and constructive thinking" (Committee on Critical Thinking)

A survey of the eighteen colleges which sent representatives to the Pittsburgh meeting had requested that the objectives from this (or another similar) list appropriate to the local program be checked. The preceding six objectives were the ones with the highest frequency. The four immediately related to subject matter (numbers 1, 2, 3, and 5) were almost unanimously selected; the remaining two were somewhat less popular. Although these objectives were taken as the basis for deciding that there should be six areas of attack and six intercollege committees, by general agreement it was left to the respective area committees to determine just what they should do.

[12] *Higher Education for American Democracy*, I, 50–58.

Following the Pittsburgh meeting the formation of the Cooperative Study was authorized and sixteen of the eighteen colleges represented at the Pittsburgh session joined the project. Three others joined within a few months, and this group of nineteen continued as participants for the entire period of the Study.

Each of the nineteen colleges was asked to decide with which of the six objectives or areas it wished to be involved. The decision was based on the interest and availability of staff members, on the stage of development of the various courses, and the financial burden imposed by travel and other expenses attendant upon participation in a committee. The number chosen by the various colleges ranged from three to all six, and varied somewhat over the period of the project.[13] With very few exceptions, the faculty members chosen were truly interested and active in the venture and demonstrated thereby that considerable care had been used in selection. At the request of the college administrators, the Director of the project had visited each campus prior to the formation of the intercollege committees. This was done so that the project could be presented directly to the faculty, and so that the project Director might have an opportunity to become acquainted with programs and with individual faculty members. These visits also enabled him to participate in the selection of intercollege committee representatives.

Two things were clear (to the Director, at least) from these early visits: (1) that teaching faculty were generally interested but somewhat less concerned about evaluation than were the administrators; and (2) that general education objectives and programs at the practicing level do not correspond well with the descriptions of them given by administrators or individual devotees of general education.

In fact, some faculty members (a minority) evidenced very definite disagreement with the implication that evaluation was necessary. One comment made several times in different places was to the effect that evaluation results are valid only when they confirm the considered expert judgments of those who set

[13] Although Harvard University was ably represented on the Committee on Measurement and Evaluation by Dr. David Owen, it did not send representatives to any of the intercollege committee meetings.

up the program. A larger group of general education instructors was inclined to be somewhat dubious of objectives other than knowledge of content. Pushed for a definite stand many would admit to a belief that most general education objectives such as critical thinking depend upon knowledge and follow automatically out of it.

Thus, in an atmosphere charged with some enthusiasm but containing reasonable proportions of doubt and skepticism and a dash of antagonism, the activity of the Cooperative Study of Evaluation in General Education began. In general, by the proclivity of the Director and the committee members, the project was inclined to de-emphasize philosophical discussions of objectives in favor of operational and behavioral descriptions; to evade arguments about course content and program organization in favor of the development of instruments or of teaching techniques usable in any program; and to substitute work for discussion. The extent to which such a course was held to and was justified by results is recorded in the following chapters.

The General Plan of Operation

The actual operations of the Study involved four distinct types of activity on the part of the intercollege committee members: committee meetings during the school year, summer workshops, individual and subcommittee activities, and local campus activity. Each of these phases of activity contributed heavily, although somewhat differently, to the program.

Committee meetings.—Initial committee meetings were held in March and April, 1950, in Cleveland, Ohio. At these sessions each committee met for three days and attempted to map out the problems to be attacked and the procedures to be used in so doing. This was accomplished with varying facility and success by the six committees. The Director of the project served as chairman of each committee session, attempting to permit the committee the greatest freedom of exchange of ideas, but also encouraging a synthesis of ideas and the definition of common but nonetheless major significant issues for attack.

Subsequent midyear committee meetings, held in Cincinnati and East Lansing, filled somewhat different roles. Review and reconsideration of activities and plans laid in the summer workshops, study of the individual contributions of committee members and colleges, and formulation of further and more specific commitments for further contributions became the major activities of these later sessions.

Summer workshops.—Summer workshops of from one to two weeks in length were held in the summers of 1950, 1951, and 1952. The first and third were held in August, the second in June. These sessions provided the committees with a period for concentrated work during which the materials contributed by individuals during the year were criticized and assembled into an instrument, report, or plan. Full committee sessions, subcommittee sessions, and individual projects coupled with occasional full workshop sessions to discuss matters of common concern resulted in participants working from early morning until late at night. A twelve-hour day was the rule rather than the exception.

Every attempt was made to supply consultants, reference materials, and the like which were requested by workshop participants. Such expediting steps coupled with the enthusiasm and assiduous efforts of the participants made the workshops the major item in forwarding the work of the Study.

Individual and subcommittee activity.—Occasions arose frequently when further development of a plan of a committee project required extensive work on the part of a few individuals. Where this involved only a few days up to a week, it was possible for the Study by paying expenses—travel and maintenance—to arrange for the persons involved to come to the central office for this work. In one case arrangements were made for a small group to work together for several days on the campus of another of the cooperating institutions, but more commonly such small working groups assembled at the central office. The time and effort thus contributed played a significant role in moving along various phases of the Study. Had the Study budget permitted it, much more of this type of activity would have been carried on.

Local campus organization.—It was quite apparent at the beginning of the Study that the central staff could not satisfactorily function in reference to the many members of committees on each of the given campuses without some coordination being provided at that level. At the start of the Study, then, each cooperating college was asked to name a local liaison officer. In some cases these liaison officers were active participants in one or more committees; in others their role was that of maintaining a general awareness of the entire scope of activities of the Study and meeting frequently with individuals and with the group of people working on various phases of the Study projects. These liaison people tended to be persons having administrative responsibilities for the general education program, although occasionally they were chairmen of evaluation or research committees or the evaluation officer himself.

Many of the colleges further organized local faculty committees related to each of the intercollege committees in which the college participated. Usually, although not always, the chairman of this local committee was the designated representative to the intercollege committee. In this way the person serving on the intercollege committee reported viewpoints from a definite group on his campus, and was also in a position to secure opinions and contributions from his committee in carrying out the work of the Study as planned by the intercollege committee. The significance of such local organization was pointed up by the difficulties found by those intercollege committee members having no such committee in obtaining a hearing or in arousing interest upon their return home after each of the meetings.

At all stages of the Study the cooperating colleges had complete autonomy, not only in the committees selected, but also as to the extent to which they contributed to any phase of the work of a committee. For example, the Communications Committee was concerned with all the communication skills, but on some campuses speech is not included in the freshman course. In such cases no contribution could readily be made and none was expected. Deviation from the planned program of a committee was not necessarily in the direction of abstention from certain activities. In a number of cases individuals developed an idea related to the committee planning or proposed some additional step which they carried out independently of the committee. The number of such individual projects was not as large as originally expected simply because specific commitments of individuals to the committee program when added to their full teaching load left little time for additional endeavors.

SUMMARY

The general education movement originated as a reaction against overspecialization and compartmentalization. Objectives have played a prominent role in the development of general education and have provided some degree of commonality among very diverse manifestations of the movement. Three reasonably distinctive emphases have been noted:

1. Content orientation wherein the primary concern is with the importance of the materials selected and the task of education is to expose students to these materials.

2. Intellectual orientation wherein attention focuses on certain intellectual objectives, and subject matter is selected in part because of its relevance to the attainment of these objectives.

3. Student orientation wherein the primary value is the total development of each individual and wherein experiences are developed or selected with this end in mind.

These variations in viewpoint and associated variations in materials and methods suggested the need for experimentation and evaluation to determine whether one approach is better than another. Recognition of this challenge resulted in the formation of the project here reported upon.

The six intercollege committees working on six objectives accepted by all or most of the colleges undertook to define the objectives more carefully, develop evaluation techniques, and collect evidence on student achievement. The major portion of this volume is devoted to a report of the procedures and the results of this committee work, but a brief examination of the concept of evaluation which in part controlled, and in part, developed out of the work of the committees is a desirable prologue.

2

RATIONALE OF THE STUDY

THE INITIAL chapter briefly examined the origins of general education and indicated why both the proponents and opponents of general education might feel that general education needs to justify itself. It was suggested that the task thereby implied is an extremely difficult one. As the committees of teachers representing the various general education courses and programs entered upon their deliberations, it also became apparent that, to them, an attempt to evaluate general education seemed altogether premature. Evaluation to many of these teachers carried an implication of finality—a judgment of goodness or badness which they, being dedicated to general education goals, were uninterested in and unwilling to make.

There was, in most cases, no hesitation about admitting that their present efforts at general education might be inadequate and that some indications of adequacy or inadequacy were needed. There was, however, less interest in such evidence than in the inferring from it and from the attempts to collect it, what steps should be taken to improve existing programs. Evaluation regarded as a judgment of the worth of general education was also deemed premature in that most of the committee members felt that the full significance of general education objectives was not yet realized and that certainly the means for appraisal of their achievement was not yet available. Quite obviously some individuals viewed evaluation as a personal threat in that it might reveal course or personal inadequacies which would be used against them. Assurance had to be given that intercourse and intercollege comparisons would be made at the discretion of the participants and would be kept confidential if revealed to the staff of the Study. The use of the preposition "in" rather

18

than "of" in the title of the Study carried significant and meaningful overtones for most of the participants.

Having assimilated and accepted the point of view implied by the preposition "in," the committees readily turned their attention to the development of an evaluation program. Naturally, most of the participants were neophytes in evaluation and were concerned with achieving an understanding of the nature of evaluation and the possible purposes which the process might serve. A review of some of the thinking in this regard will make clearer the concept of evaluation finally attained and afford a basis for appreciation of the efforts reported in later chapters.

POSSIBLE PURPOSES OF EVALUATION

The following possible purposes of evaluative activity were identified in the early committee deliberations:

1. Clarification and possible redefinition of the objectives of general education.
2. Development of more adequate and reliable means of measurement.
3. Appraisal of the development of students.
4. Adaptation of courses and programs to the individual student.
5. Motivation of student learning through continual self-evaluation.
6. Improvement of instruction.

The clarification of the objectives of general education might appear to be an inappropriate purpose to associate with evaluation since evaluation is presumed to begin with a previously determined set of objectives. However, such an objective as "attainment of a satisfactory emotional adjustment" is so unspecific that as one undertakes to define it and to evaluate student attainments in regard to it, the very attempt brings greater insight into the objective and modifies some of the preconceptions about it.

The second of these purposes is really only a step in evaluation or a means to that end, but it is particularly relevant to general education because it is with respect to objectives descriptive of behavioral outcomes other than knowledge that the most difficult measurement problems arise. Unquestionably, the lack of adequate and reliable techniques of measurement has impeded greatly the placing of suitable emphasis on such goals. In part, this may be a result of the common pattern that things not tested for are apt to be ignored; in part, it may be that our inability to measure reflects our lack of understanding of just what it is that we want.

The third purpose—appraisal of the development of students—is one often talked about in education but seldom dealt with adequately. The question of how and how much students change as a result of their educational experiences requires an extensive program of pre- and post-testing over a period of time such as one, two, four, or more years. Such appraisals of progress are difficult because they involve very careful experimental designs if extraneous factors are to be so controlled that conclusions can be drawn. They also involve technical problems in the proper interpretations of test score gains.

The fourth purpose, that of adaptation to the individual student, at the simplest level, was seen to involve the pre-testing of students for sectioning or for appropriate placement in courses. At a more complex level, it may involve assignment of students to special services or the development of individualized courses and assignments.

The motivation of student learning through self-evaluation is a purpose based upon one of the accepted principles of learning. As objectives become understandable and important to students and as information regarding achievement is available to them, an increased desire for further improvement results from more precise goals and from the satisfaction of realizing that some improvement has taken place. Self-evaluation is a potent learning incentive and a procedure too seldom exploited. The lack of simple yet reliable and valid evaluative evidence with regard to certain objectives and the tendency to view evaluation as separate from teaching may account for much of this neglect.

The improvement of instruction was seen by the committees as a major purpose of evaluation. This purpose disturbs some teachers, for it seems to imply that instruction is poor, whereas the implication need be only that instruction may be improved through study of the instructional process and through determination of the effects of it on students. It should not be implausible that instruction—particularly that aimed at certain previously ignored general education objectives—is less than perfect and that therefore it might be improved by conscientious teachers who have developed new insights into what they are doing. Accepting this view, evaluation becomes a technique highly significant in modifying and improving instructional practice through relating it more directly to previously stated outcomes.

All of these six purposes at one time or another were considered by all committees and some contribution was made to all purposes. However, the initial emphasis in every case was placed on the first two purposes: selection and clarification of one or more objectives and development of evaluation procedures or devices. The third purpose, evaluation of student development, was regarded as the next logical step following the first two, and the fourth and fifth purposes were touched upon only incidentally. The sixth purpose, improvement of instruction, ultimately came to be regarded as the most important of all to the committee members who as teachers were vitally concerned with that process. The gradual move toward this emphasis will be apparent in the activities of the four subject-related committees.

CHARACTERISTICS OF THE EVALUATION PROCESS

Evaluation, as contrasted with measurement, embraces a wider range of technique and evidence. Evidence of increased participation in cultural activity can be accumulated on a simple counting basis by recording the attendance of students at concerts, lectures, and art exhibits; evidence of increased ability to judge critically such activity may require essays, interviewing, or simply subjective appraisals by teachers based on class discussions. The primary concern is that the best—the most valid—possible evidence be collected, and the techniques of evaluation are selected to this end. Certainly the restriction to objective tests—a common complaint of teachers—is unnecessary and is by no means characteristic of the best-conceived evaluation programs. Early in the Study the Director suggested a series of questions to be faced in entering into an evaluation of general education:

1. What does this objective mean in terms of definite and concrete action, feeling, or behavior on the part of the individual? Faced

with a group of individuals of unknown educational background, what would distinguish between those who have and those who have not attained the objective?

2. What are some of the specific situations, problems, or experiences which confront individuals and in which the type of behavior described by this objective is necessary or desirable? What is the range of situations in terms of type, complexity, involvement of other factors, etc., in which this objective is involved?

3. At exactly what point, or to what elements, in the problem or situation is the described behavior applicable?

4. What other types of behavior seem to be involved in many, or most, situations in which the desired behavior is applicable?

5. Is the desired behavior sufficiently distinct to be noted separately, or must it be noted only as it occurs in conjunction with some more involved, and perhaps more meaningful, behavior pattern?

6. Does this conjunction of behaviors and possible inability to separate the particular one in question suggest a redefinition of the original objective, or a grouping-together of several related objectives?

7. Should this objective be related to others, or considered simultaneously with others in evaluation on the basis of logic, reality, or convenience, even though separation is possible?

8. Is the desired behavior a totality of more specific behaviors which may not be closely related to one another?

9. Is it possible to place before students, or to place students in, the real or true-to-life situations which have been considered? If not, what modifications must be made, and on what basis?

10. Is it desirable to construct a less realistic situation in which achievement with respect to this particular objective is more easily noted and is more clearly separated from other objectives and from random elements?

11. What kind of record is to be kept of the student's behavior in the situation? How is the record to be analyzed? What is to be done with the results?

12. Of those individuals who are observed to handle adequately a situation supposedly involving a certain behavior: (a) Do all show that behavior? (b) Do they show it in varying ways and amounts? (c) In what ways do they differ? (d) Do some show complete absence, or almost complete absence, of the behavior?

13. If presence of the desired behavior is not found to be necessary for success in the total situation, what are the alternative patterns of behavior which succeed, and to what knowledge, experience, interests, attitudes, etc., are these due?

14. Is the desired behavior, even though not necessary, deemed desir-

able on aesthetic, ethical, or other grounds? Another way to ask this is: Is a certain process, behavior, or activity considered *good* in itself, even though not necessary for satisfactory handling of situations in which individuals find themselves?

15. What are the specific classroom experiences—readings, demonstrations, discussions, activities, or lectures—which are thought to contribute to the growth of the individual with regard to the objective?
16. Do the classroom experiences add measurably to the growth of the individual as compared with other individuals who have not had these particular experiences? If not, is this due to lack of, faulty, or inadequate classroom experiences, or is it simply that growth with regard to the objective is so slow and complex as to be hardly noticeable?
17. Do the analysis of the objective and the discussion of situations involving it suggest any additional activities which might be carried on in the classroom, or any different way of teaching? To what extent are the evaluation exercises also usable as learning devices or instructional techniques?
18. Do the clarification of the objective and the accumulation of evidence of growth with regard to it provide any basis for greater student motivation?
19. What relations exist between growth with regard to this objective and such factors as (*a*) intelligence; (*b*) status at beginning of a course; (*c*) grading of the students?
20. What is the optimum growth which may be expected for various kinds of students with regard to this objective.[1]

These questions were not used point by point in the deliberations of any of the committees nor were they intended to be so used. The scope of the questions does fairly reflect the many issues to be faced in careful study of an objective, and the questions demonstrate also that no artificial limitations are to be placed on the nature of evidence solicited nor on the ways of obtaining it. Finally, they indicate that evaluation and instruction can very profitably be thought of as inseparable.

Approached in this way, it was apparent that evaluation must be a cooperative enterprise—cooperative in many ways for many reasons. The more complex behavioral outcomes require cooperation between teachers and evaluators in developing procedures and

[1] Paul L. Dressel, "Evaluation Procedures for General Education Objectives," *The Educational Record,* April 1950, pp. 97–122.

in collecting evidence—cooperation of administrators, personnel workers, and of the students themselves—if time is to be found, if a broad range of evidence is to be collected, and if students are to be properly motivated. Student motivation through cooperation is particularly important. Evaluation which has grading as its purpose provides an immediate motivation, although one conducive to fallacious results in that the answers of students frequently represent an attempt to guess the intent of the teacher, rather than an honest statement of their own individual viewpoints. Evaluation which has no such competitive motivation may be met with indifference by students unless the purposes and the relation to the course or programs are made clear. Similarly, evaluation done by evaluators without the full cooperation of teachers is apt to be misunderstood and even rejected. Research involving human beings cannot be a cold, calculated procedure disregarding the emotions of those involved.

The preceding questions imply that evaluation is concerned with the utility and utilization of results. A purely research orientation may be more efficient in obtaining results but—for reasons just noted—it may be ineffective insofar as acceptance and resultant change are concerned. Some lag between research results and practice is to be expected, but the gap presently existing between psychological investigations and much of instructional practice is an undesirable state of affairs. Evaluation seeks to remedy this situation.

The complexity of some of the questions suggests that the use of evaluation in improvement of the educational process cannot be a single-shot proposition, but rather it must be an ongoing process in which evaluation and instruction interact and continually modify each other. So regarded, evaluation is a state of mind as much as it is a process. The instructor who critically regards his practices each day, who seeks to find in his students evidence of the effect of his instruction and of their own endeavors in terms of progress toward accepted educational goals, will find that evaluative-centered thinking is a continuing, rewarding, and integral part of his teaching. On the contrary, evaluation which is periodic or spasmodic is usually not well conceived and has very little effect other than the development of a distaste in both teacher and students for such ventures.

ATTITUDES TOWARD THE ROLE OF EVALUATION
IN GENERAL EDUCATION

Ruth Eckert[2] has provided a stimulating and provocative statement regarding the status and the possible role of evaluation in respect to general education. In doing so, she has outlined also some of the major issues wherein experimentation or evaluation is needed. These are classified broadly as follows: (1) research on the aims of general education; (2) studies of students who take general education courses; (3) studies of different types of general education programs; (4) studies of instructional methods used in general education; (5) studies of out-of-class experiences in their relation to general education; (6) studies related to the staffing of general education; and (7) studies related to methods of evaluating outcomes of general education. The scope of this list—for many specifics were listed under each of these headings—suggests how little we know about educational processes. Many of the points of this list correspond to and confirm the possible purposes of evaluation identified by the committees of the Study.

The extent of these recommended studies suggests a major, even a central, role for evaluation in general education and one which has not been much in evidence in practice. Although not a subject of formal deliberation, the question of why evaluation has not played such a role was discussed informally and repeatedly with committee members, faculty members, and administrators. Lack of facilities, expense, and lack of trained personnel were frequent complaints, but actually appear less important than the disinterest and even antagonism of many teachers toward evaluation. The role of evaluation in general education is likely to be whatever teachers and administrators assign to it. Even in cases where much in the way of evaluation has been done, there may be little apparent effect in the general education program unless the results are understood and accepted by the faculty.

There appear to be three distinctive attitudes toward evaluation which are identifiable in teachers. One of these completely rejects evaluation other than the judgment of the teachers themselves. Discussion with those holding this viewpoint reveals that they view

[2] Ruth Eckert, "Evaluation in General Education," in *The Fifty-First Yearbook of the National Society for the Study of Education, 1952, Part I—General Education* (Chicago: University of Chicago Press, 1952), pp. 250–78.

many of the outcomes of instruction as intangible in nature and assessable only by the instructor as he is in close contact with a student over a period of time. These outcomes may differ markedly—these teachers say—from instructor to instructor and are not readily communicable to others. Certainly these intangible objectives are not amenable to evaluation processes as viewed by adherents of this viewpoint. Rejection of evaluation is apparently quite common among humanities teachers but is not limited to them. Subjectively it seems that a majority of this group are also strongly content-oriented in the actual conduct of their courses. They are inclined to favor essay testing but may use some objective achievement tests which are more often than not largely factual in nature and based on recall more than on understanding. An extreme reaction from this group is exemplified by the actual although paraphrased comment that evaluation is a waste of time, for it either confirms the judgment of those who developed the course or the evaluation itself is in error.

A second attitude toward evaluation found among teachers recognizes the need for it, but feels that the exigencies of teaching make it impossible to do much about results. The size of classes, the teaching load, and the amount of material to be covered are cited as factors which force the teacher into the use of formal and traditional instructional procedures which—they may admit—probably are not particularly conducive to student development other than in factual knowledge. Many teachers will add to this that the low ability and poor attitude of many students admitted to college nowadays make unrealistic any attempt to develop intellectual skills or to use group dynamics procedures which might be more conducive to development of social understandings, attitudes, and values. Most of the teachers who feel this way must be regarded as either content-oriented or intellectually oriented, but the classroom practices of even the latter group commonly regress to the content orientation. Such individuals frequently exhibit interest in evaluation procedures and results and they are usually much interested in extending the range of their own testing to include more of understanding and application as an antidote to overemphasis of rote recall. They are not ordinarily much concerned with evaluation of broad general education goals transcending their own courses, nor do they, with the many pressures upon them, see much opportunity for adaptation of their courses to individual needs. In many cases their generally favorable attitude toward evaluation can be utilized in initiating evaluation activity which will, as it becomes productive of new insights, result in replacing the somewhat dubious and pessimistic view regarding the utility of evaluative practices by a positive and even enthusiastic endorsement. Perhaps because of their generally open-minded and scientific attitude, science and social science teachers are particularly likely to be found in this second group.

There are some general education faculty members, and the number is increasing, who have had formal measurement and evaluation training or who have had sufficient practical experience in educational research to be reasonably facile in planning and executing an evaluation project. The Study was extremely fortunate in finding in each of its committees a few individuals who had carried out significant studies in connection with their own courses or in relation to the total educational program. There would seem to be—judging from the experiences in working with such individuals—a positive but not perfect correlation between active interest in the broader problems of evaluation and concern for introduction of a greater degree of student orientation into the general education program. More such individuals must be identified or developed, for in them lies the hope for truly significant developments in general education.

The existence of some of these reactions to evaluation suggests that general education faculties are not, to a man, breathlessly awaiting the opportunity to join in an extensive evaluation of general education or in a critical restudy of their own courses. However, the actual opposition is probably less than it at first appears to be, for those most opposed to evaluation are also the ones who are likely to express themselves strongly on the matter. The vocal antagonism of such a group, especially since it has the support of a long tradition of independence on the part of individual college teachers in their classroom procedures, is a major difficulty to overcome in beginning any basic evaluation or self-study venture. Despite such opposition, there is, as indicated by experiences in the Study, a sufficient number of persons already evaluation-minded so that, assuming administrative support, some action can be initiated.

With the committees in our Study containing many evaluation-minded individuals, it might be expected that the full range of major issues suggested by Ruth Eckert would be attacked, but only in a limited sense was this true. At the present moment in the development of general education most teachers are concerned with evaluation as it relates to their immediate responsibility in teaching a course, a state of mind which does not quite appear to coincide with that of professional researchers and evaluators. Hence, the question may be raised as to just what teachers do want from evaluation. In a sense, the later chapters of this report provide the answer because the committees of the Study were largely self-directed; they made their own plans and they attempted to carry them out. The lack of single-mindedness in some of the committees betrays the presence of differences in viewpoint about education and about the role of evaluation. There are present, nevertheless, certain evidences of common desires and hopes as to what evaluation may do. We shall attempt to synthesize these into a point of view about evaluation which may be a reasonable picture of what general education teachers desire. It is certainly a description of the most pervasive point of view about evaluation represented in the Study.

A Point of View about Evaluation

The student orientation approach to general education starts with the concern that, as the result of general education experience, the individual be different—not just in knowing more, but different in the way he thinks, believes, and behaves. This concern that education make a real difference in people is not a crass utilitarian view but one which arises out of the commonly observed tendency of individuals to compartmentalize the various areas of behavior either because they do not see or are unwilling to see any connection. College graduates—particularly the specialists—frequently do not apply in their activities as citizens the knowledge and skills learned in the classroom because little relationship is seen between the mundane problems of living and the cloistered academic situation. In an attempt to develop improved programs which will bridge this chasm between theory and practice, it is necessary to seek for every imaginable type of evidence about student backgrounds, student reactions, and student performances. Even the reactions, interactions, and teaching practices of the teaching staff are fit subjects for study and change. This broad conception of the possible significance of evaluation may be acceptable to many teachers, but it is just too remote from their immediate problems to arouse much enthusiasm.

The instructor is concerned with instruction, and evaluation must make direct contribution to this if it is to be of interest to him. Typically he has some objectives but is not quite certain what they mean. He is interested in an operational approach to the definition of these objectives, an approach which makes it possible to detect the presence or absence of the implied abilities or characteristics in his students. He realizes that because objectives are not clear, they have commonly played little part in the selection of course materials and experiences which are likely, therefore, to have been selected on the grounds of personal judgment as to their intrinsic worth. Similarly, his techniques of instruction are commonly highly traditional and bear little relation to the desired outcomes. His hope is that evaluation can become the means for drawing together into an integrated whole these elements of the curriculum which too often are fortuitously determined rather than systematically planned.

As objectives are clarified, it often becomes equally clear that certain objectives may have been slighted or even ignored entirely in the course as offered. The efforts to develop tasks or to devise means of observation which will give information about the objectives as revealed by student behavior may suggest new experiences, new materials, and new ways of presenting them which relate directly to the objectives. The historical cases in science suggested and developed by Dr. Conant represent such an attempt to select science material which particularly well exemplifies what science is and how scientists operate. The attempt of the Committee on Evaluation of Objectives in Science to evaluate student ability in the reading of current science articles led to an analysis of what is involved in such reading, to the selection of appropriate readings, and to the specification of what reactions might be appropriate to each selection. The resulting materials were immediately utilized by many of the committee members for instructional purposes.

Methods necessarily become important as emphasis is placed on behavioral objectives. The social science teacher who is concerned with good citizenship as an outcome and who accepts some responsibility for it beyond basic knowledge will wish his classroom to provide some experience in democratic participaton. He may also become concerned that students have a number of relevant experiences because he feels that these experiences are more conducive to growth with regard to the objectives of the course than were his former practices. He has already made a subjective evaluation justifying this change; he may wish a more objective evaluation which will test the implied hypothesis. In the past and in many general education courses at present the matter of method—except for such decisions as whether there shall be a laboratory—is left to the individual teacher. Any attempt to change this may seem to be a move in the direction of standardizing the individual teacher; in a limited sense, it is. In passing, it may be noted that certain kinds of standardization are already in evidence, since classes are scheduled at certain hours and, for multiple section courses, common materials of instruction are usually specified. Unless each general education course is offered as a discrete course by a single instructor, some degree of standardization is inevitable; the only issue is how far it should go. In regard to method many difficulties arise. A method which works with one instructor may not work with another. The instructor who is required to conduct discussions despite dislike and ineptness in so doing may not achieve the hoped-for results. If the time arrives when research demonstrates that certain desired results can be achieved only through discussion, it may be conceivable that all instructors should be required to develop some proficiency in handling discussions. At the moment we have no such evidence.

The selection of technique or method cannot be by fiat nor can it be coldly scientific. The enthusiastic and reasonably able teacher who undertakes to use a new classroom technique and who makes it evident to students that he is doing so in order to help them learn more, may obtain better results simply because of his enthusiasm and the student response to it. What a teacher does is probably less important than the frame of mind with which it is done, for the reaction of students is as much to the intent as to the acts of the teacher. The preceding comments lead to the conclusion that no simple or universal answers about the worth of specific materials or specific methods are possible. Effective teachers will probably vary both in their materials and their techniques with different classes and possibly with different students. Since, to date, the extensive attempts to evaluate teaching effectiveness have not had any significant results, it is doubtful that research on methods of instruction in general education will soon present valid answers.

However, evaluation does provide some suggestions about method, suggestions which may not be scientifically validated but which nevertheless have a degree of logical validity. For example, the attempt mentioned above to evaluate the ability to read current science materials resulted in a finding that textbook materials and popular scientific articles are quite different in nature. If it is really desired that students learn to read the latter, the introduction of a series of such experiences into the course seems appropriate. Particularly is this true if the habit of reading such materials is to be developed. The use of such materials does not have behind it the weight of tradition, but in respect to the purposes stated, it has as much logical validity as exists in the use of a textbook. Hence, there is no reason to ask nor to expect that a teacher await the results of an extensive research study before modifying his teaching to include such materials.

A related point is that much of general education instruction has been so traditional that few distinctive and well-organized instructional approaches can be found for comparative evaluation. The slight modifications found are like fresh frosting on a stale cake; the appearance is improved but the essential character is unchanged. Much more needs to be done in the devising of new materials and new techniques with general education objectives in mind. The various committees of the Study found that their attempts to clarify objectives and to develop ways to evaluate them led to the development of problems and materials which—almost without exception—were appropriate and better means for instructing or for giving students practice and experience conducive to growth with regard to the objectives. The developing pattern of activity in each of the six committees of the Study over their three-year period of operation exhibits an increasing concern with the instructional implications of their work on evaluatory procedures. This concern even superseded the original, rather strong, interest in the evidence accruing from pre- and post-testing with the instruments developed. At first thought this may appear regrettable but it was actually a decision—not entirely a conscious one—of considerable wisdom. Preliminary evidence pointed to the fact that rather small gains, if any, were present. Careful review of the instruments and the mode of development provided an assurance of validity. Study of classroom activity and the reactions of students to whom the instruments were administered indicated a paucity of experience in the classroom directly related to the objectives under study. Since the evaluation activity in itself suggested ways to introduce a relevant set of experiences, it appeared more important to spend some time on these matters than to devote it all to assessing changes in students with regard to objectives which had been largely ignored in the classroom.

Evaluation has frequently been defined as the placing of value *on* an educational experience. It is equally true that evaluation activity may suggest ways of placing more value *into* the educational experience. In the present state of general education it seemed more important to those involved in this project to emphasize the latter point of view without, however, entirely neglecting the former.

3

OBJECTIVES IN SOCIAL SCIENCE

Intercollege Committee on Social Science Objectives: WENDELL
BASH, Colgate University; HARRY D. BERG, Michigan State College;
JAMES A. BURKHART, Stephens College; ALFRED COPE, Syracuse
University; GOLDA CRAWFORD, Kansas State College of Agriculture
and Applied Science; LYNN CURRAN, Boston University; PAUL
HANNA, University of Florida; EDITH M. HUDDLESTON, Educational
Testing Service; NORBERT R. MAHNKEN, Oklahoma Agricultural
and Mechanical College; GEORGE H. MCCUNE, University of
Minnesota; DOYLE MIKESELL, Drake University; H. T. MORSE,
University of Minnesota (Consultant); GEORGE NEEL, Muskingum
College; ARTHUR REYNOLDS, Colorado State College of Education;
BENJAMIN F. ROGERS, Florida State University; VERNE SWEEDLUN,
Kansas State College of Agriculture and Applied Science; MEYER
WEINBERG, Wright Junior College

ALMOST ALL SOCIAL science courses, regardless of whether they
are historically oriented, problem-centered, or surveys of certain social science disciplines, postulate some common objectives. Teachers in such courses would like their students to be
able to apply knowledge and social science techniques to current issues and problems. They would like their students to sense, know,
and understand interrelationships existing between social science
areas and other branches of human knowledge. Quite naturally they
want their students to put into practice in everyday life those
skills, abilities, ideas, and the knowledge accumulated in the classroom. Perhaps their most commonly held hope is that students of
social science courses will be better citizens than individuals who
have not had such educational experiences. Thus, the development
of the various traits incident to good or effective citizenship is listed
more frequently than any other of the objectives of social science
courses.

At its first meeting the Intercollege Committee on Social Science Objectives considered many such objectives, seeking to find some common interest. The deliberations of this committee during its organizational meeting throw into relief a number of issues of concern to any group struggling with the problems of preparing meaningful educational experience in the social sciences.

The question of course content is a difficult one. If general education is conceived of as "those phases of nonspecialized and non-vocational education that should be the common possession, the common denominator, so to speak, of educated persons as individuals and as citizens in a free society,"[1] there is some logic in seeking to establish common course content. Such a goal, however, is contrary to the diversity so necessary in colleges serving a nation as large as this one. Nevertheless the Social Science Committee gave careful consideration to the development of a project to determine what items of content should be included in a general education course. Such an inquiry was rejected chiefly on the ground that it would be inappropriate in an evaluation study and also because of apparently extreme institutional differences.

However, the possibility was open of investigating means by which courses might be more closely integrated within themselves and with other curricula of individual institutions. While eventually the Study provided insights which might furnish means for integrating general education, the time was not right for such a development at the beginning of the Study. Methods of teaching, the relationship of individual courses to other general education courses, the relationship between social science courses and advanced specialized courses, and making of social science courses more meaningful in preparation of students for life might all be involved. While such a project appeared intriguing, differences between institutions and the almost impossible task of assembling requisite information upon which to base judgments conspired against undertaking the inquiry. Further, decisions derived from a search for integrating techniques might be viewed as too prescriptive in nature for a cooperative undertaking.

[1] *A Design for General Education* (Washington: American Council on Education, 1944), p. 7.

Having rejected these possibilities, discussions returned to the development of good citizenship. A number of studies about the development of good citizenship characteristics were noted.[2] None of these has satisfactorily defined what good citizenship actually is. Defined one way, good citizenship consists merely of the practice of certain rudimentary mechanisms incident to a democratic government. Such things as voting, knowing the provisions of the Constitution, and keeping abreast of current events are exemplary of this minimal definition. At the other pole lies the conception of citizenship as synonymous with the democratic way of life or the corpus of Christian ethics. Viewed in this latter light, citizenship can no more legitimately be claimed as the exclusive province of the social sciences than of the natural sciences, the humanities, religion, or any other aspect of college life. If good citizenship were defined narrowly, the only possible measure of achievement would be to obtain evidence of how many times graduates voted, went to town meetings, contributed blood, or wrote letters to editors. Such a follow-up study as this would involve ways and means obviously impossible for the resources and tenure of the Cooperative Study. Conceived in broader terms, evaluation of good citizenship would involve such a wide variety of tests of knowledge, attitudes, values, and beliefs that their mere development was clearly beyond the hopes of attainment by the Social Science Committee.

CRITICAL THINKING AS AN OBJECTIVE

Citizenship appears to demand one skill above all others. Even in voting for prospective office holders, the citizen must be able to analyze the candidate with respect to the issues of the particular election and the demands of the office. The good life in a democratic society also seems to rest fundamentally on one's ability to think critically about the problems with which he is confronted. The essence of the democratic creed is that each person possesses potentialities for discovering his own problems and for developing

[2] Thomas H. and Doris D. Reed, *Evaluation of Citizenship Training and Incentive in American Colleges and Universities* (New York: The Citizenship Clearing House, 1950). Studies have also been carried on by Citizenship Education Project, Teachers College, Columbia University; Citizenship Education Study, Detroit Public Schools and Wayne University.

personally satisfactory and socially acceptable solutions to them, so that he has no need to defer completely to the will of an authority, although he is perfectly willing to make use of expert opinion when relevant.

In view of the importance of critical thinking in citizenship, the Intercollege Committee on Social Science Objectives elected to develop a project involving this skill. However, numerous important questions were raised. (1) Is critical thinking teachable without reference to any particular body of knowledge? If so, is critical thinking a legitimate objective of social science courses or is it rather the responsibility of courses in logic or syllogistic reasoning? (2) Is critical thinking merely the intelligent use of knowledge? If so, should courses make explicit an objective which is assumed to be merely a concomitant of acquisition of knowledge? (3) Granted that social science courses might legitimately concern themselves with critical thinking, is it possible for a cooperative evaluation project to assess such a trait? Possibly the creation of test situations with a priori "correct" answers is antithetical to truly critical or effective thinking? (4) Another issue is the relationship between critical thinking and creative thinking. The concept of critical thinking is certainly not a new one. The Socratic method of dialectic, the logic of Aristotle and of Bacon are exemplifications of it. Another tradition is, however, equally operative. If individuals were to be evaluated in terms of their ability to apply essentially critical skills, creative but perhaps chaotic minds exemplified perhaps best by Rousseau would be penalized. Preoccupation with critical thinking conceivably might fetter rather than free the minds of students.

The nature of critical thinking can be determined only by research. While the Study accumulated some relevant evidence, it remains a crucial issue.

The suggestion that a "test" of critical thinking with "correct" answers is antithetical to genuine critical thought implies that any evaluation is likely to be inadequate. Indeed, the in-school evaluation of any outcome of education must be artificial, for the final proof of the efficacy of education rests in the subsequent history of individuals affected. Although limited by existing techniques of measurement and the materials with which students are commonly familiar, some approximations of the effectiveness of education are possible and estimates of changes with respect to critical thinking can be accumulated.

Critical thinking frequently begins when the individual becomes aware of an obstacle between himself and some personal goal. His effectiveness may be inferred from the way in which he analyzes this problem and hypothesizes and tests solutions to it. Critical thinking in this sense is a highly personalized ability which defies precise measurement. However, certain intellectual problems of concern to students can be posed to determine how well the students can solve them. A test can rarely pose problems possessing emotional impact comparable to that of personal problems; yet test situations possessing sufficient emotional loading to challenge a majority of students to overcome their prejudices, biases, and preconceptions have been created.

The issue of creative thinking was regarded as important but outside the province of the committee to resolve. The committee was unwilling to take sides as to any differences which might exist between the creative act and the critical act. Rather, the committee chose to assume that there was room in the college curriculum for both creativity and criticism. Further, the committee was willing to accept, for purposes of compromise at least, the hunch that creativity and criticalness might be merely differing degrees of the same essential process.

Thus far the concept of critical thinking has not been defined nor analyzed. During the early deliberations of the Social Science Committee, the members talked at some length about a project in critical thinking on the assumption that other people were generally aware of what was meant. This assumption was proved erroneous, for while various definitions were suggested, all proved too abstract for evaluation or teaching purposes. The only recourse was to define critical thinking as the sum of certain rather specific behaviors which could be described and which could be inferred from student acts. These abilities which were developed a priori by the members of the committee are indicated below. This list is the result of modifying earlier lists in terms of behaviors observed in classes and from study of test items.

THE CRITICAL ABILITIES

1. *To identify central issues.*—One of the basic skills in critical thinking is the ability to identify the central issue or main theme. The thesis may be perfectly clear; it may be hidden in a mass of verbiage; or it may be unstated. Until the student has identified the central issue, an analysis of the information cannot proceed on a sound basis.

2. *To recognize underlying assumptions.*—An argument is always based upon certain assumptions. These assumptions may be generally accepted; they may be subject to grave doubt; or they may be absolutely untenable. The validity of many arguments depends upon the validity of the assumptions upon which they are based. An individual whose analysis does not go beyond the argument and into the assumptions will seldom arrive at a truly satisfactory insight into any social science issue.

3. *To evaluate evidence or authority.*—

    a) *To recognize stereotypes and clichés.*—Social science materials contain abundant illustrations of faulty thinking in the form of stereotypes and clichés. Everyone is familiar with the popular concepts of "the American clubwoman," "the tired businessman," "the absent-minded professor," "100 percent Americanism," and "the good old days." Many people who accept these at face value may be victimized by skillful propaganda techniques.

    b) *To recognize bias and emotional factors in a presentation.*—The validity of any presentation should depend only upon such factors as the soundness of its reasoning and its factual basis. Many presentations, however, neglect reason and fact and substitute highly colored words or appeals to prejudice. This practice is frequently an admission that there is very little substance supporting the presentation. Since bias refers to opinions or attitudes based on prejudice and preconception rather than upon fact and reason, it bears no constant relation to truth and is as likely to be favorable as it is to be unfavorable. To detect bias is not to impute dishonesty, for many biases are unconscious. Recognizing bias, conscious or not, is the important thing. Awareness of the part one's own biases may play in the process of analysis and decision is also an important factor in critical thinking.

    c) *To distinguish between verifiable and unverifiable data.*—An early step in determining the verifiability of a proposition is the distinction between material which is of a factual or verifiable nature and that which is not. Sweeping generalizations, value judgments, beliefs, and opinions are usually unverifiable. Material of a factual nature, on the other hand, is capable of proof or disproof, although frequently the data necessary to verify it may not be available.

d) *To distinguish between relevant and nonrelevant.*—To analyze social situations and problems adequately, an individual must be able to distinguish between those facts that have a bearing upon the solution and those that do not. One should ask, "Does this statement define, illustrate, or bear upon the problem?" This ability is less complex than the one which follows, because it does not require the individual to judge the degree of relevancy, but only to sort the aspects of a situation into those which do or do not have a bearing upon it.

e) *To distinguish between essential and incidental.*—Those facts which are essential to a given situation are often confused with other facts which are present but are not a necessary part of that situation. Relevant data are not necessarily essential to an interpretation and may be of only secondary importance.

f) *To recognize the adequacy of data.*—An appreciation of the connection between adequate facts and a valid conclusion is an essential ability in critical thinking. A judgment made on the basis of fragmentary evidence is likely to be of little value. In dealing with social issues, it is particularly important that judgments be based upon sufficient information. It is also important to be able to detect that significant data have been ignored or omitted. The omission may have been unintentional, but often the additional evidence has been purposely suppressed in order to strengthen the argument advanced. In many cases consideration of neglected material will destroy an argument completely.

g) *To determine whether facts support a generalization.*—Facts may be relevant, essential, and adequate but still not support a generalization. Furthermore, poorly selected facts occasionally contradict and seem to disprove a generalization. Also, in some cases the support furnished by one fact is stronger than that furnished by another.

h) *To check consistency.*—All arguments must be checked for internal consistency. Identification of a major inconsistency may invalidate a presentation, and in any case an argument cannot be considered as a logical whole when it is based upon contradictory elements. If an argument withstands the test of internal consistency, it still must be submitted to a check for consistency with other known data. Having recognized the external consistency or inconsistency of the argument, one is ready to draw a conclusion.

4. *To draw warranted conclusions.*—The drawing of a warranted conclusion involves making an inference. An inference is a truth or proposition drawn from another which is admitted or supposed to be true; a conclusion; a deduction. An individual needs to realize that certain facts not explicitly stated may be inferred as true or untrue.

It is also important to realize the limitations of the inferences which can be made from given data. Many statements at first glance appear plausible, but if the inferences are properly drawn their meanings may change.

VALIDITY OF THE LIST OF CRITICAL ABILITIES

Any group of college teachers can prepare without too much effort a similar classification which, in the abstract, is quite satisfactory. The difficult task is to prepare a classification which is internally logical and related to reality. The list developed by the Social Science Committee gained considerable validity from two quarters. The Cooperative Study Committees on Science, Critical Thinking, Humanities, and Social Science each decided independently to work on objectives involving the concept of critical thinking. Each committee proceeded quite independently; yet the respective final lists were markedly parallel. This is not a particularly startling phenomenon considering that the members of all four committees are products and exemplifications of a Baconian system of logical thought. But the similarity of their conclusions indicates that they were each dealing with a particular phenomenon which exists at least in Western culture and possesses meaning and value for teachers.

The second source of validity for the list of specifics rests with their relevance to actual, observable human behavior. After the list had been created, members of the committee were asked to find evidence of demonstration or lack of demonstration of these abilities on the part of students, and to prepare test materials and test items requiring demonstration of each one of the abilities or complexes of them. Applying such behavioral tests to any similar classification will quickly make clear those elements which are too abstract for educational manipulation. Such a behavioral test should be used to judge any proposed objective classroom practice or item of content.

The Social Science Committee had developed a list of objectives stated in behavioral terms. The question now became what to do with it. Since the Study was essentially evaluative, the area of possible activity was definitely circumscribed to an evaluation or measurement effort. The task then became to prepare techniques by which student possession or lack of possession of these behaviors might be assessed. In the course of working out such techniques the committee became faced with new issues.

SOCIAL SCIENCE COURSE CONTENT

The first of these involved a matter already touched upon—the element of course content. Fifteen of the nineteen participating institutions were represented on the Social Science Committee. Each of these institutions possessed certain social science courses which, judging by the titles, differed from each other as much as night does from day. Would it be possible for such a heterogeneous group of courses to use the same measuring instrument? A study was made of the specific content of social science courses from seventeen cooperating schools with a view to finding out whether or not they were as distinctive as their names implied.[3] Tables 1 and 2 reveal some of the findings of this survey. These data permit the generalization that there is a great deal of commonality among social science courses—much more than has heretofore been suspected.

ISSUES INVOLVED IN PREPARATION OF AN OBJECTIVE TEST OF CRITICAL THINKING

Closely allied to the matter of course content is the degree to which a test of critical thinking should also be a test of knowledge in the social science area. This issue brings into relief several points of view regarding the nature of critical thinking. There were some who believed that whatever test was developed should demand a fairly sophisticated level of knowledge of social science content. Others could visualize a self-contained test of critical thinking demanding no technical knowledge. The committee compromised and decreed that its test should not demand more knowledge in the social sciences than a majority of entering college students could be reasonably expected to possess. They decided also to find out something about the role played by knowledge in critical thinking. The test items which were eventually prepared into a

---

[3] This study, considerably expanded, has been published. Doyle Mikesell, "Social Science General Education Courses," *Junior College Journal*, January 1954, pp. 268–77.

TABLE 1

CLASSIFICATION OF SOCIAL SCIENCE COURSES OFFERED BY SEVENTEEN PARTICIPATING COLLEGES

COLLEGE AND COURSES	History		Nonhistorical			SEM. HRS.	RE-QUIRED	YEAR TAKEN
	World	U.S.	Inte-grated	Prob-lem	Com-bined			
A. Boston University								
a. Human Relations (2 yrs.)								
First Year..........................			√			10	Yes	1
Second Year......................					√	7	Yes	2
b. Political Economics................					√	9	Yes	1 & 2
B. Colgate University								
c. Public Affairs......................				√		6	Yes	1
d. American Ideas in the Modern World..		√				3	Yes	4
C. Colorado State College of Education								
e. Contemporary Institutions and Problems in Historical Perspective.......					√	6	Yes	2
D. Drake University								
f. Development of Modern Society......	√					8	Yes	1
g. An Introduction to Social Science.....			√			8	Yes	2
E. Florida State University								
h. Historical Development of Modern Society...........................	√					4	No	1
i. An Introduction to Contemporary Civilization........................				√		6	No	1-2
F. Florida, University of								
j. American Institutions..............					√	8	Yes	1
G. Kansas State College								
k. Introductory Social Science.........			√			8	No	2
H. Kansas State Teachers College, Pittsburg								
l. The American Heritage..............	√					5	?	?
m. Contemporary American Problems....				√		?	?	?
I. Michigan State College								
n. Introduction to Social Science........				√		6	No	1
J. Minnesota, University of								
o. Problems of Contemporary Society....					√	3½	No	1 or 2
K. Muskingum College								
p. Social Studies.....................					√	8	No	1
L. Oklahoma A. & M. College								
q. Challenges in American Democratic Life.............................					√	8	Yes	1
M. Stephens College								
r. Contemporary Social Issues..........				√		6	No	1
N. Syracuse University								
s. Democratic Citizenship.............				√		6	Yes	1
t. Problems of American Democracy....					√	6	No	2-3
O. Wright Junior College, Chicago								
u. Social Science.....................				√		6	Yes	1
Total..........................	3	1	3	7	8			

form of a test were screened and all terms which seemed even remotely technical were used as the basis for a separate vocabulary test. The Test of Critical Thinking in Social Science and the Vocabulary Test were administered to the same students to test the hypothesis that knowledge of terminology was essential for critical thinking but not sufficient of itself to ensure success in critical thinking. The several studies, to be reported later, thoroughly supported the hypothesis. Students with low scores on the Vocabulary Test were unable to do anything with the critical thinking test. Equally significant, however, was the fact that some students with good vocabulary scores did very poorly on the critical thinking test.

Two other issues had to be faced at this time. The first of these involved the limitations of existing testing techniques. Many individuals contend that ability to do critical thinking cannot be assessed by means of objective-type test questions. They feel that the presentation of several responses "gives away much of the show." Their solution to a measurement problem would be to ask students to respond orally or in writing to a problem situation. This solution, however, has two serious limitations. Scoring of students' written or oral responses poses such a formidable task as almost to preclude dealing with large numbers of students. The second

TABLE 2

TOPICS MOST FREQUENTLY TAUGHT IN SOCIAL SCIENCE COURSES
IN SEVENTEEN PARTICIPATING COLLEGES*

Categories	A		B	C	D	E	F	G	H	I	J	K	L	M		N	O		No. of Courses	No. of Colleges
	a	b	c	d	e	f	g	h	i	j	k	l	m	n	o	p	q	r	s	t	u		
Social Processes																							
1. Nature of social science	√	√			√		√		√		√	√	√		√			√			√	12	11
2. Culture concept	√		√		√		√	√	√		√		√	√		√		√		√	√	12	12
3. Scientific method and social science	√	√	√		√		√		√		√		√	√	√		√	√	√		√	12	12
4. Formation of personality	√				√		√			√											√	5	5
Social Institutions																							
1. Family	√				√		√		√	√	√		√	√			√				√	11	10
2. Education	√		√		√		√	√	√	√		√	√	√								10	10
3. Religion	√			√	√	√	√	√	√									√				8	6
4. Community	√	√	√		√						√	√	√					√		√		8	7
5. Social groups	√	√			√						√	√	√				√			√		7	6
Political Institutions																							
1. American form of government		√	√	√	√		√		√	√	√		√	√	√	√	√	√	√	√	√	17	15
2. Nature of government	√			√	√	√	√	√	√		√	√	√	√	√	√	√	√	√		√	16	13
3. Government and business	√	√		√		√		√	√		√	√	√	√	√	√	√	√	√	√	√	16	15
4. Political parties and elections	√	√		√		√		√	√		√	√	√	√		√	√	√	√	√	√	14	13
5. Pressure groups and propaganda	√	√		√		√		√	√		√		√	√		√	√	√	√	√	√	14	12
Economic Institutions																							
1. Forms of business organization		√	√		√		√	√	√		√	√	√	√	√	√	√	√	√	√		16	15
2. American capitalism	√	√		√		√		√	√		√	√	√	√	√	√	√	√	√	√		15	14
3. Production	√			√		√	√	√	√		√	√	√							√	√	11	11
4. Personal income distribution	√			√		√		√	√	√	√					√	√			√	√	9	9
5. Money, banking and credit	√				√		√	√	√	√	√					√			√	√	√	9	9
6. Business cycles	√					√		√	√	√			√			√	√				√	8	8
7. Marketing and price	√				√			√		√			√								√	7	7
Topics or Problems																							
1. International affairs	√	√		√	√	√	√	√	√	√	√		√	√	√	√	√	√	√	√	√	19	15
2. Labor		√	√		√		√	√	√	√	√		√	√	√	√	√	√	√	√		16	14
3. American values	√	√	√	√	√	√		√	√	√	√		√	√		√			√	√	√	15	12
4. Comparative systems	√	√	√	√	√		√	√	√	√		√	√		√	√	√		√		√	15	13
5. Race and minorities	√		√	√	√		√		√	√	√	√	√	√			√		√	√	√	14	12
6. Civil liberties	√	√	√	√		√		√	√	√	√	√	√				√		√	√	√	14	11
7. Agriculture		√			√		√	√	√	√		√			√						√	9	9
8. Public finance		√			√		√	√	√	√		√		√			√				√	9	9
9. Population	√			√		√		√	√	√		√					√		√			9	9
10. Social security		√				√		√	√	√	√					√			√			7	7
11. Consumer problems							√	√	√	√	√		√		√			√				6	6
12. Urbanization	√				√		√		√		√	√				√			√			6	6
13. Crime						√		√		√						√			√		√	5	5
14. Mental abnormalities	√				√		√		√							√			√			5	5
15. Natural resources and conservation				√		√		√							√				√			4	4

* Column headings refer to the institutions and courses indicated in Table 1.

limitation lies in the unreliability of appraising written and oral responses. This unreliability is heightened further as test questions attempt to go beyond the mere assessment of factual knowledge and enter into the domain of the more abstract intellectual skills. The committee finally decided to prepare an objective test, in full awareness that certain elements important in critical thinking were not adaptable to objective testing techniques.[4] It is possible to present an examinee with a paragraph and ask him to detect the central issue of the argument by means of an objective-type question, but the fecundity with which an individual can invent hypotheses to fit a particular problem is outside the scope of an objective-type test. To test this latter trait might require the examinee to list many possible hypotheses which could explain a given situation.[5]

The second issue involved a concern as to whether classroom teachers, for the most part inexperienced in the theory of test construction, could produce respectable evaluation instruments dealing with relatively complex intellectual skills. It was felt that, with some help from experts, classroom teachers possessing insight into their subject and into the student mind, could develop appropriate evaluation and research methods. One of the correlative values of the Cooperative Study has been the in-service training in testing techniques for a goodly number of classroom teachers.

Since the development of evaluation materials for the assessment of behavioral outcomes is relatively new in higher education, a description of how the Social Science Committee proceeded may be helpful in the understanding of results reported later. As has already been indicated, the objective of increased critical thinking was defined by specifying some of its behavioral attributes. This specification is the first step in the evaluation process, but scanning the critical abilities listed above will quickly reveal that they are still far removed from practical evaluation and teaching situations.

---

[4] This decision did not rule out completely a concern with essay testing. Toward the end of the Study the members returned to a consideration of essay testing, and crystallized their thoughts in *Critical Thinking in Social Sciences* (Dubuque, Iowa: Wm. C. Brown Co., 1954).

[5] The Psychological Corporation has produced several forms of a test involving testing for creativity, George K. Bennett, *Test of Productive Thinking*. Guilford and his associates have also done considerable research along similar lines.

Evaluation of the ability "to sense or to define a problem" requires thorough understanding of what people *do* in demonstrating this trait. The practicing educator cannot trace the actual psychological or physiological process. Indeed, it is doubtful if experienced clinicians can do this. The teacher can only infer the existence or absence of the trait from the activities in which students engage. Thus the task of developing evaluation techniques becomes one of cataloguing various kinds of overt student acts from which can be inferred demonstration of whatever traits are immediately relevant.

CRITERIA FOR SELECTION OF PROBLEM MATERIALS

Clearly the social sciences are rich in materials which can serve as provocative stimuli for problem-solving activity. The available data with respect to communism, socialized medicine, euthanasia, pro- or anti-vivisection, or tidelands oil, typify the wealth of such information. However, not all materials impinging on these topics are equally adaptable for testing purposes so that in selecting materials several criteria must be applied:

1. A problem situation should be meaningful in terms of the student's own experiences. It would be possible to construct a test of critical thinking making use of highly abstract or even nonsense symbols. For some purposes this is appropriate, but for a test in the social sciences, material more relevant to the everyday world should be sought. Furthermore, test items must have considerable intrinsic interest if students are to put forth their best efforts. This same principle of relevancy also rules out some highly specialized areas of the social sciences which would be of interest to the specialist but of little concern to a freshman or sophomore college student.

2. Materials selected should be short enough for students to study in a relatively brief period of time. A reading passage, for example, should contain a great deal of information in a paragraph or so. Tabular or graphic information should be brief yet complex enough to present a significant task.

3. Problem situations should involve a certain degree of emotion for most persons working with the material. Human beings can be objective and critical about problems which are purely academic, whereas this remoteness is considerably more difficult to

attain if the problem is one which involves the individual emotionally. It would be impossible to find test materials which would involve emotionally all students but it is possible to pick out situations which will prove stimulating to the majority.

4. Materials should be intelligible to students.

Experienced teachers often know what problems appeal to students, what they find challenging, and what they can solve. Teachers with less insight can obtain equally good results by asking students for their opinions about materials and by trying out materials in a variety of ways on students.

These two techniques were utilized by the Social Science Committee in obtaining problem situations. The members solicited their colleagues for appropriate materials, worked these materials into trial testing situations, and administered them to their own classes. Students were asked to solve the problems and to indicate their opinions about the activities in which they had been required to engage. Their answers and opinions provided one basis for revision of materials.

Criteria for Development of Test Items

The creation of plausible alternative responses to an objective-type question is always a difficult task. Perusal of student free-response statements about the materials under consideration frequently proves to be a source of good ideas for possible alternatives. After test items have been developed, they may be evaluated by the test writer or by other competent persons using questions such as the following:

1. Does the item appear to you to measure what it purports to measure?
2. Does the item seem to you to be realistic and practical?
3. Is the language of the item appropriate to the educational level at which it is expected to be used?
4. Is the item or group of items capable of standing independent of all other items of the test in which it is to be used?
5. Does the item contain unnecessary details or purposeless elements of confusion?
6. Does the item appear to you to measure possession of only one fact, principle, concept, skill, or ability?

7. Does the item contain irrelevant details which might reveal the correct response to the students?
8. Does the item require greater knowledge than most of the students could be expected to possess?
9. Does the stem of the item present a clear problem to the students?
10. Is the stem of the item free from ambiguities?
11. Does the stem present its problem as briefly and as clearly as possible?
12. If the stem employs the negative form, are the negative words or phrases emphasized?
13. Do the foils make sense when compared with the stem of the item?
14. Are the responses to the items free from ambiguities?
15. Are the responses stated as briefly as possible?
16. Do the foils sound realistic and plausible?
17. Are there more than the intended number of correct responses?
18. Is the item free from grammatical and punctuational errors?
19. Is the item free from typographical errors?
20. Do you agree with the keyed response?
21. Does this item seem worth keeping for further work?

DEVELOPMENT OF THE TEST OF CRITICAL THINKING IN THE SOCIAL SCIENCES

The preceding discussion has suggested two possible dimensions for test items. One of these dimensions might be called a skills dimension and the other a subject or content dimension. In planning and assembling an examination, it is useful to have a two-dimensional grid as a kind of blueprint for the test builder to follow. One axis of the grid lists the specific skills with which the test is concerned, in this case the list of abilities involved in critical thinking. The other axis lists content areas within which the skills are to be operative. Naturally, the content axis of the Social Science Committee was derived from their survey of course content.

With such a grid the test builder can decide a priori how he would like to balance his final examination. The grid brings to the conscious level decisions which are commonly made without conscious attention and therefore without any rationale. The existence of the grid does not require that an equal number of items be assigned to each cell. The test builder may decide that he would like to have one item for each skill for each content classification, or he could decide to skew the distribution in whatever direction

CRITICAL ABILITY CONTENT AREA	Identify Central Issues	Recognize Underlying Assumptions	Evaluate Evidence or Authority	Recognize Limitation of Data	Establish Relationships	Draw Warranted Conclusions
CULTURE CONCEPT (10%)						
ECONOMIC AFFAIRS (40%) Systems Business Organizations Labor Problems Agriculture Consumer						
POLITICAL AFFAIRS (40%) Systems Government & Business Civil Liberties International Relations						
SOCIAL AFFAIRS (10%) Family Education						

FIG. 1.—GRID FORM FOR THE CONSTRUCTION OF THE TEST OF CRITICAL THINKING IN SOCIAL SCIENCE. The aim of the Social Science Committee was that the number of items for each ability would be approximately equal.

he desires. The Test of Critical Thinking in Social Science was eventually prepared by the Social Science Committee on the grid presented in Figure 1. In this case the committee aimed at approximately equal numbers of items for each ability, but planned to have about four times as many items dealing respectively with political and economic affairs as with the culture concept and social affairs. Some modification of these intentions was enforced later by the difficulties in building good test items.

The process of developing good test items, particularly those measuring traits beyond simple recall of information, by no means stops when the draft items have been prepared. Items ought to be reviewed critically by competent colleagues before being administered to students. These colleagues should judge the items in terms of scholarship and relationship to whatever trait they were intended to measure. Items withstanding this critical scrutiny can then be consolidated into trial tests and administered to groups of students. At that time, students can be asked their candid opinions about the test materials. Student responses to the items can be treated statistically to determine their relative efficiency. Still further insight may be obtained by asking students to verbalize their thought processes for recording as they solve problems.

All of these procedures were used in developing the Test of Critical Thinking in Social Science. Even so, the test went through several revisions before reaching its present form. This test was designed to sample each of the behaviors shown on the grid but was to yield a total score which could serve as an index of students' general critical thinking ability in the social sciences. At the point of putting together the final test form the committee had to resolve an issue which constantly intrigues anyone working with tests dealing with a complex of abilities. There appears to be a strong temptation to try to obtain multiple subscores from a relatively short test. Teachers are prone to say, "Wouldn't it be nice if we could find out in which of these skills our students are strong and in which weak?" Once having thus verbalized this hope, they are nudged almost irresistably toward creating subscores, often unreliable and ordinarily not used. The Social Science Committee, after having been faced with this temptation, decided that it would use only a total general index of critical thinking ability.

Typical Test Items of Critical Thinking
in Social Science

The following items are presented as illustrative and contain some explanatory comments as to the skills they purport to measure. They are similar to the ones included in the Test of Critical Thinking in Social Science. Consider, for example, the following items:

> The average American consumer, if he thinks in terms of economic self-interest, will give primary consideration in judging the desirability of the sales tax as a means of raising federal revenue to the fact that
> 1. many people own no property to tax.
> 2. income and corporate taxes account for a major part of the federal revenue.
> 3. customs taxes have declined as a source of federal revenue.
> 4. the sales tax generally falls most heavily on those least able to pay.

This item requires the student to do more than recall some generalizations made by a book or a professor. He must analyze the concept of "average American." Then he must consider the relevancy of the alternative responses to the economic self-interest of this hypothetical person. Clearly response four is the only proper one for this item.

Dealing with a different skill is the item:

> Which of the following does NOT offer support for the generalization, "Man is a social animal"?
> 1. All his life man is guided by group customs.
> 2. Prestige is a major motivating force in human activity.
> 3. As an infant, a child, an adolescent, and an adult, man's conduct is molded by influences which are outside the individual.
> 4. Human nature is mostly learned behavior.
> 5. Structurally man resembles other animals.

This is an item designed to test the ability to determine which of given facts tend to support a generalization. Able students, in reading the stem, may formulate in their own minds possible facts and will then look among the responses for one statement of a different order from the ones they thought of. Such an item requires even the poorer students to reflect. They will generally attempt to discover the correct answer by a process of elimination —which is not a bad intellectual technique.

Although requiring considerably more factual information than the previous item, the next one still goes far beyond mere factual knowledge.

> The due process clause of the Fourteenth Amendment
>   1. adds nothing to the due process clause of the Fifth Amendment.
>   2. strengthens the Fifth Amendment by exactly duplicating its terms and meaning.
>   3. adds to the due process guarantee by placing a federally enforced prohibition on state action in violation of due process.
>   4. weakens the due process guarantee by limiting the prohibition on state action in violation of due process.

A student might answer this correctly by knowing that the Fourteenth Amendment acts on states. On the other hand he might, and this is more likely, solve the problem by making an analysis somewhat in these terms:

It isn't likely that the Fourteenth Amendment adds nothing to the Constitution, else it never would have been ratified. By virtue of the same point, response 2 is wrong because a law is a law and doesn't gain any force by mere repetition. Response 4 implies a weakening of the Federal Constitution. If I remember my history, the Fourteenth Amendment was written at a time when state rights were on the wane. This leaves only response 3 which, now that I think of it, is a point of fact.

Frequently test writers find it desirable to present students with certain written, tabular, or graphic material to provide a basis for testing reading and thinking abilities. The passage below is followed by five questions designed to do this.

> Read the following paragraph. Then answer the questions which follow.
>
> If "peace" is conceived in its broad meaning, as the "tranquillity of order," it is clear that if any individual nation or group of nations is to attain that happy condition, its primary task is the repression of violence. Here the analogy with the domestic law of the state is

not only suggestive but compelling. Long ago it was recognized that there can be no peace within the state if each citizen is to be allowed to take the law into his own hands and enforce his claims by his own armed might. Violence is forbidden him, and any resort to it is unlawful and punishable even though it should subsequently appear that the claim itself, by the judgment of the courts, was a just one. To the extent that the law of the state defends existing personal and property rights, it protects the *status quo;* and it does so even when, on occasion, there is reason to believe that abstract justice might call for a different decision. As between citizens, so between nations, the repression of violence must be the paramount obligation of the international community, to which all others are subordinate. Under no circumstances must a nation be permitted to take the law into its own hands; and if it should do so, it must find ranged against it the organized community of nations which will see in its act of violence an attack upon the principle of law and order and, therefore, an attack upon each member of the community individually.

1. The author of the statement above holds that the fundamental requisite for the establishment of the "tranquillity of order" to which he refers is the
    1. establishment of just laws by the international community.
    2. elimination of aggression by single states or groups of states.
    3. reduction of national states to mere administrative districts.
    4. elimination of violence within national states.

2. The sentence beginning with which of these words contains the key idea of the paragraph?
    1. "Here the analogy with the domestic law . . ."
    2. "Long ago it was recognized that . . ."
    3. "To the extent that the law of the state . . ."
    4. "As between citizens, so between nations . . ."

3. A basic assumption underlying the author's contentions is that
    1. national self-interest must be the chief motivating factor in international relations.
    2. national armaments inevitably lead to war.
    3. a threat to the peace anywhere is a threat to it everywhere.
    4. the maintenance of the *status quo* may be identified with abstract justice.

4. Which of these concepts would be *least* in harmony with the author's viewpoint?
    1. Arbitration.
    2. Diplomatic immunity.
    3. Neutrality.
    4. Treaties.
5. The general principle which is advocated by the author is known as
    1. collective security.
    2. balance of power.
    3. imperialism.
    4. multilateral agreement.

The first item requires students to see that the author equates "tranquillity of order" with "peace." Then he must scrutinize the responses in terms of what is *fundamental* to peace in the eyes of the author. In the passage the author talks about just laws, but in two places the remark is made that violence must be eliminated. This points to response 2 as the correct answer.

The second item demands the student be able to sense the crucial element of the paragraph, but in addition to recognizing this central problem the student should be able to detect the assumptions upon which the central idea rests. The third item requires the student to do this.

Then, as a further check on student understanding, he is asked to equate the point of view of the author with an appropriate technique of international relations. He must know the meaning of these techniques to see that neutrality is least in harmony with the notions being considered. The last item requires the student to be able to so paraphrase the general principle enunciated by the author as to be able to apply an appropriate generic term to it.

Items requiring demonstration of critical thought may be based on various kinds of quantitative data. Data are supplied and students are asked to interpret given statements in the light of the data or they may be asked to bring previously acquired information to the interpretation of the material. The table and items given below require interpretation without recourse to outside information. This entire series is designed to test students' ability to recognize the adequacy of data to support certain generalizations.

Examine the table below which shows percentage distribution of marriage choices in Amsterdam, Holland, during two selected periods.

Period	Bachelors with			Widowers with		
	Spinsters	Widows	Divorced Women	Spinsters	Widows	Divorced Women
1905–1909......	96.1	2.4	1.5	62.0	31.4	6.6
1926–1930......	95.2	1.3	3.5	59.9	26.8	13.3

Period	Spinsters with			Widows with		
	Bachelors	Widowers	Divorced Men	Bachelors	Widowers	Divorced Men
1905–1909......	92.0	5.9	2.1	41.6	53.9	4.5
1926–1930......	90.2	5.2	4.6	29.7	55.7	14.6

On the basis of the information contained in the table, select from the key below the best judgment about each of the following statements.

     1. The statement is *justified* by the data in the table.
     2. The statement is *contrary* to the data in the table.
     3. There is *not enough information* given in the table to either justify or contradict the statement.

1. More men were married in the period 1905–1909 than in the period 1926–1930.
2. In the period 1926–1930, spinsters were about four times as likely to marry widowers as bachelors were to marry widows.
3. About three-fifths of the remarrying widowers selected women who had never been married before.
4. The number of widows was greater than the number of widowers.
5. Widowers were more likely to marry widows than widows were to marry widowers.
6. In both periods, more than half of the remarried widows were married to widowers.
7. There was a marked increase between 1905–1909 and 1926–1930 in the tendency of widows and widowers to marry divorced persons.
8. The divorce rate was higher in the second period than in the first.

SUMMARY OF RESEARCH DATA CONCERNING THE TEST
OF CRITICAL THINKING IN SOCIAL SCIENCE

Reliability and Validity

In preparing the final form of the Test of Critical Thinking in Social Science, studies of item analysis, reliability, and the validity of the test instrument were carried out. The detailed results of this work are described in an instructor's manual prepared to accompany the test.[6] Some summary of those findings is necessary, however, to aid in the proper interpretation of research findings reported.

The test has proved adequately reliable for purpose of group measurement of college freshmen and sophomores. Depending on the size of the group tested and the technique used to estimate the reliability, coefficients centered about the .80 magnitude. In view of the length of the test and the nature of the trait it purports to measure, such statistics were considered satisfactory. Item analyses, by which the difficulty and the discriminative characteristics of test items are estimated, yielded highly satisfactory results.

The validity of the test rests primarily on the judgments of the committee, but a number of other techniques were used to confirm this judgment. These included comparisons of the test scores with (1) those of other appropriate instruments; (2) course grades; (3) outside estimates of student possession of the relevant skills; and (4) student demonstration of critical thinking by other means. The unequivocal conclusion of all of these when combined with expert estimate of the test's potentialities is that the test measures a complex of traits which can be legitimately described as critical thinking in the social sciences.

Student Growth and Development in Critical Thinking
in Social Science

In the early fall of 1951 the Social Science Committee completed a satisfactory form of its test and proposed spending the next year (1951–52) finding out the capabilities and limitations of the instrument. The length of the Study, however, made it desirable to engage in some research beyond that involved in test analysis. To

[6] Copies may be purchased from the Educational Testing Service, Princeton, N.J.

combine these two purposes, a simple research program was prepared to be carried on during the academic year 1951–52. The purpose was stated as a study of growth and achievement in social science, as measured by the Test of Critical Thinking in Social Science, in relation to performance on the Test of Critical Thinking, Form A, and the several tests of beliefs and attitudes.

One major concern has been to determine something of the nature of the critical thinking skill. Some evidence on this is revealed in Tables 3 and 4. Critical thinking is positively related,

TABLE 3

COEFFICIENTS OF CORRELATION OF THE TEST OF CRITICAL THINKING IN SOCIAL SCIENCE WITH OTHER TESTS

TEST	COEFFICIENT OF CORRELATION			No. OF COLLEGES	No. OF STUDENTS
	Lowest r in Any College	Highest r in Any College	Average r*		
Pre-Test					
ACE Psychological Examination..	.34	.71	.59	12	2,171
Critical Thinking, Form A.......	.47	.66	.59	12	2,171
Inventory of Beliefs............	− .10	.46	.30	12	2,171
Problems in Human Relations...	.16	.41	.27	11	1,853
Post-Test					
ACE Psychological Examination..	.41	.64	.51	5	743
Critical Thinking, Form A.......	.55	.67	.62	5	743
Inventory of Beliefs............	.24	.63	.35	5	743
Problems in Human Relations...	.27	.42	.33	4	505

* Quinn McNemar, *Psychological Statistics* (New York: John Wiley & Sons, 1949), pp. 123–24.

although not perfectly so, with intelligence. The degree of this relationship is emphasized by considering the lower order of magnitude of the correlations involving the Inventory of Beliefs and the Problems in Human Relations tests, which are measures of more affective traits.

Critical thinking in the social sciences, as measured by this test, is also apparently related to knowledge of social science content. Correlations between knowledge tests such as course final examinations and the Test of Critical Thinking in Social Science are in the range from .69 to .74—about the same magnitude as those between academic aptitude and critical thinking. Further information on this point is to be found in comparing student achievement on the Critical Thinking in Social Science Test with achievement on a vocabulary test containing technical or quasi-technical terms found in the critical thinking test. Due to the simplicity of the vocabulary items, most students scored high on them, regardless of their score on the critical thinking test. However, there were sufficient low scorers to present an interesting pattern. Some high scorers on the vocabulary test scored high on the critical thinking test and some scored low. Some students scored low on both tests. No students, however, scored low on the vocabulary test and high on the critical thinking test. These data, derived from three different studies, support the generalization that knowledge of the content of the social science area is not of itself sufficient to guarantee success in critical thinking.

Scores of the Test of Critical Thinking in Social Science are positively related to grades in general education courses in social science at about the same magnitude as are tests of knowledge or intelligence. Coefficients range from .53 to .68 and are in general slightly higher than similar statistics for academic aptitude tests and course grades. Perhaps as a by-product, the test may show a way toward better prediction in this area. One comparison was made between critical thinking scores and grade-point averages for all general education courses and for all non-general education courses taken by a particular group of students. The r's of .41 for the former and .30 for the latter are interesting, especially in the light of the fact that critical thinking is made explicit in the objectives of those general education courses but not in the specialized courses.

Further relationships also have been studied to show more of the nature of the trait critical thinking. An r of .73 was obtained between a reading test especially designed for general education[7] and the Test of Critical Thinking in Social Science, an r of .56 was obtained between a final social science course examination and the Test of Critical Thinking in Social Science, and an r of .71 was obtained between the General Educational Development Test (High School)[8] and the critical thinking test. At one large institution the test was administered to a group of new students which

[7] East Lansing, Mich.: Michigan State College Board of Examiners; copyright 1951.

[8] Tests of General Educational Development, High School Level (Princeton, N.J.: Educational Testing Service; copyright 1945 by American Council on Education).

also took a placement test sampling materials from a full year's course in social science. The r's from two comparable groups were .67 and .61.

Including some of the coefficients just mentioned, as well as others, Table 4 contains a large number of r's reported from vari-

TABLE 4

COEFFICIENTS OF CORRELATION BETWEEN THE TEST OF CRITICAL THINKING
IN SOCIAL SCIENCE AND OTHER MEASURES*

Test	N	r
Inventory of Beliefs	145	.16
Problems in Human Relations	145	.21
Inventory of Beliefs	150	.28
Problems in Human Relations	150	.28
Grade-point average (non-general education courses)	39	.30
College Entrance Examination Board Test of Scholastic Aptitude		.37
Test of Science Reasoning and Understanding, Form A	145	.40
Grade-point average (general education courses)	39	.41
ACE Psychological Examination (Total Score)	352	.49
M.S.C. Reading Test (Paragraph Comprehension)		.50
Test of Critical Thinking, Form A	101	.51
ACE Psychological Examination (Total Score)	342	.53
Final letter grade (freshman social science)	318	.53
Critical Analysis in Reading and Writing	145	.54
ACE Psychological Examination (Total Score)	308	.57
M.S.C. Reading Test (Total)	342	.61
Social Science Placement Test	342	.62
Final letter grade (freshman social science)	318	.66
Test of Critical Thinking, Form A	300	.67
Final grade (social science course)	150	.67
Social Science Placement Test	352	.67
Social science course grade	298	.68
Test of Critical Thinking, Form A		.68
Nelson-Denny Reading Test (Total)	145	.68
ACE Psychological Examination (Total Score)		.68
Social Science Vocabulary Test		.68
Test of Critical Thinking, Form A	150	.69
Social Science Achievement Test	300	.69
Social science course grades	150	.70
Social science final examination		.70
General Educational Development Test (High School) Social Science		.71
M.S.C. Reading Test (Total)	73	.73
ACE Psychological Examination (Total Score)	55	.74
Social Science Vocabulary Test	300	.75

* The number of cases involved in some of these computations is unavailable.

ous cooperating colleges, arranged in increasing order of magnitude.

Effect of Socioeconomic Background on Critical Thinking

The belief was voiced that the socioeconomic background of students might be influential in determining ability to think critically. The reasoning runs that students from the upper socio-economic levels, by virtue of their broader experiences and richer cultural level, should do better than less fortunate students. To test this reasoning, biographical data were collected about each student examined in the fall of 1951. These data were treated by

TABLE 5

MEAN GAINS OF STUDENTS ON CRITICAL THINKING IN SOCIAL SCIENCE POST-TEST, CLASSIFIED ACCORDING TO PRE-TEST STANDING

COLLEGE	INITIALLY LOW GROUP		INITIALLY LOW-MIDDLE GROUP		INITIALLY MIDDLE GROUP		INITIALLY HIGH-MIDDLE GROUP		INITIALLY HIGH GROUP		TOTAL GROUP		
	Gain	N	Gain	N	Gain	N	Gain	N	Gain	N	Mean Pre-Test	Mean Gain	N
Pre-Test Range..	4–17		18–21		22–25		26–31		32–48				
1.......	14.00	1	5.67	6	5.89	9	5.57	21	1.64	76	34.13	3.04	113
2.......	7.38	29	4.91	44	3.64	39	1.98	55	1.94	53	25.84	3.56	220
3.......	5.85	40	4.67	30	2.08	24	2.08	24	3.00	13	22.03	2.95	144
4.......	9.15	65	7.76	66	6.42	64	6.62	76	3.60	55	24.06	6.81	326
5.......	13.69	13	11.43	21	9.22	18	8.44	34	5.05	22	25.68	9.09	108
6.......	5.11	91	4.43	77	3.50	58	2.61	28	0.86	7	20.03	4.17	261
7.......	5.86	21	5.04	27	4.10	29	4.79	28	1.84	25	24.65	4.29	130
8.......	5.95	38	3.55	49	1.58	38	1.30	47	0.81	42	24.55	2.59	214
9.......	12.50	4	9.00	5	1.33	3	6.08	13	3.59	49	32.64	4.78	74
10.......	6.53	15	4.69	13	2.50	8	3.12	17	0.87	15	24.66	3.60	68
11.......	6.29	24	3.90	30	2.24	17	2.38	13	−2.00	10	21.85	3.37	94
Total 11 colleges	6.89	341	5.48	368	3.68	320	4.20	356	2.26	367	24.64	4.49	1,752

analysis of variance and yielded the generalization that socio-economic differences were statistically significant at the .01 level of confidence in accounting for differences in test achievement for male students. No significant variance was isolated for female students. By the same technique it was discovered that there were some differences between students grouped according to their proposed major field of specialization, although these also were slight.

One-Year Gains on Critical Thinking in Social Science

Of much more importance in considering what affects ability to think critically are the data contained in Table 5. These data indicate how students from different colleges gain over a year's time with respect to critical thinking ability. Students from each institution are classified according to their pre-test performance.

It is at once apparent that, in general, students who score low on the pre-test record the most significant gains on the post-test. Whether this phenomenon only illustrates the familiar regression toward the mean which seems to pervade all testing, or whether it has more fundamental significance, is a debatable point.

Table 6 presents mean gains for students of different ability levels who were divided according to their pre-test scores. The numbers to the left of the table represent quartile ranking on the ACE Psychological Test, with "First" representing the lowest and "Fourth" the highest. The numbers at the top of the table represent quartile ranking according to pre-test score on the Test of

TABLE 6

MEAN GAINS OF STUDENTS ON CRITICAL THINKING IN SOCIAL SCIENCE POST-TEST, CLASSIFIED ACCORDING TO QUARTILE RANK ON THE ACE PSYCHOLOGICAL EXAMINATION AND THE CRITICAL THINKING IN SOCIAL SCIENCE PRE-TEST

ACE PSYCHOLOGICAL EXAMINATION QUARTILE RANK	QUARTILE RANK ON CRITICAL THINKING IN SOCIAL SCIENCE PRE-TEST								TOTAL	
	First (low)		Second		Third		Fourth			
	Gain	N	Gain	N	Gain	N	Gain	N	Gain	N
First (low).........	11.88	17	9.30	10	12.00	6	....	..	11.12	33
Second.............	14.62	8	9.83	12	9.90	10	7.33	3	10.79	33
Third.............	14.20	5	9.67	6	7.28	7	5.21	14	7.91	32
Fourth.............	17.00	3	13.60	5	9.56	9	6.75	16	9.48	33
Total group	13.36	33	10.21	33	9.62	32	6.15	33	9.84	131

Critical Thinking in Social Science. The larger gains for each pre-test quartile are made generally by the more apt students.

There may be some justification for the belief that some portion of the larger gains of the lower-scoring students reflects the orientation of most general education courses in social science. Designed as most such courses are, to provide a common educational experience for larger and larger numbers of students, they may be taught at a level most effective for the less well prepared students. However, any interpretation of these results must also recognize that larger gains for initially high-scoring students are made less probable by the smaller number of items available to them for demonstration of improvement.

Another generalization needs to be emphasized in view of the earlier discussion of the nature of critical thinking. Students from all schools involved showed gains on the test although these gains differ from institution to institution, even when such things as academic aptitude are held constant. The cause of these variations is largely conjectural, although some of the subsequently described studies may provide insight on this matter.

Critical Thinking Performance of More Advanced Students

For the most part, students whose scores were included in the preceding data took social science courses in their freshman year. The resulting gains, while generally not large, were of the kind to be expected. It then became desirable to find out what happened to those students during the next year of college. To determine this, identical cases were selected who had been tested in the fall of 1951, spring of 1952, and spring of 1953 with the Test of Critical Thinking in Social Science. Arranged in this order the data in Table 7 reveal what happened.

Replication studies were made at several other institutions, the results of which are included in Tables 8, 9, and 10.

From these data emerges the fact of considerable importance that scores on the Test of Critical Thinking in Social Science continue to increase, or at least remain constant, during the second year. Forgetting of knowledge begins almost immediately after a

TABLE 7

RETEST OF SOME STUDENTS TESTED IN TABLES 5 AND 6
ON CRITICAL THINKING IN SOCIAL SCIENCE

Testing Date	N	Mean Score	S.D.
Fall 1951..................	81	25.12	7.85
Spring 1952...............	37	34.54	6.08
Spring 1953...............	81	34.94	7.24

TABLE 8

PERFORMANCE OF MATCHED GROUPS OF STUDENTS ON TEST OF
CRITICAL THINKING IN SOCIAL SCIENCE

Group	N	EQUATED BY ACE PSYCHOLOGICAL EXAMINATION TOTAL SCORE		ACHIEVEMENT IN TEST OF CRITICAL THINKING IN SOCIAL SCIENCE	
		Mean	S.D.	Mean	S.D.
Pre-freshmen 9/51.........	55	118	19	26.6	7.7
Pre-sophomores 9/51.......	55	118	19	29.0	6.5
Post-sophomores 6/52......	55	118	19	31.5	7.2
Seniors 5/52..............	55	118	19	35.8	5.7

learning experience.[9] Perhaps the more fundamental skills such as critical thinking have a more lasting effect. The problem still remains, however, of increasing the magnitude of the residual ability.

In interpreting these figures it may be well to inquire as to the

TABLE 9

TEST AND RETEST SCORES ON CRITICAL THINKING IN SOCIAL SCIENCE OF SIXTEEN STUDENTS

Testing Date	N	Mean Score
Pre-test, September 1951	16	28.38
First post-test, April 1952	16	34.69
Second post-test, March 1953	16	35.38

practice effect on scores of students taking the same test three times. Several studies have been made testing students from the same population who had and who had not been previously tested with the same instrument. The slight difference in scores led to the conclusion that a test such as this one could be used as a pre-test and as a post-test with confidence. Apparently over a nine- or eighteen-month period there is insufficient practice effect to make any significant differences in test scores.

TABLE 10

TEST AND RETEST SCORES ON THE TEST OF CRITICAL THINKING IN SOCIAL SCIENCE

Group	Fall 1951	Spring 1952	Spring 1953	Gain
43 students who had fewer than 10 semester hours in the social sciences	23.2	24.7	28.7	5.5
41 students who had more than 10 semester hours in the social sciences	23.2	27.4	31.2	8.0
Total 84 students who took the test all three times	23.2	26.1	29.9	6.7
41 students taking the test for the first time in the spring of 1953	....	....	28.3	...

Studies Involving Different Course Patterns or Teaching Techniques

In order to study more carefully some possible factors which might influence growth with respect to critical thinking, several

[9] Ernest R. Hilgard, *Introduction to Psychology* (New York: Harcourt, Brace & Co., 1953), pp. 262–63.

analyses have been made comparing students at the same institution who had different but relevant course experience. The results from this research have suggested that minor variations in course experience make no appreciable difference in student achievement. At one institution a class was divided into six groups, each of which carried out a different set of activities, some of which involved use of audio-visual aids and some of which did not. While the differences in gains for the various groups were not statistically significant, the experimenter felt that the use of richer course materials did improve the quality of class work as assessed by more subjective means.

At another institution pre-test and post-test mean scores were

TABLE 11

PRE- AND POST-TEST MEANS ON TEST OF CRITICAL THINKING IN SOCIAL
SCIENCE FOR SELECTED GROUPS OF STUDENTS

Group	N	Pre-Test Mean	Post-Test Mean	Adjusted* Post-Test Mean
Completed general education social science course...................	94	26.47	30.14	29.65
Completed introductory history.....	42	23.00	25.67	28.11
Neither social science nor history....	66	26.91	29.61	28.75

* Adjusted means compiled by Snedecor method of adjusting post-test means to equate groups on pre-test means.

compared for three groups of students: (1) those having taken a general education social science course, (2) those having taken an introductory history course, and (3) those having taken neither social science offering. No significant differences between groups were found, although the group taking no social science course made smaller gains than the other two groups. Table 11 indicates this.

Still another institution provided data showing comparisons between three groups of students divided on the basis of the pattern of general education courses they took. These data revealed no significant differences between students who had and those who had not taken the general education social science courses.

At another institution one member of the Social Science Committee attempted to use a series of special teaching techniques with one section, while only the more customary ones were used in two other sections of the same course. His purpose was to determine whether or not these special techniques appreciably affected students' achievement on the Test of Critical Thinking in Social Science. Unfortunately he did not teach the control sections (2 and 3 in Table 12); hence the results are open to question. Table 12 suggests that at least the particular technique employed did not make much difference in test achievement.

TABLE 12

COMPARISON OF RESULTS OF DIFFERENT TEACHING
TECHNIQUES IN THE SAME COURSE

Section	ACE Psychological Examination Total	Pre-Test, Test of Critical Thinking in Social Science	Post-Test, Test of Critical Thinking in Social Science
1.................	109.09	31.32	36.18
2.................	101.17	30.61	34.06
3.................	92.06	26.18	32.76

At one institution a general education course is offered which makes a deliberate attempt, by means of class work and rather comprehensive testing, to develop skills of critical thinking within the context of the course content. Comparisons of students taking this course with those not taking the course revealed significant differences on test scores, although all students made some gain. These data are somewhat at variance with the other studies cited, although rationalization is possible. The period of instruction was longer, and there probably were some differences in the thoroughness with which techniques of instruction had been developed.

While course differences such as those identified above do not seem to be particularly effective as determiners of scores on the Test of Critical Thinking in Social Science, who the instructor is does seem to be important. Table 13 presents some comparative data for students from one institution taking the same course but from different instructors.

The evidence presented is by no means conclusive for any single point nor could such definitive conclusions be expected from a project organized as this one was. The findings and experiences of the Social Science Committee have, however, resulted in raising some highly provocative questions on which future research is needed and have focused attention on the significance of the kind and quality of collegiate teaching.

The evidence shows that there is growth, over a period of a year, and over a period of two years, with respect to the traits assessed by the Test of Critical Thinking in Social Science and that different groups grow at different rates. This suggests that it is possible to plan learning situations so as to facilitate development of critical

TABLE 13

COMPARISON OF RESULTS OF CLASSES OF DIFFERENT TEACHERS ON TEST OF CRITICAL THINKING: PRE-TEST AND POST-TEST MEANS

TEACHER	PRE-TEST		POST-TEST		MEAN GAINS
	N	Mean	N	Mean	
A................	52	26.5	50	30.0	3.5
B................	70	23.7	69	26.1	2.4
C................	21	25.4	46	26.0	.6
D................	50	22.9	43	24.6	1.7
E................	22	22.9	48	22.7	— .2
F................	58	23.0	66	27.0	4.0
G................	21	23.1	11	23.7	.6
H................	84	24.7	51	28.3	3.6
Combined Groups..	378	24.1	384	26.4	2.3

thinking ability. How this might be accomplished is still largely conjectural, although some clues have been provided.

DEVELOPMENT OF AN INSTRUCTIONAL HANDBOOK

As the Social Science Committee worked through the steps in the evaluation process, its members became aware of some of the limitations of existing teaching practice. The problems developed for tests were good ones, requiring a high degree of intellectual skill; yet when the problems were compared with what students were required to do in classes, they proved that little was being done to teach for critical thinking. Such an awareness caused the members to view the project in which they were engaged in a new light. And they began to seek ways by which their activities might be more intimately related to the classroom. As a visible manifestation of this concern a handbook was prepared describing various ways by which critical thinking abilities might be taught for in social science courses. This book presents a point of view which might be worth summarizing.[10]

The basic assumption is that critical thinking may be developed more fully by requiring students to practice the skill frequently within the context of social science content. If the desired skills are represented by the tasks posed by the test questions, then such problems can as well be utilized in teaching as in evaluating. Such adaptation, however, should not take the form of mere drill on the solving of test questions, but should seek to develop in students a facility for handling a variety of problems. The process of critical thinking, not the answers to specific questions, should be the goal of instruction.

The impact such a point of view will have on college teaching is, of course, unknown. However, there is some reason to suppose that those people who actively participated in the Cooperative Study developed an increased awareness of the limitations of their teaching practices and some insight into other ways of approaching their tasks.

SUMMARY

After considering a number of objectives frequently claimed for general education courses in social science, the Intercollege Committee on Social Science Objectives selected critical thinking for its area of particular inquiry. The meaning of critical thinking in social science was specified in a List of Abilities and was then exemplified by test situations and examples of student behavior. After the members of the committe were convinced of the validity of their conception of critical thinking in social science and had tried out on students various kinds of appraisal techniques, an objective-type Test of Critical Thinking in Social Science was developed, revised, and printed in a final form. This test was administered to a great many entering freshmen at a number of participating colleges, and to these same students or to comparable groups at the end of the freshman year and at the end of the sophomore year. The changes in test scores over these time intervals were studied with a view to determining their magnitude and the

[10] *Critical Thinking in Social Science, A Handbook for Evaluation and Teaching* (Dubuque, Iowa: Wm. C. Brown Co., 1954).

factors associated with them. In general, it was found that students gained in ability to think critically in social science over a period of a year, although the size of these gains varied widely, depending on the institution that students attended. Attempts to teach critical thinking in social science by making minor changes in particular courses did not appear to result in greater growth than was found in courses not making overt attempts to teach this skill. Attempts to relate growth in critical thinking ability to course organization or to specific teachers suggested that both of these were highly important, although the research could not identify specific factors which seemed to be operative.

Feeling that more attention should be given to the teaching of critical thinking in the context of social science, the intercollege committee prepared a handbook describing the teaching and evaluation of this trait in social science courses. This handbook outlined a rationale of thought and presented many examples of testing or teaching situations which might be adapted to almost any social science course. The experience of the intercollege committee members suggests that explicit attention to critical thinking can result in a much richer, more varied approach to teaching, with the possibility of infinitely greater student growth.

4

OBJECTIVES IN COMMUNICATIONS

Intercollege Committee on Communications Objectives: JAMES I.
BROWN, University of Minnesota; JAMES CALLAHAN, Kansas State
College of Agriculture and Applied Science; W. KENNETH CHRIS-
TIAN, Michigan State College; WILLIAM E. COFFMAN, Educational
Testing Service; J. E. CONGLETON, University of Florida; PAUL
DIEDERICH, Educational Testing Service; DONALD DIKE, Syracuse
University; THOMAS DUNN, Drake University; WILLIAM C. HUM-
MEL, Kansas State College of Agriculture and Applied Science;
MARY ELIZABETH JOHNSON, Muskingum College; FLORENCE
LEAVER, Drake University; THOMAS R. LEWIS, Florida State Uni-
versity; RALPH LEYDEN, Stephens College; JEAN McCOLLEY,
Kansas State Teachers College at Pittsburg; CHARLES SCHWERIN,
Boston University; ROBERT ZETLER, Pennsylvania College for
Women

A S AN INTEGRAL part of the general education movement,
numerous courses have been developed to replace the
customary offerings of rhetoric or freshman composition.
While such courses are assigned any of a variety of names such as
Written and Spoken English or Communication Skills, and organized according to any of several possible patterns depending on
staff interest, competency, and the institution's tradition of acceptance of general education, they all have a common concern for
better accommodating the needs of their students. They are based
on the conception that students should be adept in all of the
principal skills of communication—not just a restricted one of
writing or speaking or reading. The precise methods by which the
skills of reading, writing, listening, and speaking are developed
range from treating each in a separate course at one extreme, to

attempts to provide a completely unified or integrated course including all skills.[1]

This common concern is reflected in statements of specific course objectives which were accepted, at least in principle, by representatives of institutions participating in the Intercollege Committee on Communications Objectives, although not all those institutions possessed unified courses. All agreed that students should understand sentence structure and how it reflects relationships of ideas; that students ought to be able to listen with concentration and judgment; and that they should understand the role language plays in influencing social behavior. They also agreed that students should develop skill in logical thinking; that they should be able to read with critical comprehension; and should be able to engage in group discussions or face-to-face conversations with profit to themselves and others.

The committee made a brief survey of the present state of evaluation activity in communications and found that:

1. Effective testing of reading ability is important and much already has been done about it. However, virtually nothing has been done on a large scale to determine growth in reading ability as a result of collegiate experiences.

2. Most testing of reading ability in the past has been restricted to questions about what an author explicitly said or what could be logically inferred from his remarks. There have been some attempts to appraise sensitivity to nuances, overtones, and values in literary works. In addition, there is need: to assess the ability to analyze fairly complex arguments; to recognize assumptions, hypotheses, reasons, and conclusions; to detect lack of evidence, fallacies, and loopholes; to estimate relative strength of arguments; and to see how arguments can be refuted. At this point the committee was clearly concerned with what other committees identified as aspects of critical thinking.

3. Ability to write effectively is usually appraised through evaluation of written work, but objective-type devices have been used to measure this skill. Each technique possesses inherent weaknesses.

[1] Earl J. McGrath (ed.), *Communication in General Education* (Dubuque, Iowa: Wm. C. Brown Co., 1949).

If writing is judged, the chief problem lies in the subjective evaluation of the reader. If an objective technique is employed, it must be established that the results are relevant to skill in writing. Both problems are far from solution, and perhaps no general solution exists.

4. In appraising writing ability most attention is given to: (*a*) content and organization, (*b*) mechanics, and (*c*) effectiveness of expression or style. Scarcely any efforts have been made to develop techniques for evaluating constructive thinking, creative imagination, or the ability to get ideas.

5. At present there is some dissatisfaction with the methods of judging oral communication. There is a need for improved methods of evaluating individual speech performance, and there is a critical lack of techniques for appraising speech effectiveness in a group situation. The possibilities for interdisciplinary research between communications workers and group dynamicists are great.

6. In view of the increasing impact of the audio-visual techniques of mass communication, general education must prepare its products to listen effectively and to evaluate what they see and hear. The field of evaluating listening is a relatively new one with immense research possibilities.

Obviously, significant work could not be done on all of these questions. Although its activities touched most of the issues, the members of the Communications Committee decided to select one for initial inquiry. The one selected involved perhaps the most crucial problem confronting general education and the field of communications—the problem of identifying common elements in separate subject-matter disciplines.

The Critical Incident Study

Although the membership of the committee represented diverse types of courses—some restricted to speech, some restricted to composition, and some integrated—there was much interest in exploring the concept of communications and whether it could best be taught and evaluated as a single entity or in its separate parts. Was it possible that communication was in essence the same act, regardless of the medium? Or was the more traditional view—that the separate aspects of communication should be regarded as discrete skills which as such had to be taught independently of each other

—the more valid one? Would it be feasible to develop devices for evaluating effective or ineffective communication regardless of whether oral or written symbols were employed?

Some work done by psychologists during and since World War II appeared to possess potentiality in this regard. Faced with the need for evaluating the effectiveness or ineffectiveness of individuals in various kinds of work situations, Dr. John C. Flanagan, of the American Institute of Research, developed a new technique for approaching such a problem known as the "Critical Incident Technique."[2]

The basic data of the technique consist of descriptions of effective and ineffective behavior reported by supervisors who have been observing the workers and making judgments about the effectiveness or ineffectiveness of their behavior. The reports are examined and the "critical" behaviors are separated from other descriptive materials in the incident. Next, a classification system is derived which will facilitate the grouping-together of similar behaviors. The third step is to study carefully each critical behavior and classify it under one of these categories. The final step is to write descriptive statements which accurately summarize the behaviors within each category. It is often necessary to revise the classification system and repeat the ordering of data until the resulting statements are of a nature appropriate to the purposes of the study.

It seemed to the committee that Flanagan's approach might be suitable for determining the critical requirements for effective communication. If a sufficient number of critical incidents, descriptions of effective or ineffective behavior of students in communication situations, could be collected and classified inductively without direct reference to the logic of either speech or writing subject matter, some indication might be given of the degree of unity of the communication process.

During the spring of 1950 teachers at participating institutions were asked to collect critical incidents either of writing or of speech. Incidents of effective or ineffective listening and reading were excluded because of technical difficulties; however, as a side project some data were obtained concerning student listening. To

[2] John C. Flanagan, *Critical Requirements for Research Personnel* (Pittsburgh, Pa.: American Institute for Research, 1949).

ensure uniformity of collection, detailed instructions were mimeo-graphed for teachers participating in the project and special cards distributed upon which incidents were to be recorded. Regardless of whether they taught in communication courses or in some other area, teachers were informed in writing:

The next time you have an opportunity to examine the writing of students, look for incidents in the writing which make you decide that their communication is especially effective or unusually ineffective. As soon as possible after you have made the selection, describe the ob-served incident on one of the 4 × 6 cards provided with these instruc-tions. Fill in the requested background information necessary to identify the source of the incident, using the key provided. In reporting the incidents, give special attention to the following points:

1. The incidents you report may be taken from samples of writing which are generally good or generally poor, or they may be taken from samples which are generally mediocre but which contain some specific instance of *especially effective or unusually ineffective communication.* The committee is not interested in reports of conventional types of errors or lack of errors as such. Instead, they wish only reports of errors of the type which are critical in the sense that they interfere with effective communication or, at the other extreme, types of writing which facilitate effective communication and result in very clear state-ments. You may pass over a number of papers without observing any-thing which you consider critical in this sense and then come to one paper which makes you feel like shouting, "This is it!"

2. Samples of written communication may be taken from any source available to you—assigned themes, essay examinations, term papers, etc. In fact, the committee hopes that some people will use one source while others use other sources. Be sure, however, to provide sufficient information so that the committee can identify the situation, since writing which is effective in one situation might not be effective in another.

3. Report behavior rather than generalized traits. Do not report, "Organization good" but rather, "An outstanding example of organiza-tion in that the student presents argument in three steps, each devel-oped in a separate paragraph and identified by a topic sentence."

4. Report not more than twenty incidents. A large number of people are cooperating in this study and nobody is asked to contribute many incidents. If you have difficulty in finding twenty really critical inci-dents, report fewer.

Volume-wise the response from teachers was successful. How-ever, the resulting 1,300 incidents had many qualitative defects attributable chiefly to teacher inexperience, such as: (1) lack of sufficient detailed description to make clear the basis of judgments reported; (2) reporting of evaluative statements only ("Organization poor," "misspelled"); (3) no identification by the instructor of what he considered the critical behavior; (4) incidents which led to the inference that the instructor was reporting behavior critical for determining a grade in "English Class" or "Speech Class" rather than behavior which was critical with respect to communication; and (5) sets of incidents which suggested that instructors were sacrificing quality of incident to quantity and reporting insignificant incidents in order to complete twenty cards.

Although the collected incidents were not as free from error as had been hoped, they were analyzed and classified by the entire committee. To fill major gaps which seemed to exist in the categories thus established and to verify the rubrics already determined, a second collection of incidents was made with greater care being exercised in schooling teachers as to what they should seek. The thus augmented file of incidents was then reclassified into two tentative lists—one of examples of effective and one of examples of ineffective communication. Items were included regardless of whether they had been discovered in the context of speech or of writing. While some of these clearly represented their origin, enough referred either to speaking or to writing as to suggest the interdependence of the two skills. Unfortunately, it is much easier to find incidents of ineffectiveness than the converse; hence the positive side is perhaps insufficiently represented.

EFFECTIVE AND INEFFECTIVE BEHAVIOR IN SPEAKING AND WRITING

Effective Behavior	Ineffective Behavior

I. ADAPTATION TO THE COMMUNICATION CONTEXT

A. Adaptation to the Requirements of the Assignment

The student	The student
Limited subject in relation to time available.	Chose subject too broad for time available.
Selected novel topic related to the situation: spoke about "public speaking at the turn of the century" in a speech class.	Failed to observe time limits.
	Failed to develop subject sufficiently to use time available.
	Copied material without giving references or using quotation marks.

Effective Behavior	Ineffective Behavior

Failed to include original thinking as required by the assignment.

Included "value judgments" in a list of "details objectively verifiable."

Submitted selected quotations where précis was assigned.

Developed irrelevant topic after clearly stating major thesis.

Failed to treat subject in accordance with stated focus of the assignment.

B. Adaptation to Audience and Occasion

The student	The student

Effective:

Handled personal subject with unusual objectivity, dignity, and directness.

Distinguished between feelings and their occasion.

Dressed for the occasion.

Related material to everyday experience of audience.

Coordinated verbal and visual elements in speech.

Made sketch on blackboard before class began so that there was no interruption of communication.

Used vivid figures of speech (avoided clichés).

Used an effective (appropriate) attention-getting device.

Ineffective:

Used excessive negative criticism irritating to audience.

Used offensive material—vulgar story, sentimentality.

Chose subject which embarrassed himself—unable to complete talk at first attempt.

Dressed inappropriately for occasion.

Laughed with audience when "poker face" was appropriate.

Apologized for performance.

Bragged.

Misspelled one word four different ways.

Submitted mussy paper.

Wrote illegibly.

Affected emotion—paid attention to style rather than meaning.

Failed to allow audience to "set" before beginning speech.

Used clichés and trite phrases.

Failed to integrate demonstration: stopped talking to make sketch; passed pictures and lost audience.

C. Adaptation to the Immediate Situation

The student	The student

Effective:

Was not disturbed by interruption of speech.

Used manner directly in contrast to preceding speaker.

Related talk to preceding one.

Used visual aid presented by opposing speaker to make own point.

Ineffective:

Forgot speech when interrupted.

Memorized and failed to change as required by immediate context.

Forgot memorized talk.

II. Structure
A. Ordering of Material

Effective Behavior	Ineffective Behavior
The student	*The student*

Suited organization to purpose:
  summary first in inspection report.
  topical ordering for essay examination.
  general to specific.
  interrelated sequence.
  climactic.
  psychological.
  logical.
  several points of view.
Adopted unusual method of organization.
	Arranged material in random order:
	  rambled.
	  no organization apparent.
	Adopted inappropriate organization:
	  chronological order required but not used.

B. Paragraph Unity

The student	*The student*
Fitted quotation into development so that relationship was clear.	Related random series of details as a "paragraph." Included irrelevant material in paragraph. Switched from one idea to another in a single paragraph. Wrote two paragraphs where there should be only one. Failed to order sentences logically in paragraph. Included copied material without showing its relationship to central idea.

C. Sentence Structure

The student	*The student*

Used skillful subordination.
Used variety of sentence structure.
Used effective parallelism.
	Used involved sentences:
	  words scrambled like vegetables in a soup.
	  words, words, words meaning nothing.
	Used sentences of single pattern so that relative importance of ideas was not made clear.
	Used faulty parallelism.
	Used dangling participles.

Effective Behavior	Ineffective Behavior
	Used pronouns and demonstrative adjectives which lacked clear referents.
	Wrote sentence fragments.
	Misplaced modifiers so that meaning was confused.
	Introduced more details than could be clearly related in a single sentence.
	Included two apparently unrelated ideas in a compound sentence.
	Misplaced sentence parts so that meaning was confused.
	Failed to show relationship of sentence parts.
	Appended idea to a sentence rather than integrating it into the sentence.
	Made errors in punctuation.

D. Divisional Relationships

The student	The student
Used special devices to guide reader: underlined subtopics. numbered points.	Provided no transition between paragraphs: ideas presented like "clothespins on a line."
Effected transition by repeating key words of two paragraphs in connecting sentence.	Provided no transition between large sections.
	Wrote faulty linking sentence.

III. DEVELOPMENT

A. Development of an Introduction

The student	The student
Had adequate introduction to communication.	Made introduction too long to be consistent with rest of paper.
Defined key words in many ways.	Assumed specific knowledge which could not be expected of audience.
Gave essential background.	Used references without antecedents (in introduction).
Anticipated possible misinterpretations and dealt with them.	Used a beginning which worked counter to central purpose of essay.
Used personal experience to introduce subject.	

B. Development of an Ending

The student	The student
Had adequate summary: restated main points.	Had no summary where one was needed.

Effective Behavior	**Ineffective Behavior**
	Stopped without adequate ending: said, "That's about all."

C. Selection of Supporting Thought Groups

The student	*The student*
Covered subject completely: included all essential subtopics.	Failed to include essential subtopics.

D. Integration of General and Particular

The student	*The student*
Supported generalization by specific example: used quotation to support generalization. used "real examples." Used specific details to build up organization. Selected pertinent evidence to support judgment.	Stated generalization without supporting facts, illustrations, or examples. Gave details without pointing to their meaning. Failed to give reasons to substantiate judgment. Failed to indicate central idea to which illustrations were related. Assumed a cause and effect relationship but presented no evidence for the existence of such a relationship.

E. Harmony and Relevancy of Details

The student	*The student*
Used pertinent details. Used carefully selected, realistic details: used statistics. used apt quotation. Identified key factors and related others to them. Used details to focus on one aspect of the subject. Used unusual distinguishing details.	Used insufficient pertinent details. Used excessive details (boring). Failed to select and emphasize: all details given equal weight. faulty relation of material to central purpose. Failed to distinguish main ideas from subordinate thought.

F. Reasoning and Originality

The student	*The student*
Selected from his experience pertinent materials to make his own points. Presented fresh or original ideas about the subject. Made clear limitations of his arguments and qualified his opinion. Noted significance of lack of data to support a particular point of view.	Failed to distinguish between facts and opinions. Used faulty reasoning: argued by applying labels. a *non-sequitur*. Reasoned from the specific to the general without proving the validity of such reasoning. Made illogical inference leading to

Effective Behavior	**Ineffective Behavior**
Made a key distinction between symptom and cause.	faulty coordination of causal classes.
Asked pertinent question which focused the discussion.	Developed argument on the basis of an unqualified assumption.
	Failed to show relationship of new idea to material already presented.
	Stated verbally a logical connection which did not exist in fact.

G. Use of Maps, Charts, and Visual Aids

The student	*The student*
Used model to facilitate technical explanation.	Failed to provide needed demonstration.
Used visual aids.	Failed to show relationship of demonstration to topic.
Used pertinent demonstration.	
Made demonstration with real props.	

H. Adequacy and Recency of Sources

The student

Stated views at variance with facts readily available.

Used invalid source material:
out of date.
questionable authority.

IV. Skill in Expression
A. Word Choice

The student	*The student*
Used specific words to convey sense impression.	Used words with wide general meaning to convey narrow personal meaning.
Used exact words.	Used vague general words:
Selected words which supported one another and conveyed a single impression.	used "something" in place of exact word.
Used proper connectives to indicate transition.	Used incorrect connective: "nevertheless" for "in addition to."
Used clear, racy diction.	Misused word:
Used "double-edged" vocabulary to express irony.	"undertakings" for "activities."
Adapted diction to subject matter.	"turbine" for "turban."
	Misspelled word so that meaning was distorted.
	Used word to express meaning word does not usually express:
	"story" for "essay."
	"bring forth" for "express," etc.
	Used many words where a few would do the job better (wordiness).

SCALE FOR EVALUATING SPEAKING AND WRITING

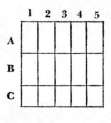

I. ADAPTATION TO COMMUNICATION CONTEXT

A. Adaptation to the requirements of the assignment—evidence of clear conception of purpose in relation to limitations of time and background; appropriate form of discourse; continuity of development.

B. Adaptation to the audience and occasion—suitability of language, topic, and dress; evidence of common courtesy through legible writing, consistency of spelling, clear articulation; coordination of supplementary aids; etc.

C. Adaptation to the immediate situation—evidence of flexibility through use of preceding and immediate incidents.

II. STRUCTURE

A. Ordering of material—evidence of adoption of some underlying order—logical, chronological, analytical, etc.

B. Paragraph unity—selection and arrangement of pertinent ideas to convey unified impression; exclusion of extraneous material.

C. Sentence structure—use of proper grammatical construction, pronoun reference, sentence variety, subordination, punctuation, and voice to convey clear meaning.

D. Divisional relationships—showing transition between paragraphs and sections by structures, position, or explicit transition devices.

III. DEVELOPMENT

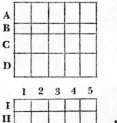

A. Development of an introduction—using anecdotes, definition, or review; relating topic to audience; length in relation to total communication.

B. Development of an ending—using summary or other ending devices; effecting ending through cumulative arragement of parts; length in relation to total communication.

C. Selection of supporting thought groups—including sufficient thought groups to develop topic; excluding irrelevant thought groups.

D. Integration of general and particular—supporting generalizations with convincing details; drawing generalization from particulars where necessary.

E. Harmony and relevancy of details—selecting from available details those which contribute to development of central idea; exclusion of unnecessary details.

F. Reasoning—employing logical processes to support argument; creating original synthesis of materials.

G. Use of maps, charts, and visual aids—pertinency of aids in relation to topic (cf. I-B where concern is with mechanics of using aids).

H. Use of sources—adequacy and recency of sources and bibliography; avoidance of bias in use of sources.

IV. SKILL IN EXPRESSION

A. Word choice—exactness and economy in word uses; regard for emotive effect of words; spelling and pronunciation which eliminate confusion of meaning.

B. Rhythmic devices—cadence, meter, alliteration, assonance, and sound symbolism.

C. Voice quality—variation of tempo, volume, pitch, etc., beyond minimum judged as punctuation in II-C.

D. Gesture and body posture—integration of body posture and movement with thought; eye appeal; articulatory gestures.

I. Adaptation to Communication context

II. Structure

III. Development

IV. Skill in Expression

Key: (1) outstanding, (2) effective, (3) routine, (4) ineffective, (5) unsatisfactory.

Directions: Make judgment concerning each aspect of the speech or theme and record by placing a check mark in the appropriate box. Draw a line through the boxes opposite category which you do not wish to rate. Fill in identification information below.

This is a rating at .... Date ....

....

Fig. 2.—Scale for Evaluating Speaking and Writing

Effective Behavior	Ineffective Behavior
	Misused words so that the reader was amused in a serious situation.
	Repeated words and phrases unnecessarily.
	Misspelled many common words: conveyed impression of illiteracy through misspellings.
	Used pronunciation inappropriate to situation: "candidate," "dose."
	Failed to understand connotative meanings of common words.

B. Rhythmic Devices

The student
Used onomatopoetic words.

C. Voice Quality

The student	*The student*
Used soft, well-modulated voice.	Used mechanical speech.
Used voice to support sense value of words.	Spoke too loudly.
	Spoke inaudibly.
	Mumbled.
	Spoke too rapidly.
	Spoke with excessive hesitation.
	Spoke with excessive dramatic pauses.

D. Gestures and Body Posture

The student	*The Student*
Maintained active body.	Used distracting bodily movements.
Used natural gestures.	Used artificial gestures.
Had "sparkling eyes and lighted face."	Had no bodily activity.
	Lacked eye contact.

After the categories were established, the next step was to write descriptions of each which would encompass all of the incidents under each heading and at the same time provide a generalized base for classifying additional incidents and making judgments about the quality of products. Following this, the task became that of developing some form or forms of rating scales which might be tested by application to new speech or writing situations (see Figure 2). In order to explore whether or not speech needs were essentially different from writing needs, two forms of the check list

Student _____   Subject _____

1. Adaptation to the communication situation:

SUPERIOR 14 13	EXCELLENT 12 11	GOOD 10 9	AVERAGE 8 7	FAIR 6 5	POOR 4 3	VERY POOR 2 1

A. Suited to the assignment: follows assignment- stays within set time limits
B. Suited to the speaker: ethical justification- well prepared- desire to communicate
C. Suited to the audience: clear articulation- correct pronunciation- visual aids where necessary- neatly dressed- poised in body and facial expression- eye contact- conversational tone- variation in pitch, rate, and loudness- subject appropriate

II. Structure of the speech:

SUPERIOR 14 13	EXCELLENT 12 11	GOOD 10 9	AVERAGE 8 7	FAIR 6 5	POOR 4 3	VERY POOR 2 1

A. Introduction: captures attention- focuses attention on subject- leads to stated or implied purpose- establishes mood of speech- proper length for balance
B. Body: subject analysis pattern clear- all divisions subordinate to purpose- each division a separate unit- division by one principle only
C. Conclusion: restates purpose and summaries- uses additional element (pithy epigram or reference to previous illustration, etc.)- proper length for balance
D. Transition elements: verbal bridges between divisions clear
E. Sentences: correct structure- varied structure- effective parallelism

III. Developmental materials:

SUPERIOR 14 13	EXCELLENT 12 11	GOOD 10 9	AVERAGE 8 7	FAIR 6 5	POOR 4 3	VERY POOR 2 1

A. Originality of material: selection of material from many sources- initiative in gathering data- no hint that the material is paraphrased from book or magazine
B. Freshness of material: uses personal experiences- avoids outdated data- adapts old facts to new contexts

C. <u>Accuracy of material</u>: uses honest details- qualifies opinions- uses specific support- avoids questionable authority

D. <u>Adequacy of material</u>: sufficient details- sufficient illustrative devices- use of statistics or apt quotations when such are available

E. <u>Relevancy of material</u>: details pertinent- details realistic - connection between examples and generalization demonstrated

IV. <u>Skill in expression:</u>

SUPERIOR	EXCELLENT	GOOD	AVERAGE	FAIR	POOR	VERY POOR
14 13	12 11	10 9	8 7	6 5	4 3	2 1

A. <u>Extemporaneous delivery</u>: speaks without notes- minimum of vocalized pauses- effective use of unvocalized pause- adaptation to audience reactions- rapport with audience

B. <u>Use of language</u>: avoidance of clichés- sense of sentence rhythm- exactness in word choice- recognition of connotative value of words

C. <u>Use of voice</u>: voice modulated to verbal symbols- pleasant tonal quality

D. <u>Use of body</u>: projects alert body tone- purposive movement- coordinated movement- natural and spontaneous gestures

V. <u>Overall evaluation:</u>

SUPERIOR	EXCELLENT	GOOD	AVERAGE	FAIR	POOR	VERY POOR
14 13	12 11	10 9	8 7	6 5	4 3	2 1

Directions: Indicate your rating on the five aspects of the speech by drawing a circle around the number which represents your rating in each case.

Name of student making the rating _____

FIG. 3.—SCALE FOR EVALUATING SPEAKING

were prepared, and a modification developed for speech rating exclusively (see Figure 3).

Each of these two scales provided a means by which every behavior listed might be judged qualitatively. It was hoped that the large number of specific behaviors listed on the scales would not prove frustrating to users by their very number and that they would enable a rater to render a more reliable judgment about the act he observed.

The items on either rating scale (Figures 2 and 3) will not appear appreciably different from those found on any similar a priori established device. However, by virtue of their empirical origin, the categories provide a valid criterion with which to compare other devices based more on logic and deduction. These rating scales have not been used extensively either by members of the committee or by other interested teachers, although they have been used in a few institutions. There are several reasons why this has been so.

1. In spite of the effort to conceive of communications as a single phenomenon, members of the committee came to feel they would wrench meanings of categories on the scale if they were to be applied either to speech or to writing. Speech-oriented members argued that the original check list ignored important aspects of the speech act. The composition-trained persons felt that the scale was so burdened with technical phases of speech as to cause irritation and frustration in a writing context. Perhaps both groups erred in not seeking a more generic classification. Thus, the incidents "dressed for the occasion," "related talk to preceding one," "made sketch on blackboard," and "used visual aids," clearly bear on speech evaluation. Yet each could be modified so as to apply to composition or still further modified so as to be appropriate for either kind of communication. Dressing for the occasion might involve the same principle as selecting the appropriate form for recording a theme; both are factors external to the communication but that nevertheless affect it. Dressing in a sloppy pair of jeans and sweater to give a formal speech is much the same ineffectiveness as writing an essay on Gibbon on varying sized sheets of paper. Relating a talk to the previous one appears to be of the same order as relating the paper either to point of view expressed in a text or

by a teacher or classmate. They all involve utilization of an appropriate device to give the communication perspective for the reader or listener. At any rate, considerably more research than has thus far been attempted is in order before such possibilities can be rejected.

2. The check lists are long and somewhat more difficult to use than the kind usually found in college courses. Compare, for example, the length and complexity of the two critical incident rating scales with the following two in use at one of the participating schools:

Speech Rating Scale	*Theme Rating Scale*
1. Fluency	Conventions of grammar
2. Physical and vocal control	Sentence structure
3. Organization	Diction
4. Content	Organization
5. Sense of communication	Content

Such check lists will appear much more convenient than will the longer ones to busy classroom teachers facing 150 students each week. Yet there is a price for such convenience in the form of unreliability of rating. For example, the two short scales were used by ten pairs of raters, each pair judging twenty-five themes. The correlations between raters in each pair ranged from .30 to .90, with the average falling at about the .55 level. A partial reason for this relative unreliability lies in the relative abstractness of the rating scale. Because the behaviors to be judged under each major rubric have not been specified, each teacher is free to interpret the concept as he will. This free interpretation can be rectified by providing each pair of raters with several discussion periods to coordinate their meanings before themes are actually rated. A longer, more specific scale attempts to accomplish the same end by different, more economical means.

3. There was some feeling on the part of committee members that perhaps the entire critical incident approach was inappropriate to the area of communication because of the invalidity of a basic assumption. The technique was originally developed in the context of activities for which existed clearly demonstrable criteria of success. Activities or incidents could be selected on the basis of whether or not they affect success. The criterion for fighter pilot

success is whether he shoots down enemy planes and is not shot down himself. The criterion of success for a surgeon is whether his patient lives and recovers health. Criteria of success for processes of communication are not so clear cut. If formal excellence of a piece of written work is the criterion, then certain incidents such as grammatical use are relevant. If, however, the criterion is rejected, as it is by many theorists about communication, knowledge of grammar loses some of its potency. This position is expressed in an evaluative statement submitted by one member of the committee:

The critical incident method of Flanagan is inadequate for any valid use in discovering essential characteristics of communication in a sufficiently large number of pieces of communication to be of any real use. Only in a small proportion of examples does any *one* aspect of behavior make the difference between effective and ineffective communication, and even in these cases the one aspect is always a phenomenon in a unique situation of the total context. In reality, the critical incident is always the complex of relationships in the whole communication. One "incident" or aspect of behavior may render a communication effective in one context and ineffective in another. Hence a generalization, which is implied by the identification of an incident deemed critical, would be exceedingly misleading.

This point of view certainly has validity and cannot be lightly disregarded. Yet to assume that the absence of perfect criteria of success prevents effective measurement precludes any evaluation at all. A major task of workers in the field of general education is to develop acceptable criteria. At an abstract level these have been codified in various publications, for example, the *Report of the President's Commission on Higher Education*. A major purpose of enterprises such as the Cooperative Study is to assign meaning to these abstract symbols. Failure to classify criteria in one or many attempts should not support a presumption that the task is impossible. As a matter of fact, the emphasis found in the critical incidents to adaptation to the specific communication situation underscores a criterion which until recently was disregarded—the doctrine of appropriateness.[3] Further collection of incidents might

[3] C. Merton Babcock, "A Rationale for Communication Skills," *School and Society*, July 11, 1953, pp. 4–6.

direct attention to other criteria accepted in practice if not in theory.

4. One reason why the critical incident materials were not employed more extensively falls under the heading of public relations. Teachers were asked to collect the critical incidents by means of a mimeographed letter and instructions. This device did not properly convey the nuances and implications of the study without which the collection of data would seem to be just busywork. Then when the final list of categories and the final check lists appeared with some gaps suggested by logic, teachers became convinced that further work on the project would be a waste of time.

In the light of these reasons the Communications Committee reached the conclusion that the critical incident attempt to study communication was not successful. The attempt did, however, have important by-products in the form of other committee activities.

The Theme Analysis Handbook

In order to practice using the critical incident check lists, the Communications Committee collected representative study themes from each of the participating schools. The idea was that these could be reproduced and each member of the committee could rate each theme by means of the rating scale. As members began this work, however, it became apparent that individuals approached theme rating from many diverse points of view regarding the process of theme evaluation. It further became clear that these differences regarding the nature of the rater's role made significant differences in the value assigned a particular paper. To reconcile these divergent orientations, the committee members began to study the process of theme rating.

From this discussion emerged a set of principles or a rationale governing evaluation of student written work, the effectiveness of which could be demonstrated on the themes collected. These principles attained increased significance in the eyes of the committee members when they realized that in spite of handbooks of usage and training in writing, few teachers approached theme reading from a consistent frame of reference. Thus, a project designed to provide assistance to the committee members alone came to be viewed as having importance for all communication teachers, particularly new staff members. These principles have been embodied in another publication[4] which presents them and then demonstrates their applicability to a collection of themes, each of which was critically analyzed and judged by the entire committee. Since they do represent the mature judgment of the committee with respect to one of its major concerns, they are also included in this report.

Some Principles of Theme Analysis

1. *External motivation.*—Any writing occurs in a context of which it is a part and from which it should not be separated. A student theme is no exception. It should be read in the light of its external motivation—the audience and assignment to which it is addressed. It should be judged, not by inflexible standards, but by the success with which it meets the requirements of that audience and assignment. This, of course, challenges the teacher to make assignments that will stimulate a response and provide a sufficiently defined frame of reference to make possible an evaluation of the writing. Probably classes do their best neither when totally uncued nor when faced by too restrictive assignments.

2. *Internal motivation.*—The good theme reader should try to understand what may be called the internal motivation of the theme: what the writer has tried to do, whether in response to a specific assignment or in a free situation. Once discovered by analysis, the intention of a theme guides and informs the reader's appraisal of it. If the theme intention is kept in mind, it will give the reading a direction and unity which will enhance its value, both to the instructor in his evaluation and to the student, who learns best when his purpose has been appreciated.

The purpose of a theme is not likely to be discovered unless the instructor can read it genially and humanistically, less concerned to criticize negatively than to help with his intelligence and imagination. This attitude, however, need not commit him to a program of milk and honey. It is more important that his responses be direct, intelligent, and attentive than that they be superhumanly

[4] *Handbook for Theme Analysis* (Dubuque, Iowa: Wm. C. Brown Co., 1954).

tolerant. Nor does the fact that the teacher can realize the intention of a theme automatically earn it credit. That intention may be worthless. Once recognized, however, the special aims that govern the writing should be considered as part of the total performance to be evaluated.

3. *Unrealized potentialities.*—The reader of a theme should be aware of its unrealized potentialities, its opportunities wasted or used without imagination. His evaluation should consider not only what has been done but also what might have been done with this or that detail, image, and argument. Not only does this obligation on the part of the reader add a frame of reference complementary to the preceding two; it also gives a valuable stimulus to the student as he reads over the criticism of his work.

Suggestions two and three, both touching on constructive criticism, need to be modified by the warning that their successful adoption requires considerable tact and caution. If the instructor follows the second suggestion without this caution and attempts to reconstruct the internal motivation of a theme, it is quite possible that he will credit the student with and impose upon him ideas which the theme never contained. Likewise, an engrossing interest in the unrealized possibilities of the writing may make the teacher lose sight of what *has* been achieved; may make him substitute for the student's theme an imaginary essay with an alien point of view. Although it is difficult to know how consciously an author is aware of the intention of what he is writing, nevertheless the theme reader should avoid the risk of distorting another's work; he should stick to concrete evidence.

4. *Interdependence of parts.*—The teacher should remember that the paper he is reading is not a set of miscellaneous details but a single theme whose parts are interdependent. Their significance arises from their belonging to a particular order of verbal events and from their relation to one another within this order. To see them accurately is to see them in action; issuing from and leading to; doing things. They cannot properly be taken from their whole and assessed in isolation.

However obvious this may seem, it cannot be too strongly urged. Despite lip service paid the proposition that every element of a theme is one term in a relation or in a number of relations, the temptation in critical practice is to deal with these elements separately as they are encountered in the reading. The reader usually does not hold in his mind the entirety of the theme he is appraising because he has time to read it only once. Nevertheless, the attempt to reread should be made lest the final evaluation be made on only a fragment of the original theme.

The structural importance of the large elements of a theme—of introductions and conclusions, of paragraphs and key sentences—is clear. They can hardly be seen except in connection with the developments to which they contribute. Yet matters of diction should also be examined in terms of the context in which they occur. Logic, grammar, and semantics allow the observation of relationships between things named, the union of word to word, and the relation of word to thing or to the concept of a thing. The good theme reader will also be concerned with questions of the harmony of phrasing—the way words fit with each other and with the total tone and purpose.

5. *Psychological interrelation of parts.*—Since a theme is the activity of a single mind, its several properties are probably related. The way it attacks different problems, its various successes and failures, its excellences and deficiencies presumably are connected. The reader must discover these connections and infer the tendencies that govern them. The better he can gauge a piece of writing as a single though complex mode of behavior and the better he can relate apparently different characteristics and see them as variations of a dominant trait, the greater value will his reading possess, both for evaluation and instruction. What is being recommended is not the easy generalization so often found at the end of a theme. A good theme reader's analysis ends instead by getting to the roots of a complicated process.

The difficulties and risks of such an analytical process are obvious. If there were more evidence available that certain kinds of communicative acts are connected and often appear in clusters, the validity of the belief that a theme is a psychological whole would be strengthened. Yet it seems true that the teacher who has read a number of themes by the same student, written over a period of time, is the one most likely to detect a pattern in the student's expression. The suggestion just made consequently applies to the reading of a sequence of themes as much as or more than it does to the reading of a single one.

Often instructors who inquire closely into the psychological bases for imagery, metaphor, and other verbalizations feel tempted to regard a piece of writing as almost a set of data for a case history rather than as a series of expressions. Although such an inquiry may yield valuable insights into the origins of difficulties and the sources of achievement, it should be remembered that such insights are valuable to the student of communication only if they can help him improve his writing.

6. *Attention to details.*—It follows from the earlier suggestions in this section that the reading of a theme should be as painstaking and as attentive to detail as possible. Although the committee shares the current tendency to rate mechanical errors as not highly important in themselves, it does believe that all minor details, mechanical or otherwise, deserve critical examination. Such details may be significant in two ways: they may markedly interfere with or help the writing (a misspelling sometimes stumps the reader and a casual figure of speech may light up an entire subject), and they may be related to more distinguishing features of the communication, expressing a controling tendency or revealing a characteristic habit of thought.

In practice, the theme reader must be selective in his notes on student papers because he is pressed by time and because he must not confuse his students. After a full reading of the theme, he will probably wish to focus his commentary on those elements which show interconnections and relationships, and which are parts of the major patterns of the theme.

7. *Reciprocal relations of discovery and judgment.*—The reader starts to lay the groundwork of his concluding judgment at the beginning of his analysis. It is at first a mere impression—to be checked, amplified, and corrected by rereading. Although discovery of the qualities of the theme logically precedes the appraisal of it, the two activities make up an indivisible process; hence, a consistent separation between description and evaluation should not be expected. The vocabularies of these processes are to some extent

interchangeable, so that a description may be worded in the language of values and the statement that a certain thing has been done may imply a judgment.

The concluding judgment on a theme should be specifically related to its subject matter and should clearly follow from the running commentary. This is not to imply that the final evaluation should be merely a mechanical summary of points already established; rather, by its consideration of the total performance it has opportunities for making additional and perhaps invaluable contributions.

When the theme being analyzed is a good one, there is a temptation to limit the observations to minor flaws and conclude with a message of congratulation to the student. But a full and conscientious reading must take account of successes as well as failures. The commentary itself on such a theme should be nearly if not entirely as full as on one which is unsatisfactory; the general comment must do more than merely congratulate or condemn. The idea of theme reading which governed the work of the committee on this project was not one which merely fathoms the depths of error with some standard lead and line. It instead challenges the adequacy of a uniform lead and line and disputes the accuracy of listed soundings. It invites the reader to grasp the communication as a total action and to attempt an analysis that reflects the direction and ends of its subject matter.

The *Handbook for Theme Analysis* was originally intended as a means by which teachers could improve the quality of their evaluation activities. Used either for individual study or as a basis for staff discussion, the principles of theme analysis and the accompanying themes could provide insights hitherto unrealized. However, a rather nasty question emerged. The principles demanded a thoughtful consideration of an entire theme and its interacting parts. The way themes are typically graded and returned to students provides little opportunity for students to profit from careful scrutiny of their work. Generally themes are read, assigned a grade, and returned to students with a few blue pencil hieroglyphics referring the student to a rule book. The student, more interested in the grade than anything else, may or may not seek to correct the few mechanical errors of spelling or use brought to his attention by the teacher. Rarely is the student required to reconsider his theme as a total product which has genuine strengths but also definite limitations. Using the *Handbook for Theme Analysis* as an adjunct to teaching might prove a way of rectifying this condition.

Several uniformly successful experiments were made using the *Handbook* as a teaching device. Students were given copies of the book and asked to study the principles. Then the themes themselves and their criticisms were discussed as showing how some students had succeeded or failed with respect to their assignment. In another class, analyzed themes were extracted from the book and shown on a screen by means of an opaque projector. After a discussion of the analyses, other unanalyzed themes were shown and the class was asked to make a similar critical analysis and judgment. In still another class, discussion of analyzed themes preceded asking members of the class to evaluate written work of their peers with equal thoroughness. All of these activities rested on the assumption that the act of criticism and judgment was positively related to increased ability to write effectively. In the experience of the users of the *Handbook* this assumption was warranted.

SPEECH ANALYSIS

Comments from the initial users of the *Handbook for Theme Analysis* were so uniformly favorable that the Communications Committee decided to prepare a similar work dealing with speech analysis. Again the basis for the project was the critical incident rating scale. To test the validity of the scale for speech rating, a number of student speeches were recorded on wire and played back to the committee members. However, the committee members felt that it was unrealistic to rate such speeches without being able to see the speakers, for the total presence of an individual and of his audience are essential components of whatever the rater should judge. This belief led to the preparation of a sound motion picture film of students giving speeches under classroom conditions.

One class of the third term of Written and Spoken English at Michigan State College was selected for the film. This class met several times in the college television studio to become acclimated to the apparatus and activity of such a place. During this trial period students gave speeches before the television camera but no pictures were made. Then at a time unknown to the students, kinescopic films were made of certain students giving different types of speeches. Since the speakers were unaware that they were being photographed, the resulting ten filmed speeches had an air of realism not to be found in acted speech situations. Five of these ten speeches were edited into a fifteen-minute film with an introductory statement, prefatory remarks for each speech, and camera shots of the class responding to each speaker.

The plan called for the speeches to be transcribed in a booklet and each speech to be followed by a detailed analysis of the presentation in terms of the particular assignment made. It was believed that copies of the film and the companion volume of speech evaluation and analyzed speeches could be used in ways similar to those involving the *Handbook for Theme Analysis.*

Unfortunately, the design failed because of technical difficulties. The kinescopic technique for filming student performance is excellent from the standpoint of preserving naturalness and probably can achieve the quality needed. However, in this case, the copies made from kinescopic negatives did not record either the sound or the images with sufficient fidelity for the uses anticipated. In a rather small room the sound portion emerges clear and distinct, but as volume increases to provide for rooms the size of a typical classroom, the words of the speakers become blurred and inaudible. While some of this difficulty might have been alleviated in subsequent trials, the Cooperative Study could not underwrite further effort on what promised to become a rather expensive project and one not envisaged in preparing the budget.

In spite of the technical deficiencies of the film, some members of the Communications Committee attempted to analyze the speeches as a pilot study to determine whether a more concentrated effort might be warranted. The unanimous conclusion of those who worked with the material was that there was a need for a film and handbook such as had been proposed and that, given adequate financial support, these materials could be developed.

The *Handbook for Theme Analysis* and the proposed project dealing with speech have been criticized on the ground that they were not by their nature intrinsic to general education. This point of view was based on the belief that communication activities in general education should be more closely integrated and more intimately related to student or adult life. The contention was advanced that the speeches in the film and the themes were essentially no different from student performance in more traditional speech or rhetoric courses.

To such remarks several answers are possible. It is true that the specific performances were fairly formal in their design and that viewed solely by themselves they represented nothing particularly new. To so judge them, however, would be to miss the quality which gave them validity as part of the thinking of general education. The committee members were seeking to find ways of improving teaching and evaluation of all aspects of communication. They attempted to do this by means of a single rating scale. When that technique did not prove as successful as they wished, they attempted to accomplish the same ends by other means. As a matter of fact, at one time there was considerable discussion of preparing an entire battery of devices for measuring speaking, reading, listening, and writing—all in the context of the same subject. The scheme did not materialize because of a variety of factors. However, the intention illustrates that these efforts in the fields of speaking and writing were not discrete but were interdependent. Thus, the intentions and the approach place the theme and speech analysis activities squarely within the province of general education.

In part, however, the contention is valid and must be accepted as just. In spite of course names implying a general education orientation and in spite of a few exploratory ventures such as the critical incident approach to evaluation, fairly old wine of traditional speech or rhetoric is being offered in new bottles, or perhaps even in some old bottles with new labels. The facility with which the separate theme and speech projects were accepted evidences this tie with tradition. Particularly does this become apparent as one visits communications courses. With almost no exception, much of what is being done with students in respect to writing could have been observed in college classes fifty years ago. Apparently the integrating factor for the communication skills has either not been found or is not yet being implemented, and this needs major study.

Perhaps emphasis is too much on the process of communication and not enough on the preparation for it. One possible integrating factor—the thought process, about which we shall say more in chapter x—is largely ignored in preoccupation with the characteristics of the process.

Objective Testing in the Communications Area

While the Communications Committee was exploring the idea of a coordinated battery of evaluation devices, it had occasion to review the most recent test developments in several of the participating schools. Several hundred different tests were reviewed and a few selected for recommendation because of their relevance to the objectives of the committee. These tests, which may be obtained from their parent institution, have been described briefly in Appendix II.

The Communications Committee reached the conclusion that some effort testing for a student's ability to analyze reading passages and to render mature judgments about them would be appropriate. Particularly did this appeal because inherent in it was the possibility of involving several communicative skills, a major concern of the committee.

Plans were made, however, to attempt to test, with one instrument, students' ability to do rather mature discriminating reading and to write effectively. The attempt to appraise writing effectiveness was based upon the assumption that a good judge of style and expression will be better able to express himself than will a poor one.

The test which was ultimately developed—the first version of the Test of Critical Analysis in Reading and Writing—was based upon prior work done by Dr. Paul Diederich, now of the Educational Testing Service, in preparing a test for the United States Armed Forces Institute. Part I of the test gave students three reading passages, each dealing with the subject of the good life from a somewhat different point of view. Then, by means of objective questions, students are required to demonstate a full understanding of the selections from *The Sermon on the Mount, The Rubáiyát,* and Thoreau's *Walden.* They were asked to be able to see each point of view in other contexts and to interpret various literary allusions.

The several items given below are illustrative of the kind found in the test.

1. Who is represented as the speaker in Passage III?
   1. Lincoln
   2. Jesus
   3. Thomas Aquinas
   4. Homer

2. Which of the following descriptions of *man's role in life as* conceived in these passages is most accurate?
   1. I: Man is a tool-using animal.
   2. II: Man is the master of his fate.
   3. III: Man is a child of God.

3. Which passage agrees with the thought expressed in the following quotation?

   > "Life's but a walking shadow, a poor player
   > That struts and frets his hour upon the stage,
   > And then is heard no more; it is a tale
   > Told by an idiot, full of sound and fury,
   > Signifying nothing."

   1. Passage I
   2. Passage II
   3. Passage III
   4. None of them

These items clearly indicate that the test demanded a high degree of reading ability plus an equally high level of analytical thinking. They also refute by example the often-made contention that objective-type test questions can only measure knowledge.

The second part of the test consists of a reproduction of a student analysis of the preceding three passages and questions concerning the way in which the theme was written. This portion of the test was designed to measure writing ability by means of such questions as:

In items —— to ——, assume that the student's purpose was to show that *success in work is important*.

1. In the light of this purpose, to show that success in work is portant, his review of the passage is
   1. adequate, for he covers their chief objections to regarding success in work as important.
   2. adequate, for he points out that the only fundamental objection is to dishonest success in work.

    3. inadequate, for he includes only what is relevant to his purpose.

    4. inadequate, for he neither recognizes nor refutes important objections.

2. Lines —— to ——. Which is the most accurate interpretation of what Passage I meant?

    1. People are often hurt.

    2. Workmen are injured.

    3. Investors are defrauded.

    4. Lives are used up.

RESEARCH DATA FROM THE TEST OF CRITICAL ANALYSIS IN READING AND WRITING

The test was prepared in a preliminary edition and administered in the fall of 1951 to a large number of students and again in the spring of 1953 to the same students, with a twofold purpose in mind. The first objective was to obtain evidence as to the effectiveness of the test from a technical point of view. The second purpose was to find out as much as possible about how students developed with respect to these skills over a year's period.

Making use of item analysis procedures, studies of reliability, and a variety of means for appraising validity, studies of the test revealed several important facts. (1) The test was a difficult one—almost too difficult for use with college freshmen. (2) While the items were difficult and the scores low, the test appeared to yield a significant pattern of growth when pre-test scores were compared with post-test scores. The test also appeared to be most appropriate to students in the upper levels of undergraduate college work. (3) Reliability of the test was not as high as might have been desired, although the low coefficients were explainable by the difficulty of the test and the consequent narrow range of scores. (A final form of the test was prepared which made items easier and also made use of a greater number of items.) (4) The validity of the test was studied by comparing it with other relevant mental measures, by studying gain or growth patterns of different groups of students, and by comparing test scores with relevant student behavior. The results of these studies allow a strong presumption of test validity.

After the initial testing with the instrument, the item analysis data suggested that the test was much too difficult for freshman students. Regardless of the capabilities of students taking the test, their scores were extremely low and somewhat less related to level of academic aptitude than were other Study tests. From these data members of the committee reached the conclusion that perhaps the test was so difficult that students would give up without trying on the test. In one situation, for example, a group of students was administered a four-hour battery of tests with the Critical Analysis in Reading and Writing Test given last. The same battery was given to a similar group of students with the exception that the Critical Analysis Test was given first. The group taking the Critical Analysis Test last demonstrated a marked decline in morale, and a number of students failed to finish the test. The group taking it first reacted differently, possibly because they took the test when they were considerably fresher, but there can be little doubt that many students are discouraged by the unfamiliarity and difficulty of the tasks posed for the students.

This somewhat pessimistic view toward the potentialities of the test caused a number of individuals to refrain from carrying on studies designed to show how ability in critical analysis might be affected by college classes. A few persons, however, either because of curiosity or need to employ the test, regardless of its capabilities, made further studies which, to some extent, controverted the first conclusion. A doctoral candidate working with the Critical Analysis Test in Reading and Writing, the Critical Thinking Test, and the Inventory of Beliefs demonstrated that over a year period, differences between pre- and post-test means of a large group of freshmen were highly significant at the 1 percent level of confidence.[5] He further demonstrated by analysis of variance of gains that students' academic preferences as expressed in their selected major were significantly related to differences between gains, again at the 1 percent level of confidence.

The Evaluation Office at another institution administered the Critical Analysis Test to matched groups of beginning freshmen, beginning sophomores, and seniors, and reached the conclusion

---

[5] Victor Horowitz, "A Study of Selected Interest Factors as Related to Outcomes of the Program of General Education at Michigan State College" (Unpublished doctoral dissertation, Michigan State College, 1954).

that there were statistically significant gains made on this test in the freshman year and again sometime between the end of the freshman year and the senior year. Since these were matched cases on the basis of academic aptitude rather than identical cases tested and retested with the same instrument, there could be no practice effect. Still further data were obtained. Identical students at one institution were tested at the beginning of the freshman year, the end of the freshman year, and the end of the sophomore year. The tabulation below indicates the gradual rise in these students' scores. Since these students took their formal training in communications during the first year, the gains recorded for their sophomore year are understandable.

	N	Mean	S.D.
Pre-freshmen	78	14.92	3.80
Post-freshmen	75	18.17	4.14
Post-sophomore	78	18.88	4.45

These data suggested to the committee that although the test was extremely difficult, it was assessing a kind of skill difficult to master but nonetheless valuable. The mature, deliberative sort of reading which the test seemed to demand of students represented an attempt to deal with an important outcome of general education. In addition, it provided, by its very difficulty, an instrument with which growth over a long period of time might be measured. To produce such long-term data, a test either must be quite difficult or else carefully graduated.

Committee members then attempted to adapt the rationale of the original test to a completely new instrument. In place of using the belles-lettres type of reading material in the original test, more utilitarian selections were adopted. A letter to an editor, an extract from a newspaper, another from a magazine article, and a short contemporary poem were used as the basis for forty-five reading questions. The writing aspect of the original test was eliminated. This test did not prove to be appreciably easier than the original, and the item analysis data and correlations with course grades and other tests did not prove nearly so satisfactory as for the former instrument.

In view of this failure, and in view of the approaching terminal date of the Cooperative Study, the committee was faced with the alternatives of either dropping the objective test project or revising either the original or the newer form of the test. After careful deliberation, the committee elected to modify the original test because, in the opinion of the members, this test best exemplified the sophisticated kind of reading ability which they hoped to develop in college students, although they quickly agreed that at the

TABLE 14

MEAN GAINS OF STUDENTS ON CRITICAL ANALYSIS IN READING AND WRITING TEST, CLASSIFIED ACCORDING TO PRE-TEST STANDING

COLLEGE	INITIALLY LOW GROUP		INITIALLY LOW-MIDDLE GROUP		INITIALLY MIDDLE GROUP		INITIALLY HIGH-MIDDLE GROUP		INITIALLY HIGH GROUP		TOTAL GROUP		
	Gain	N	Gain	N	Gain	N	Gain	N	Gain	N	Mean Pre-Test	Mean Gain	N
Pre-Test Range..	3–12		13–14		15–16		17–19		20–36				
1........	5.40	43	1.69	39	1.09	35	0.68	37	0.80	35	15.84	2.06	189
2........	4.15	53	1.87	45	1.11	44	1.35	49	−0.58	35	15.39	1.77	226
3........	5.65	46	2.53	49	2.05	56	1.42	48	−0.02	56	16.08	2.31	245
4........	3.24	25	−0.73	11	−0.80	5	−0.34	6	−3.57	7	13.91	0.78	54
5........	5.96	144	3.88	126	2.60	113	1.54	96	0.44	66	15.00	3.32	545
6........	4.89	28	1.41	22	0.25	20	−0.95	19	−5.50	4	14.16	1.43	93
7........	5.52	23	3.52	23	0.50	18	−0.57	21	0.79	29	16.53	2.00	114
8........	5.48	23	5.43	14	2.37	27	1.10	29	0.53	32	17.18	2.52	125
9........	7.60	5	4.00	7	2.56	9	4.18	22	1.61	33	19.83	3.08	76
Total 9 colleges	5.33	390	2.89	336	1.81	327	1.22	327	0.25	287	15.71	2.47	1,667

present time few students are given the kinds of experiences to qualify them to do this sort of reading. As has been indicated earlier, the test was again revised by changing the order of some of the items and replacing some of the more difficult items with somewhat easier ones, and lengthening the test by ten items.

Some research has been carried on with the Test of Critical Analysis in Reading and Writing which may be appropriate to report here. Table 14 presents data with respect to gains made in the test over a year period by different college groups. Each institutional group was divided into five approximately equal subgroups based upon their pre-test score on the test. The figures included in the table show the pre-test mean of each one of these five school groups and the mean gain made by each such segment. One conclusion from these data, paralleling that found elsewhere, is that the initially low groups for all schools make greater gains than the initially high groups. Since several possible interpretations of this phenomenon have been discussed in other chapters, there is no further need for analysis here except to underscore the point that Institution 5, whose students showed the highest possible gain, was an institution having an administratively independent general education program required of all students. This may be a major part of the explanation of the greater gain for these students. Another possible explanation, however, might be that that institution also maintains a full-time board of examiners who prepare tests of a nature similar to that of the Critical Analysis in Reading and Writing Test which are taken by all students in the general education program. It may be that familiarity with this type of testing could account for the differential gains made by the students from that institution.

To show how the Test of Critical Analysis in Reading and Writing related to several other tests of the Cooperative Study, Table 15 below is presented. Perhaps the most significant factor

TABLE 15

COEFFICIENTS OF CORRELATION OF THE TEST OF CRITICAL ANALYSIS IN
READING AND WRITING WITH OTHER TESTS

TEST	COEFFICIENT OF CORRELATION			NO. OF COLLEGES	NO. OF STUDENTS
	Lowest r in Any College	Highest r in Any College	Average r*		
Pre-Test					
ACE Psychological Examination..	.16	.73	.50	8	1,397
Critical Thinking, Form A.......	.17	.60	.44	8	1,397
Problems in Human Relations...	.11	.39	.27	8	1,397
Inventory of Beliefs............	.27	.45	.36	8	1,397
Post-Test					
ACE Psychological Examination..	.26	.44	.40	6	994
Critical Thinking, Form A.......	.34	.46	.41	6	994
Problems in Human Relations...	.22	.38	.30	4	430
Inventory of Beliefs............	.04	.31	.21	6	994

* Quinn McNemar, *Psychological Statistics* (New York: John Wiley & Sons, 1949), pp. 123–24.

evolving from this table is that the correlations between the Test of Critical Analysis in Reading and Writing and other intellectual measures is typically somewhat lower than similar correlations between other Study tests such as the Critical Thinking Test or the Test of Critical Thinking in Social Science. Why this should be true we are not prepared to answer, other than that it may be partly due to the lower reliability of the reading and writing test.

SUMMARY AND IMPLICATIONS

This chapter began by sketching the crucial problem facing communication people. Can communication be conceived of, taught, and evaluated as an entity, or must the separate skills continue to be regarded as discrete? The problem still exists, although the experiences of the committee may have shed some light on it, even if only to underscore its complexity.

The critical incident categories revealed some of the dimensions of communication as illustrated by what students actually did. The theme analysis principles revealed more of what teachers might look for in judging themes. The descriptions of the traits purportedly measured by various institutional tests added to the composite. Finally the specifications of the Test of Critical Analysis in Reading and Writing pointed to other facets of the communicative act.

As we lay these various aspects side by side, a pattern begins to emerge which, although it requires much empirical validation, may well be the integrative factor necessary to link all phases of communication into a meaningful whole. The basic element of communication appears to be the ability to think critically. The process of reading, writing, speaking, or listening can be described as the process of determining the existence and nature of a problem, the posing of hypotheses concerning it, and the testing of these hypotheses by various means to arrive at a conclusion. Cardinal Newman told us long ago that "Thought and speech are inseparable from each other. Matter and expression are parts of one; style is a thinking into language." Curricula designed to teach effective communication must first advance the idea that the essential need is the solving of problems—to divine what an author's meaning is —to clarify one's thought so that a problem stands clear in one's own mind prior to being communicated—to listen to what is relevant and to discard the chaff. By acceptance of such a view, differences among speech and composition teachers may be resolved.

5

OBJECTIVES IN SCIENCE

Intercollege Committee on Science Objectives: NELLY BOSMA, Wright Junior College; CHARLES F. BYERS, University of Florida; BERNARD S. CAYNE, Educational Testing Service; DONALD DECKER, Colorado State College of Education; JOHN L. GREINER, University of Florida; M. J. HARBAUGH, Kansas State College of Agriculture and Applied Science; LOUIS HEIL, Brooklyn College (Consultant); CLEMENT L. HENSHAW, Colgate University; LELAND P. JOHNSON, Drake University; COLIN H. KERR, Boston University; L. COLEMAN KNIGHT, Muskingum College; OLIVER LOUD, Antioch College; WILLIAM H. MATTHEWS, Kansas State Teachers College at Pittsburg; CLARENCE NELSON, Michigan State College; LEONA SUNDQUIST, Western Washington College of Education; WILLIAM C. VANDEVENTER, Stephens College; A. L. VAUGHAN, University of Minnesota; EARL K. WALLACE, Pennsylvania College for Women; I. EUGENE WALLEN, Oklahoma Agricultural and Mechanical College

THE OBJECTIVE particularly pertinent to the science area in general education as stated in the list of general education goals of the President's Commission on Higher Education is: "To understand the common phenomena in one's physical environment, to apply habits of scientific thought to both personal and civic problems, and to appreciate the implications of scientific discoveries for human welfare."[1]

This objective was accepted by all of the colleges as suggestive of their hopes with regard to a general education science course. However, preliminary discussions suggested that several vital concerns about evaluation problems were not resolved by the accept-

---

[1] *Higher Education for American Democracy, Vol. I—Establishing the Goals* (Washington: Government Printing Office; and New York: Harper & Bros., 1947), p. 52.

ance of this very general statement. Some of the issues raised were:

(1) Should not the phrase "knowledge of the nature and structure of science" be added to the objective? (It was not added on the grounds that this is implied by understanding and application, and that even appreciation at any level other than ingenuous fascination presupposes some knowledge.) (2) Does the objective give enough emphasis to the impact of science on our culture? (This was resolved as being a matter of interpretation of the objective.) (3) In view of this concern about the implications or the impact of science, a concern which also involves the social sciences, should not other than scientists be involved in working on this objective? (This was considered highly desirable and an attempt was made to arrange for such participation.) (4) What areas of science should be represented in the committee membership and would one committee suffice?

Perhaps the most critical question was that of the number of committees necessary. Personal visits of the Director with prospective committee members elicited some strong arguments for two separate ventures, the key point being that physical and biological science courses are commonly offered separately and by distinct teaching staffs. However, a majority felt that a composite venture should be attempted, since the objective of immediate concern transcended the usual course divisions. Also in favor of the latter plan was the expressed hope that the project might do something to encourage the interaction of all general education teachers, regardless of their instructional area. After the first meeting the sentiment was clearly for a unified science committee. Although the physical and biological science teachers occasionally divided for work on special tests, they did so as subcommittees to carry out a task decided upon by the larger committee. Not only did the two groups work well together, but there was even clear indication that this experience encouraged a considerable degree of cooperation and commonality in thinking at the local level on several campuses.

The generality of the objective accepted at the beginning of the project has been noted. The following more specific problems were suggested by the committee early in the first session:

1. Evaluation of the ability to apply science knowledge to new problems and situations.

2. Evaluation of the ability to analyze scientific data summarized in maps, tables, curves, charts, graphs.
3. Evaluation of the ability to read and evaluate news articles and popular writing on scientific developments.
4. Evaluation of the understanding of the role—importance and limitations—of science in the modern world.
5. Evaluation of the willingness to face facts, to revise judgments, and to change behavior in the light of appropriate evidence.
6. Evaluation of the understanding of the point of view with which a scientist approaches his problems and of the kinds of things that he does.
7. Evaluation of the recognition of the need for additional science knowledge in a situation, and the ability to acquire it.

The first, third, and sixth of these problems were of greatest interest and, in fact, were accepted as including most of the ideas involved in the remaining four. There was general agreement that a single project was more desirable than three, and it was also recognized that the three were not entirely independent. A happy solution was reached by accepting news articles and popular writing on science as the source of materials for testing both the ability to apply science knowledge and the ability to demonstrate understanding of the scientific point of view. Clearly, the reading and evaluation of current science material must involve the other two abilities as well as others, although the full appreciation of the interrelationship of these abilities is a continually maturing concept.

IMPORTANCE OF THE ABILITY TO READ SCIENCE ARTICLES

The case for the emphasis thus placed on reading current news articles and popular (and semipopular) writing about science involves three factors: (1) Science is constantly developing, so that the individual who does no reading may soon find his knowledge of and interest in scientific developments virtually nonexistent. (2) There are many attempts to bring science and pseudo-science to the layman in an ever-increasing barrage of various degrees of accuracy and completeness. (3) For the individual whose formal college experience in science is limited to one or two general education courses, his further contact with science will be largely through popularized versions of scientific developments.

From these considerations, it follows that the ability to read current science materials is an important outcome of a general education science course. Even so, the ability in itself is insufficient; unless the ability is used, nothing of permanent value remains. The individual who does read and evaluate science materials is constantly enhancing his education and he is also able to function more intelligently as a citizen in the ever-expanding sphere of interaction of science and other disciplines.

The viewpoint just stated was not immediately acceptable to all members of the Science Committee. Certainly it never became acceptable to all the science faculties in the cooperating colleges. Visits to campuses and discussions with individuals and groups involved in the teaching of science in the general education curriculum revealed some indifference and occasionally even active antipathy to such an objective. One typical negative comment was to the effect that with the time available there exists no alternative to placing emphasis on coverage and, even so, so many important aspects of science are omitted as to call into question the possibility of achieving a respectable grasp of science. Another type of comment was to the effect that such outcomes as those discussed above are difficult to achieve, even with majors and graduate students, and probably impossible with freshmen and sophomores. Related to this contention is the agreement that given sufficient knowledge and understanding of science, the application of it is dependent on the individual. Associated with this is the viewpoint that it may be a concern but not a responsibility of the instructor that students continue to expand their knowledge and to apply it. The most pessimistic and even disdainful thought expressed about a general education science course (by a teacher of such a course) was that students would be more gullible in their science reading because they would have a casual but inadequate acquaintance with terms and concepts, and a consequent tendency to be impressed by any statement using them. On the other side, it might be argued that the very real possibility of increased gullibility would suggest some active attention to current science materials which might counteract that effect.

THE PROBLEM OF CONTENT

In discussing the problems of evaluation and instruction, attention had to be given to the content of the science courses. On the whole, however, the nature of the objectives chosen and the emphasis of this project permitted the issue of common content to be minimized. The lack of reference to it must not be construed as a lack of concern or as a suggestion that students can learn to apply science or read science articles without knowing any science. Rather, the justification for inattention to testing of content results from: (1) a feeling that testing of science knowledge has already been extensively and reasonably satisfactorily dealt with in standardized tests; even if other such tests are needed, they are relatively easy to develop; (2) the fact that most colleges expressed themselves as being satisfied with the present testing of knowledge or were even concerned about the overemphasis accorded it; (3) the fact that the planned emphasis of the Cooperative Evaluation Study was to be on those general education objectives regarding which little effective evaluation had taken place; (4) the fact that the variety in subject matter in the various science courses would make it difficult to establish a common denominator for subject-matter testing. The lack of such a commonly acceptable body of subject matter was not regarded, however, as an obstacle for dealing with non-subject-matter objectives. It does require that the problems posed for students contain a fairly complete statement of relevant facts and avoid the more intricate subject-matter ramifications.

Underlying these considerations is the assumption that, in general education courses, the science subject matter is a tool for attaining the science-oriented objectives of general education and not an end in itself. Regarding science subject matter in this fashion is not thereby devaluing knowledge. Rather, it is a realistic recognition that with the vast and rapidly expanding knowledge available, it is unlikely that any two courses will be identical since the interests of the instructors and the students, the variations in the communities, and resources will dictate different curricular organizations. Those of utilitarian bent find that it is impossible to predict either for an individual or for the development of science generally the knowledge that will be most valuable at some later date. There exists, then, no sacrosanct body of subject matter to be covered in a science course for general education. It is to be expected that every individual who maintains contact with science will continually find that he is confronted with the necessity of increasing his store of knowledge in order to understand a new scientific development. Lacking any knowledge of science, an individual cannot read intelligently about science. Having some knowledge of the field, some grasp of the methods and viewpoint of science, and a concern about the implications of science for the present and the future of civilization, it is at least possible that he may continue contact with science with some satisfaction to himself. These considerations provided at once a justification for the importance of the objective and a detachment of it from the problem of content selection and testing.

FURTHER ELABORATION OF THE SELECTED OBJECTIVES

As a first step, members of the committee undertook to examine such sources of materials as (1) science sections of *Time, Newsweek, New York Times, Science Digest, Reader's Digest,* and the like; (2) journals such as *Scientific Monthly, Scientific American, Science, American Scientist;* (3) government and industrial bulletins; (4) popular science books, science fantasies; (5) text and reference books, histories of science, encyclopedias. The purpose was that of locating cases or excerpts which would typify the kind of material which teachers felt that students should be able to handle and which might serve as a basis for the development of a series of questions. The decision to include texts, reference books, and the like resulted from a decision to broaden the scope of possible materials, in view of the fact that timeliness or relevancy is not always a matter of being current. Coincidental with this, tests and test items were reviewed to determine the availability of items meeting the requirements of the specified objectives. Many of the excerpts collected were given to students to read and comment upon or write about. Likewise some of the objective test items were given and the nature of student responses summarized.

As the committee at its first workshop undertook to create test items, it became clear that the terminology involved in the objectives was too vague to give much aid. The necessity for a careful and detailed analysis of the kinds of activities to be expected of students in relation to the three stated objectives was recognized.

Members of the committee, with the able assistance of Dr. Louis Heil, the consultant, prepared such an analysis in outline form. The statement underwent a number of revisions and finally assumed the following form.

GUIDE FOR CONSTRUCTION OF EVALUATION ITEMS

1. *Problems*—ask a question which requires the student:
   a) to identify the problem to which the statement gives the answer and to recognize the central problem to which a number of statements are addressed.
   b) to indicate, with reasons, whether or not a given problem is stated specifically enough to begin an investigation of it to obtain an answer.
   c) to indicate whether certain nonscientific factors, such as value judgments or matters of faith, are contained in the problem, thereby making a scientific solution impossible.
2. *Information* (data, laws, and principles)—ask a question which requires the student:
   a) to recognize when the information he possesses is inadequate for a given problem.
   b) to indicate kinds of sources of information appropriate for a given problem.
   c) to evaluate the authenticity of given sources of information in relation to a given problem.
   d) to indicate his ability to apply information he possesses or has gathered to the solution of a given problem.
3. *Hypotheses*—ask a question which requires the student:
   a) to formulate or recognize hypotheses based on given data or situations.
   b) to identify the evidence necessary to judge the truth of a given deduction from a hypothesis.
   c) to formulate an experiment which will test the truth of a given hypothesis
   d) to recognize when observations or experimental data support or do not support a given hypothesis, and to what degree.
   e) to recognize assumptions involved in the formulation of a hypothesis.
4. *Conclusions*—ask a question which requires the student:
   a) to recognize the generalization(s) involved in an interpretation or conclusion.
   b) to detect the unstated assumptions involved in a conclusion.
   c) to recognize when evidence used in context is adequate for drawing a conclusion.

d) to recognize in a line of reasoning whether an observation plays the role of a premise or verifies the conclusion.

e) to recognize in a paragraph or statement proper or improper use of such reasoning as deduction, induction, citing authority, or analogy.

f) to differentiate fact and assumption in a paragraph or statement.

g) to recognize the difference between statements or interpretations based on scientific evidence and those which contain opinion.

5. *Attitudes*—ask a question which requires the student:

a) to recognize in a paragraph or statement proper or improper use of such concepts as causality, teleology, simplicity, consistency, tentative nature of truth, operationalism.

b) to assess a situation and recognize appropriate action in harmony with the nature of science and society.

The guide is, in a sense, a definition of the objectives in terms of behavior expected or desired from students. As such it has several uses. First, an article or extract thereof may be studied to determine to what extent it provides opportunities to raise questions possibly evocative of one or more of these behaviors. Although not quite envisaged as such, the guide thereby becomes a means of evaluating materials from the viewpoint of their significance for testing. Long reading passages providing opportunities for few questions are hardly justified. Materials which include too much information or discuss very explicitly points upon which questions might be raised must either be revised or discarded. Second, the guide was found to have implications for teaching. In preparation for a class, some teachers found it helpful to check through the guide with the purpose of planning how the day's work might be organized to involve the maximum of behavior of the type specified. Perhaps at this point there came an almost unanimous reaction that most of the science courses represented in the committee provided little opportunity for such behavior. Next, the decision was reached to attempt to deal simultaneously with both instructional and evaluation problems, not however without some dissenting votes from a few who felt that evaluation and research—rather than instructional methods—were the charge of the committee. Evaluation continued as the central concern, but with a continual awareness of the instructional implications.

The guide was regarded as defining one axis of a chart or grid of specifications for the development of a test. The other axis was to be a specification of subject matter or problem areas to be covered. Here some difficulty arose in that there was a natural desire for broad coverage accompanied by a recognition that real coverage of the materials commonly dealt with in physical and biological science was truly impossible. In a sense, the subject matter chosen was thought to be relatively unimportant since the abilities outlined in the guide could be equally well tested in many different contexts. Yet balance, interest, and avoidance of bias suggested some delineation of subject matter. Figure 4 illustrates one of the forms of the grid on the basis of which early tentative forms of tests were constructed. In this grid the cells are filled in with names identifying particular passages.

It was found impossible to cover the complete range of subject matter or problems suggested by this grid. An article sufficiently involved to permit testing any one of the abilities usually permitted testing of others, and economy of time in the sense of the relation of the time spent in reading to the time spent in response dictated taking full advantage of that fact. In other words, if ten to twelve items are posed on a single reading selection, it is clear that four or five selections is about the limit for a fifty-minute test.

Difficulties in communicating to science teachers not directly involved in the committee work indicated two further steps in clarifying the abilities. Illustrative items involving each of the subpoints of the guide were prepared, and several teaching units were also prepared indicating how the abilities might be involved in classroom activities. Some of the latter are to be found in the handbook *Science Reasoning and Understanding.*[2] The preparation of illustrative items made it clear that items which could be clearly and unequivocally labeled as involving a specific ability represented by the subpoints of the guide were difficult to find. This arises from the fact that the abilities themselves are highly interrelated and that different individuals may attack a given task somewhat differently.

[2] *Science Reasoning and Understanding: A Handbook for College Teachers* (Dubuque, Iowa: Wm. C. Brown Co., 1954).

PROBLEM AREAS \ SKILLS	I. Ability to recognize and state problems	II. Ability to select, analyze and evaluate information in relation to a problem	III. Ability to recognize, state and test hypotheses and other tentative explanations	IV. Ability to formulate, recognize and evaluate conclusions	V. Ability to recognize and formulate attitudes and take action after critical consideration
J. Human Behavior			(Race)		
I. Applied Science			(Synthetics)		
H. Growth, Development, and Interrelationships of Living Organisms			(Hormones)		
G. Heredity and Environment			(Rh factor)		
F. History of Earth and Life		(Hoyle-Littleton theory)			
E. Conservation		(Rain-making)			
D. Nature, Strategy, and Techniques of Science		(Antivivisection)			
C. Nature of the Universe		(Interplanetary travel)			
B. Energy	(Atomic energy and its effects)				
A. Health and Disease			(Diseases)		

FIG. 4.—Grid showing the skills and problem areas to be sampled in the Test of Science Reasoning and Understanding

The result of this was a reduction for practical purposes of the many specific abilities of the guide to the five noted on the grid. Even these were hard to distinguish at times, but the attempt to frame items dealing with five abilities or with the subpoints under them secures a better balance than would otherwise be the case.

THE SCIENTIFIC POINT OF VIEW

One other development in the attempt to make the three original abilities more specific was almost entirely the work of Dr. William C. VanDeventer, then at Stephens College, who was particularly concerned with the characteristics of or the assumptions implicit in the scientific point of view. While this list was not directly used in the development of evaluation materials, it did influence considerably the interpretation placed on the third objective. The list follows.

BASIC ASSUMPTIONS OF A SCIENTIST

1. Principle of Objectivity:
   A scientist cultivates the ability to examine facts and suspend judgment with regard to his observations, conclusions, and activities.
2. Principle of Consistency:
   A scientist assumes that the behavior of the universe is not capricious, but is describable in terms of consistent laws, such that when two sets of conditions are the same, the same consequences may be expected.
3. Principle of Tentativeness:
   A scientist does not regard his generalizations as final, but is willing to modify them if they are contradicted by new evidence.
4. Principle of Causality:
   A scientist believes that every phenomenon results from a discoverable cause.
5. Principle of Uniformity:
   A scientist believes that the forces which are now operating in the world are those which have always operated, and that the world and the universe which we see are the result of their continuous operation.
6. Principle of Simplicity:
   A scientist prefers simple and widely applicable explanations of phenomena. He attempts to reduce his view of the world to as simple terms as possible.

7. Principle of Materiality:

  A scientist prefers material and mechanical explanations of phenomena, rather than those which depend on nonmaterial and supernatural forces.

8. Principle of Dynamism:

  A scientist expects nature to be dynamic rather than static, and to show variation and change.

9. Principle of Relativeness:

  A scientist thinks of the world, and of things in it, as sets of relationships rather than as absolutes.

10. Principle of Intergradation:

  A scientist thinks in terms of continua; he distrusts sharp boundary lines, and expects to find related classes of natural phenomena grading imperceptibly into one another.

11. Principle of Practicality:

  A scientist expects that in any situation involving competition among units of varying potentialities, those which work best under existing circumstances will tend to survive and perpetuate themselves.

12. Principle of Continuous Discovery:

  A scientist hopes that it will be possible to go on learning more and more about the material world and the material universe of which it is a part, until eventually all may be understood.

13. Principle of Complementarity:

  A scientist attempts to incorporate all phenomena into a single, consistent, natural scheme, but he recognizes that contradictory generalizations may be necessary to describe different aspects of certain things as they appear to us.

14. Principle of Social Limitation:

  The social framework within which a scientist operates may determine and limit the kinds of problems on which he works, and the data which he collects, and may also influence his conclusions.

This list was developed by taking note of the various kinds of decisions made by scientists and attempting to identify the assumptions or principles on which these decisions are reached. The list is regarded by VanDeventer as tentative and probably incomplete. In its present form an interesting assignment for students can be developed by asking them to read scientific articles, historical cases, and the like and identify remarks or conclusions which involve or illustrate these principles. Although there will not be unanimity on the association of specific principles with particular passages, the experience is a significant one in helping students to understand the point of view of a scientist.

THE DEVELOPMENT OF EVALUATION INSTRUMENTS

Coincidental with the clarification of objectives, articles and extracts collected from many sources were used to formulate sample test items, and other faculty members were asked to and did contribute similar types of items. Most of these were reviewed and screened by a local committee or an individual on each campus. These were further screened, revised, and collected into trial forms of tests which were returned to the various campuses for administration to students and for collection of student reactions by oral or written comments. At this stage there was little concern that the trial forms be balanced tests, the emphasis being almost entirely on having sufficient data on the items to provide some objective evidence on difficulty and discrimination. Based on the experience of administering these trial forms to students, the following specifications were drawn up for the prospective tests:

1. Reading passages used should be current and/or of interest to students, but not of such momentary interest as to date the test. It was clear, however, that a test dealing with current writings could not be used more than two to four years without revision.

2. Reading passages should *generally* involve between 400 and 500 words and should be sufficiently rich as to be capable of providing a basis for approximately ten items per passage.

3. The appropriate number of test items of the type used for this test can be approximated by using the rate of one item per minute.

4. For really high reliability the test should be about two hours in length, but practically a test longer than fifty minutes (the usual class period) will not be used. The Science Committee chose the alternative of developing two similar forms so that one or both might be used depending on whether the primary interest lay in individual or group assessment.

5. Each reading passage should be followed by test items ranging from items requiring no knowledge other than that presented in the paragraph to items requiring the knowledge and use of principles needed for the solution to the problems.

Out of the mass of items, together with the accumulated subjective reaction of faculty and students and the statistical data from tryouts, Forms A and B of a Test of Science Reasoning and Understanding (Natural Sciences) were put together. These tests involved fifty items each and were based upon five or six reading passages. These forms were extensively used in the various colleges in the fall of 1951 and to some extent in testing the same students as sophomores in spring 1953. Data from these testings will be discussed in a later section. Revised Forms C and D were developed in the last year of the project. There is not as much data available on them as on the earlier forms; yet those data which were collected indicated the superiority of Forms C and D and resulted in the discontinuance of Forms A and B.

The makeup of Form C of the Test of Science Reasoning and Understanding is described by the grid shown in Figure 5. In this grid four points have been assigned to each of the fifty items and the points for each item have been divided among the five abilities on the basis of a committee judgment. The items dealing with the article on Chubb Crater are good examples of the abilities tested. The article itself is given first as in the test and then five of the nine items on the article are given with an indication of the ability tested, using the Roman numeral shown on the grid. Items 47, 48, 49, and 50 are not related to the article but are included as indications of the attempts made to get at the scientific point of view.

Illustrative Examples

Items 38—46 are related to the following selection.

Read the following selection carefully. It is adapted from *Time.*

The northwestern tip of Quebec, just south of Baffin Island, is flat, sodden tundra sprinkled thickly with little lakes. Most of them are irregularly shaped. But Prospector Fred W. Chubb noticed, while poring over an aerial photograph, that one lake was almost round and surrounded by a wall of rock. This week Dr. V. B. Meen, field geologist, Ontario Department of Mines, returned from a quick air visit to the lake and reported that it was almost certainly a meteorite crater (there was no lava or other sign of volcanic activity), and the biggest yet discovered. The lake in the crater is two and one-half miles across, compared with Arizona's famed meteorite crater, which is four-fifths of a mile across. Its

NATURAL SCIENCE TEST, FORM C	I Ability To Recognize and State Problems	II Ability To Select, Analyze, and Evaluate Information in Relation to Problems	III Ability To Recognize, State, and Test Hypotheses	IV Ability To Recognize, Formulate, and Evaluate Conclusions	V Ability To Recognize and Formulate Attitudes and Take Action after Critical Consideration
Item No. 1	4*				
2		2			2
3				4	
4				4	
The Introduction 5				4	
of the English 6			2	2	
Sparrow 7					4
(Ecology) 8				4	
9			3		1
10			4		
11		1		1	2
12		2		2	
Interplanetary 13				4	
Travel, 14	1	1		2	
Moore 15	1	3			
(Physics) 16		2		2	
17		3		1	
18			4		
19					4
20		4			
An Experiment 21		4			
on Putrefaction, 22				4	
Redi 23	4				
(Biology) 24					4
25					4
26				4	
27			4		
28			4		
29					4
30	4				
Cloud Seeding, 31		4			
Langmuir 32			4		
(Meteorology) 33				4	
(Chemistry) 34					4
(Physics) 35					4
36			2		2
37					4
38	4				
39		4			
40		4			
Chubb Crater 41			4		
(Meteorology) 42			4		
(Geology) 43			4		
44					4
45	2			2	
46				2	2
Scientific attitude 47					4
48					4
49					4
50					4
Totals	20	34	41	46	59

* A total of 4 points is allowed for each item. These may be either allotted to one category, or divided between two or more categories.

FIG. 5.—Grid showing the structure of the Test of Science Reasoning and Understanding, Form C

level is about 80 feet above that of other small lakes in the vicinity, and around it is a ring of shattered granite that rises 550 feet above the tundra. The rim is lowest on the northwest side, which suggests that the meteorite came from that direction and hit the ground obliquely.

Dr. Meen found no meteoric iron, only a reddish rock that might prove to be the peculiar stony material of which some meteorites are made. But there was plenty of other evidence that some enormous body had buried itself in the earth: shattered blocks of stone from football to freightcar size, and concentric circles in the granite around the crater, like ripples stirred up by a pebble dropped into still water. Dr. Meen estimated that the meteorite must have fallen at least 3,000 years ago, since there are no Indian or Eskimo legends about it. He named it Chubb Crater after the sharp-eyed prospector, and promised that a full-dress expedition would report on it within a year.

Directions: For each of the items 38—46 select the best answer, then mark the corresponding space on the answer sheet.

38. The basic problem which faces a scientist in the case of this lake is the
    1. shape of the lake.
    2. size of the lake.
    3. high elevation of the lake.
    4. origin of the lake.
    5. depth of the lake.

    (Ability I)

40. Which one of the following statements is *least* related to the basic problem?
    1. "The northwestern tip of Quebec is flat, sodden tundra, sprinkled thickly with little lakes."
    2. ". . . one lake was almost round, and surrounded by a wall of rock."
    3. "There was no lava or other sign of volcanic activity."
    4. "Its level is about 80 feet above that of other small lakes in the vicinity, and around it is a ring of shattered granite that rises 550 feet above the tundra."
    5. (There were) "concentric circles in the granite around the crater, like ripples stirred up by a pebble dropped into still water."

    (Ability II)

43. Which one of the following lines of study would probably furnish the most conclusive means of testing the idea of meteoric origin of the lake?

1. Compare the lake with other lakes in the immediate vicinity.
2. Accurately survey the lake and the territory immediately around it.
3. Look for other lakes like this lake in other parts of Quebec and Baffin Island.
4. Compare the lake in detail with known meteoric craters.
5. Determine the structure and composition of the rock found in the vicinity of the lake.

(Ability III)

46. According to some theories of the origin of the solar system, the earth and moon and other planets and their moons were formed at one stage by a process in which the larger fragments picked up the smaller ones as they all traveled around the sun. According to this the present occurrence of meteorites on earth is merely a vestige of the much greater bombardment which took place in earlier days. Following out this idea

1. the moon is now being bombarded as the earth was in its early history.
2. the moon's surface has retained the effects of early bombardment.
3. the role played by meteorites in the formation of the moon is not the same as in the formation of the earth.
4. the chances of a large meteorite striking the moon are considerably greater than of one striking the earth.
5. large meteorites strike the earth now only in remote, uninhabited places.

(Abilities III and IV)

According to your understanding of the scientific point of view, mark space

1—if the statement is warranted.
2—if the statement is in conflict with the scientific point of view.
3—if the statement is neither in agreement nor in conflict with the scientific point of view.

47. In spite of what he may write, a scientist does not really want criticism of his careful procedures.

48. A scientist reads carefully the results of the experiments reported by other scientists so that he can design an experiment that avoids some of their errors.

49. A scientist thinks of the laws of nature as decreed by a divine intelligence.

50. A scientist assumes that scientific laws are no more than descriptions of relationships in natural processes.

Item 47 might be regarded as involving the Principles of Objectivity and Tentativeness; item 48, the Principle of Continuous Discovery; item 49, the Principles of Materiality and Causality; and item 50, the Principles of Consistency, Causality, and Relativeness.

The Physical and Biological Science Tests

In addition to the natural science forms of the Test of Science Reasoning and Understanding, a physical science and a biological science form were also prepared. These differ from the natural science form in two ways: first, as the titles imply, the material is restricted to either the physical or biological science and, second, the level of difficulty, primarily in terms of the amount of knowledge of the field required, is greater. The abilities tested are the same and, in fact, many of the items used in the physical and biological science forms are used also in the natural science form. The special forms are somewhat more appropriate for use in courses restricted to one area of science. One difficulty faced in making such tests is that the distinctions between biological and physical science are more easily maintained in the development of courses than in current articles, many of which report on research bridging, either in purposes or in methods used, the gulf between the physical and the biological sciences. Despite the interest in and the effort put forth to develop the special forms of the tests, relatively little use of these was made by participants in the Study. Perhaps the best case for their use can be made in a situation where the teacher of a science course restricted to one of the science fields wishes to use a test to explore the abilities involved and feels that student motivation will be higher if the test is more specifically related to the course. It has been found that students exposed only to physical science and to little direct training in the abilities involved in these tests react against biological science articles as "having no relationship to the course."

Concern about Non-objective Materials

We have noted that, very early in the project, members of the committee became concerned with the problem of teaching. Only a person or two dissented from the point of view that to the extent that evaluation-oriented activity suggested new techniques of instruction, these should be explored and systematized. This concern about instruction ultimately resulted in the development of the handbook entitled *Science Reasoning and Understanding: A Handbook for College Teachers,* already mentioned. This handbook describes the Guide for Construction of Evaluation Items,[3] indicates ways of using textbook material to teach to these ends, and suggests some special teaching methods found valuable by members of the committee. Other sections of the handbook discuss sources and the selection and modification of current materials for testing and instructional purposes. The use of essays in both testing and in instruction is discussed at length in one section. The utility and the purposes of essay testing were of particular concern to the committee, first, because some of the weaknesses of objective testing were fully appreciated and, second, because there was an awareness that complete preoccupation with objective materials would very likely prejudice others against the work of the committee. The committee was concerned with essay materials in several ways:

1. *As a testing device.* No direct attack was made on this problem, but examples of superior practices were collected. There are also numerous implications for essay testing resulting from the attempts to validate objective test items by essay questions.

2. *As a teaching device.* The handbook, *Science Reasoning and Understanding,* deals with this problem.

3. *As a means of developing objective test items.* This use has already been noted in mentioning the possibility of written responses being requested to the stem of an item for which no alternative responses are listed.

4. *As a means of validating objective testing procedures.* This will be discussed as a portion of the evidence on the validity of the Test of Science Reasoning and Understanding.

[3] See pp. 108–9.

The Survey of the Use of Essay Materials

The committee undertook to survey science teachers to see in what ways essay material was actually used in science classes. In addition to the routine and well-known procedures, the following additional uses were suggested:

1. Have the student read a description as to how one scientific problem was solved and give examples of inductive steps, deductive steps, and hypotheses that were formed. The student is asked to make comparisons with other problems studied both as to purpose and general method. He is asked to give his opinion as to what would have happened to the experiment in its early stages had certain errors crept into the investigation.

2. The student is asked to write an essay in which he is to present a convincing argument supporting the validity of a certain hypothesis.

3. Another technique involves allowing cooperative effort on the part of students in writing an examination. The essay question is presented in the laboratory. Two students, four students, or the whole class may collaborate in arriving at an answer to the question. It is possible that a minority answer may be presented. Each individual writes up his own answer after the statement of the answer has been agreed upon by the group. The ideal group for this kind of examination consists of four students.

4. Essay tests are used to motivate students to cut through a lot of subject matter in order to crystallize the point of a problem, a controversy, or a process. Essays are sometimes read in class. This is done to bring out such matters as inaccuracies of analysis and thought, hazy and inadequate statements that do not come to grips with the point at issue, or questions that are implied but left unstated. Essay tests are better used for these purposes than simply to cover particular topics, chapters, and pages in a book.

5. Students are asked to write extensive papers, one at the end of the first semester, one about midway through their college career, and one just before graduation on topics that necessitate the drawing of information from all of the areas of general education. These papers are then graded by representatives of the various areas.

6. A daily report is asked for, written on the form outlined below:

Name ....
Date of Class Experience ....
Summarize the class experience *briefly:*
(*one-half page*)
Evaluate the class experience in terms of your own thinking.
(*one-half page plus back of sheet*)

The class experience reports are collected daily from the members of the group. They are scored and returned to the students.

7. The student is required to read an article. Later he is presented with several paragraphs from the same article and a quiz that has been formulated on these paragraphs based on the guide. Each item of the quiz is so constructed that an answer can be given in one or two complete sentences and only that much room is allotted for the answer.

8. A topic that is considered "top news" in the natural science area is kept before the group. This is done all through a semester, not necessarily as an assignment but as material for discussion. Near the end of the semester each student is supplied with a summary of the articles from which material was drawn for discussion. The students are allowed several days to study the material. Then they are given an essay-type examination built around the following skills: ability to recognize and state problems; ability to select, analyze, and evaluate information in relation to problems; ability to recognize, formulate, and evaluate conclusions.

The handbook, *Science Reasoning and Understanding*, includes several detailed examples of types of essay material too lengthy to include here, but the following questions indicate one form of essay question used by a number of teachers:

An intergalactic voyager reports that there exist in another universe 26 unknown elements symbolically denoted by the letters of the alphabet, A–Z. Their relative weights are given below:

A	B	C	D	E	F	G	H	I	J	K	L	M	N	O	P	Q	R	S	T	U	V	W	X	Y	Z
1	3	13	5	15	25	7	17	9	19	29	39	49	11	31	51	61	23	33	43	53	63	35	45	47	59

It was also found that these 26 elements could be classified into 6 different groups according to their chemical and physical properties as follows:

Group I	Active gases	A, C, F, M, Q
Group II	Liquids	B, E, L, P, V
Group III	Metal solids	D, H, K, U
Group IV	Transition solids	G, J, O, T
Group V	Non-metal solids	I, S, X
Group VI	Inert gases	N, R, W, Y, Z

(a) How many new elements of weight less than 63 can you predict might be found? Explain the reasoning you use to get your answer.

[2″ space]

(b) What do you predict the weights of these new elements to be?

[1½″ space]

(c) Indicate the group to which each of these predicted elements might be assigned.

[2″ space]

An Essay Approach to Validation

The following questions are from forms developed for validation purposes but have possibilities for general usage. The selection used in the first illustration (see below) is one that was taken directly from the objective test. It would also be possible to ask for an essay on the passage without structuring the response by a series of questions, but considerably less will be elicited from most students.

> At a temperature of 0° Centigrade and standard barometric pressure there are about 27,000,000,000,000,000,000 molecules in one cubic centimeter of air. These molecules are in constant motion, and have an average velocity of about one-quarter of a mile per second. This is slightly greater than the speed of sound. Under these conditions the distance traveled by a molecule before it strikes another is eight millionths of a centimeter.
>
> In interstellar space a molecule is believed to travel about 50 billion miles before it collides with another. Each molecule in space collides with another on the average of about once a year.

Questions

18. What is your opinion of the reasonableness of the numerical values given in the passage? What is the basis for your opinion?
19. What kind of reasoning would a scientist use to arrive at the statements made in the passage?
20. The numerical values given in the passage are too large or small to be measured directly. Does the scientist just assume they are true and let it go at that, or what?
21. If the passage is taken as true, what can be deduced concerning the distance a molecule moves between collisions in comparison with its size?
22. Would you say that the region between the earth and the sun is a vacuum? Explain.

The following questions do not depend on the preceding selection.

23. Does the scientist think that laws of nature cause and/or govern natural processes? Explain.
24. What do you think of the statement, "A scientist conceives his task to be that of finding laws that fit with his already established view of the world"?
25. Does the scientist expect that a new natural law will emerge from each new experiment that he undertakes? Explain.

RESEARCH ASPECTS OF THE PROJECT

Reliability

The reliability of the Forms C and D of the Test of Science Reasoning and Understanding was computed for entering freshman groups in a number of colleges. Reliabilities computed by the Kuder-Richardson Formula No. 20 were found consistently to be in the range .80 to .85. Since the test was planned for group measurement rather than for individual use, these coefficients are satisfactory. If both Forms C and D were administered—requiring 100 minutes of actual testing time—the estimated reliability for the total, by the Spearman-Brown formula, is about .90.

The careful review of items, and the revision of the tests on the basis of evidence of item difficulty and discrimination ensures a high degree of internal consistency in the test. This is related to both validity and reliability. Since evidence on the quality of the items is included in the test manual, we shall not repeat it, but simply expect that this is indirectly reflected in other evidence about the test.

Validity

There is no completely satisfactory answer to the issue of validity for tests of this type under discussion. A priori, logical, or face validity is possessed in a great measure because of the sequence of steps involved in the development of the test. The materials or selections used are those agreed upon as being ones students should be able to read; the abilities tested are those agreed upon by a group of teachers as being important abilities to develop. The case for validity rests on these judgments, but further investigations were carried on to reinforce them.

Three questions were raised: (1) Do the abilities selected really describe what competent individuals do in reading scientific articles? (2) Does the student who rates high on the ability as measured by the test actually read science articles extensively? (3) How is ability to respond on an objective test about an article related to ability to react orally or in essay form to the same or similar articles?

The first question was deemed to have an affirmative answer simply because of the techniques used in developing the tests. The second question proceeds beyond the immediate matter of validation of a test to the habits, interests, or attitudes possessed by or inculcated in the person. The concern with validity is with whether the test reveals the extent to which a person has the abilities rather than with his habit of using them. This is not a denial of the importance of such habits or of their relevance as general education outcomes, but the abilities do have to be learned before they can be used and become habitual.

A considerable amount of evidence relevant to validity was collected by essay techniques. Directed written questions of the type exemplified on page 123 were prepared for all the passages used in the objective test. These were arranged in groups which could be answered in one or two hours. The first approach using this procedure involved: (1) giving the essay test followed by giving the objective test; (2) scoring the written test, each question being judged by two raters on a 0, 1, 2, 3 basis and total scores of the two raters checked; (3) scores on the written test were then correlated with the corresponding questions and with the total score on the objective test.

The second approach, using free response essays (no questions posed), was to be treated essentially the same way, but called for somewhat more specific instructions in rating. In practice, these free responses by students were so abbreviated and crude that no one carried out this particular type of validation. Table 16 exhibits typical results showing the range of correlations found between the objective test and structured essay responses. In this table, A and B refer to the earlier forms of the objective test, while C, D, E, and F refer to the essay questions. Each set of these covered approximately one-half of the items found in the respective objective test, C and D being associated with Forms A and E, and F with Form B. In each case the essay scores are correlated with the total score on the objective test.

These correlations are reasonably good for this type of material, and suggest considerable correspondence between the two techniques. The unreliability in both scores undoubtedly results in a

TABLE 16

COEFFICIENTS OF CORRELATION BETWEEN THE OBJECTIVE AND ESSAY FORMS OF THE TEST OF SCIENCE REASONING AND UNDERSTANDING

Institution No.	N	Forms Correlated		Correlation
		Objective	Essay	
1	42	A	C	.50
2	34	A	C	.54
3	33	A	C	.50
4	15	A	C	.38
4	18	A	D	.29
4	18	B	E	.68
4	14	B	F	.64
5	17	B	E	.26
5	19	B	E	.62

lower correlation, and the true correlation might run as high as .70 to .80. Since the essay approach definitely involves an element of originality and skill in writing which are not involved in the objective test, a higher relationship could hardly be expected.

Correlations with Other Tests

The correlations of a test with other related instruments tell something of its nature. Table 17 exhibits data of this type. The ACE Psychological Examination was administered only in the fall, so that the post-test correlations are probably lower simply because of the interval between testings.

In Table 18 there are no startling results. There is little reason to believe from the results that the test is simply a test of reading ability or of intelligence—some individuals feared or predicted such a result from the approach used. The biological science final examination (item 6 in Table 18) was a semester examination involving an independent attempt to measure some of the objectives covered by the Test of Science Reasoning and Understanding. The non-general education grades in item 8 of Table 18 are heavily loaded with science courses, whereas for general education grades,

TABLE 17

COEFFICIENTS OF CORRELATION OF TEST OF SCIENCE REASONING
AND UNDERSTANDING WITH RELATED TESTS

TEST	CORRELATION COEFFICIENT			NO. OF COLLEGES	NO. OF STUDENTS
	Lowest	Highest	Mean		
	Pre-Test				
ACE Psychological Examination..	.27	.74	.56	8	1,010
Critical Analysis in Reading and Writing...................	.29	.58	.48	5	592
Critical Thinking, Form A.......	.20	.74	.54	8	1,010
	Post-Test				
ACE Psychological Examination..	.37	.62	.42	5	864
Critical Analysis in Reading and Writing...................	.28	.49	.42	3	602
Critical Thinking, Form A.......	.50	.70	.53	5	864

TABLE 18

MISCELLANEOUS CORRELATIONS OF THE TEST OF SCIENCE
REASONING AND UNDERSTANDING WITH OTHER FACTORS

FACTOR	DESCRIPTION OF GROUP	N	CORRELATION	
			For Men	For Women
1. ACE Psychological Examination	Entering freshmen in large state university			
Q score.............		439	.36	.33
L score.............		439	.60	.51
T score.............		439	.58	.50
2. CEEB Scholastic Aptitude Test	Entering freshmen in private university for men	352	.46	
3. CEEB Scholastic Aptitude Test	End-of-year freshmen in private university for men (essentially same group as in 2)	315	.60	
4. Cooperative Reading Test	Entering freshmen in private university for men	341	.57	
5. Nelson-Denny Reading Test	Entering freshmen in private college for women	137		.35
6. Biological science final examination	End-of-year freshmen in private college for women	89		.72
7. General education grades	Juniors and seniors in large state university (science majors)	42	.35 (men and women)	
8. Non-general education grades	Ditto	42	.56 (men and women)	

science approximates one-fifth of the general education work taken. These data are consistent with expectations.

Gains over the Freshman Year

As was generally true with all tests, the use of the Test of Science Reasoning and Understanding in pre-testing was far more extensive than in post-testing. Good intentions were all too frequently defeated by the difficulties involved in scheduling. Form A was extensively used over a one-year period with freshmen, and the gains made over the period are summarized in Table 19. This form

TABLE 19

MEAN GAINS FOR STUDENTS ON TEST OF SCIENCE REASONING AND UNDERSTANDING, FORM A, CLASSIFIED ACCORDING TO PRE-TEST STANDING

COLLEGE	INITIALLY LOW GROUP		INITIALLY LOW-MIDDLE GROUP		INITIALLY MIDDLE GROUP		INITIALLY HIGH-MIDDLE GROUP		INITIALLY HIGH GROUP		TOTAL GROUP		
	Gain	N	Gain	N	Gain	N	Gain	N	Gain	N	Mean Pre-Test	Mean Gain	N
Pre-Test Range...	6–19		20–22		23–25		26–28		29–39				
5........	11.08	12	6.74	23	4.19	32	3.33	21	0.89	56	26.90	3.76	144
6........	4.86	7	5.83	12	−0.10	10	2.82	11	−0.07	14	24.96	2.46	54
10........	5.94	16	6.20	5	3.75	8	2.67	9	0.43	7	22.40	4.07	45
12........	10.28	32	6.44	32	5.62	42	4.34	41	1.31	36	24.27	5.44	183
13........	4.19	90	2.63	49	−0.57	49	−1.09	46	−2.04	27	22.03	1.43	261
16........	7.05	19	6.76	21	4.54	26	2.69	13	0.29	24	24.12	4.23	103
Total 6 colleges..	6.26	176	5.16	142	2.93	167	2.04	141	0.31	164	23.92	3.37	790

of summary was chosen after several initial ventures indicated that these gains, like those found for other study tests, were correlated negatively with initial status. Variation in the academic aptitude tests used precluded adjustment based on this type of evidence. Statistical adjustment of post-test scores on the basis of pre-test scores was done by covariance analysis, but the procedure was open to some question because of the nature of the data, and the results were less understandable to teachers than the descriptive approach of Table 19.

In order to arrive at this table, all pre-test scores in colleges contributing forty-five or more pre- and post-test scores for the same students were thrown into a single distribution which was then divided as nearly as possible into five equal groups. The students for each college were then sorted into these groups. The nature of the distribution of the students among these groups for a given college reflects the ability level of the students entering that college. At the same time it is possible to compare any particular group in one institution with the corresponding group in another, since the pre-test means are essentially the same. The general pattern of decreasing gain with higher pre-test scores is apparent. The total group gains for most of the colleges represented are statistically significant, although they are not large numerically.

Institutions 5 and 10 have particularly interesting results. College 5 is a liberal arts college with a rather highly selected student body, while College 12 is a large state institution. Both show rather large gains for the low, low-middle, and middle groups. The more selective institution is no more successful with its very able students (gain of .89) than the state institution (gain of 1.31). College 13, heavily weighted with initially low students, shows only moderate gains (4.19) for this low group and the more able students actually lose ground. The variation in the gains suggests that general education programs do differ in the extent to which they promote change in the abilities measured by this test. Whether those differences are due to differences in emphasis, to quality of instruction, to the nature of the science courses, other factors, or a complex of many of them, it is impossible to say. It did appear that those institutions wherein the larger gains were registered were ones in which the class assignments and the laboratory provided experience more obviously related to the objectives than was true in the other colleges. Reading and analysis of science materials, exercises specially prepared with something very like the pattern of abilities of the Test of Science Reasoning and Understanding, and tests requiring these abilities, were more apt to be a part of the regular instructional program of those colleges making the larger gains.

It is significant that in the institution in which the largest gain was recorded, the Test of Science Reasoning and Understanding was regarded as so closely related to the objectives of the course that it was used as one-half the final examination. Furthermore, there was no comment from the students, who could not distinguish between this and other test materials developed specifically for the course.

In Table 20 are shown mean gains for subgroups determined by both ability (ACE Psychological Examination) and pre-test score on the Test of Science Reasoning and Understanding. It is evident from this, once again, that students low on pre-test make the largest gains, and it is also evident that the combination of low pre-test with high ability yields the largest gains. More significant, perhaps, is the fact that, except for one classification of high ability and high pre-test, the gains for students whose ability ranking equals or exceeds the pre-test status, are rather sizable. Small gains are largely characteristic of those whose pre-test rankings are higher than the ability level rankings.

TABLE 20

MEAN GAINS OF STUDENTS ON TEST OF SCIENCE REASONING AND UNDERSTANDING, FORM A, POST-TEST, CLASSIFIED ACCORDING TO QUARTILE RANK ON THE ACE PSYCHOLOGICAL EXAMINATION AND THE TEST OF SCIENCE REASONING AND UNDERSTANDING, FORM A, PRE-TEST

ACE PSYCHOLOGICAL EXAMINATION QUARTILE RANK	QUARTILE RANK ON TEST OF SCIENCE REASONING AND UNDERSTANDING, A, PRE-TEST								TOTAL	
	First (low)		Second		Third		Fourth			
	Gain	N	Gain	N	Gain	N	Gain	N	Gain	N
First (low)....	8.62	26	5.29	17	4.75	12	−1.00	6	5.98	61
Second.......	8.88	17	5.38	16	2.56	16	2.67	12	5.08	61
Third........	11.67	15	7.62	16	6.94	18	−1.00	11	6.85	60
Fourth.......	12.00	3	8.00	12	5.57	14	3.84	32	5.46	61
Total group...	9.61	61	6.46	61	5.02	60	2.26	61	5.84	243

Gains Related to Type and Amount of Science Taken

Study No. 1.—In one of the colleges, the freshmen were divided into groups according to the general education courses carried during the freshman year. The freshmen who took Form C of the Test of Science Reasoning and Understanding as a post-test in January 1953 were separated into five groups depending upon what general education courses they were enrolled in. The performance of these groups is described in Table 21.

To find whether these different gains could be attributed to the different course experiences rather than to the random variations in average ability of the groups, a statistical study by the analysis of covariance method was made. Based on the correlations between CEEB Scholastic Aptitude scores, Natural Science pre-test and

TABLE 21

GAINS ON TEST OF SCIENCE REASONING AND UNDERSTANDING (FORM C)
IN FIVE CORE COURSES IN A FRESHMAN CLASS

GROUP	PROGRAM	N	MEAN SCORES		GAIN	IMPROVE-MENT INDEX
			Pre-Test	Post-Test		
1	Physical science only........	17	26.2	31.8	5.8	+ .28
2	Biological science only......	9	26.9	28.4	1.5	−1.27
3	Social science only..........	99	27.5	30.4	2.9	− .23
4	1 and 3...................	78	25.8	31.0	5.2	+ .37
5	2 and 3...................	86	24.8	32.4	7.6	+ .03

post-test scores, a predicted mean for each group was calculated. The results indicate that the differences in the groups would occur by chance more often than once in twenty times, perhaps once in seven or eight. Hence there is no strong evidence that success in Natural Science, Form C, is significantly affected by any of these course combinations, although physical science alone or in combination with social science did produce somewhat better results.

Study No. 2.—At one university, comparisons were made for groups taking various science courses and no science at all. Adjusted mean scores were determined and used in the comparisons. These results, shown in Table 22, indicate that students taking either of the available general education science courses attained gains over a year which are greater than those for students taking no science or a science course for prospective teachers.

Study No. 3.—In another college, students with both pre- and post-test scores were divided into groups on the basis of the amount of science taken. Those with no science showed a mean gain of 1 point over the year, those with 9 to 18 credits in biological science

TABLE 22

COMPARATIVE ANALYSES OF ACHIEVEMENT ON THE TEST OF SCIENCE
REASONING AND UNDERSTANDING*

Students Enrolled in	Mean Pre-Test Score	Adjusted Mean Post-Test Score
Biological science 1 and 2....................	22.42	25.88†
Physical science 1 and 2....................	27.47	26.12†
General science 1 and 2....................	20.33	24.78
No science.................................	23.78	24.13
Mean for all students.......................	23.77	...

* Donald G. Wallace, "A Report of the Drake Evaluation Study in General Education" (Mimeographed; Drake University, Des Moines, Iowa, 1953).
† Significant at .01 level.

and 5 credits in physical science had a mean gain of 4.5. With one exception, there was a gradual increase in mean gain with the amount of science taken.

Study No. 4.—From Brooklyn College, Heil reported that the Test of Science Reasoning and Understanding was used as one of several instruments for comparing students in an experimental general education program with those in the regular program. For students in the two programs matched on entrance qualifications, high school attended, sex, and major field, results at the end of the sophomore year were favorable to the experimental program although the differences were not statistically significant.

Study No. 5.—One of the larger group gains reported was for 199 students enrolled in a general education science course for one semester. The emphasis in instruction was related closely to the objectives involved in the test. The mean gain on the Physical Science form of the Test of Science Reasoning and Understanding for the entire group was 7.66, with the mean gains of the eight classes involved ranging from 5.2 to 9.6. Considerable interest is aroused by the fact that the largest gain, 9.6, was obtained with a class of 28 students selected from the top 10 percent of the freshman class by use of the CEEB Scholastic Aptitude Test. The mean pre-test score of the class was about 6 score points above the other classes. This is the one case where a superior group made the largest gains. It is to be noted that they were in a special section taught by an instructor very active in the work of the Science Committee of the Cooperative Study.

Study No. 6.—In another investigation 160 students were pretested and post-tested over one semester of a physical science course. A mean gain of 5.1 was found. Interest attached to the fact that those taking simultaneously a course in practical logic demonstrated no greater gain than those not taking that course; this finding suggests that the transfer value of a course in logic may not be very great.

Study No. 7.—At one college the Test of Science Reasoning and Understanding in Physical and Biological Science was used with both the biological and physical science courses over the same year period. Both groups made significant gains on both tests, but the gain made in each course on the test related to that area was significantly higher than that in the other course. The indication is clearly that achievement of the objectives of science reasoning and understanding involve both knowledge of or familiarity with the material and ability to reason in it.

Test Performance Related to Number of Years in College

Study No. 8.—Table 23 shows for three colleges the retesting results at one- and two-year intervals. The same students were retested at the two-year interval and the one-year results are based on a subgroup of these same students. The pattern here, found in

TABLE 23

ONE- AND TWO-YEAR TEST RESULTS FOR SCIENCE REASONING
AND UNDERSTANDING TEST, FORM A

COLLEGE	PRE-TEST			ONE YEAR LATER			TWO YEARS LATER		
	N	Mean	S.D.	N	Mean	S.D.	N	Mean	S.D.
A	79	23.72	5.34	55	28.78	5.47	79	29.95	5.48
B	64	22.75	5.77	switched forms			64	28.28	5.32
C	66	24.47	4.59	66	28.77	4.86	66	29.36	6.19

other cases also, is a gain of 4 to 5 raw score points the first year, followed by a smaller gain the second year. Partly this reflects the tendency to take general education science courses in the freshman year, but it was still true to a lesser degree where science was continued for two years, thus bearing out the tendency for higher pre-test scores to be associated with smaller gains.

Study No. 9.—At another college, freshman and senior women were matched in terms of ability on the ACE Psychological Examination and the performance on the Test of Science Reasoning and Understanding. These data are shown in Table 24.

The seniors had taken a minimum of two general education science courses during the preceding four years. The difference in

TABLE 24

PERFORMANCE OF MATCHED GROUPS ON THE TEST OF
SCIENCE REASONING AND UNDERSTANDING, FORM A

Group Tested	Mean	S.D.
101 entering freshmen*	24.98	4.59
101 seniors†	31.00	5.52

* Tested September 1951.
† Tested February 1952.

means is approximately 6 points and indicates a real improvement. A similar investigation with another matched group yielded a difference in means of 7 points.

Results of Experimental Studies

Tables 25, 26, and 27 show the results of studies comparing science classes wherein the objectives involved in the Test of Science Reasoning and Understanding were emphasized with classes in which no overt attention was given to these objectives. These investigations were arranged by committee members to see whether their newly developed ideas about instruction would result in any greater change in students.

In most of these comparisons the gain for the general education course in which the instructor gave special attention to the objectives was larger than for the non-general education courses or for the general education courses with a primarily content emphasis. However, in Table 26 a class in zoology shows an adjusted post-test mean rather close to that of the general education biology course. In Table 27 a physical science course which supposedly gave no

TABLE 25
ONE-SEMESTER GAINS ON THE TEST OF SCIENCE REASONING AND UNDERSTANDING, FORM A, IN A STATE TEACHERS COLLEGE

Group Tested	N	Pre-Test		Post-Test		Adjusted Post-Test Mean
		Mean	S.D.	Mean	S.D.	
Physical science course*....	55	28.1	5.9	30.4	6.1	29.5
Biological science course†...	32	24.9	7.9	23.6	7.4	25.1

* A general education course with special emphasis on the scientific method.
† A general education course.

TABLE 26
ONE-SEMESTER GAINS ON THE TEST OF SCIENCE REASONING AND UNDERSTANDING, FORM A, IN A STATE COLLEGE

Group Tested	N	Pre-Test		Post-Test		Adjusted Post-Test Mean
		Mean	S.D.	Mean	S.D.	
Biology*.................	208	29.0	7.4	31.1	7.0	29.5
Botany..................	88	24.5	6.4	25.5	6.9	26.8
Zoology.................	103	29.3	5.3	30.7	5.8	28.9
Chemistry...............	287	24.4	6.6	25.2	7.0	26.5

* A general education course with emphasis on scientific method.

TABLE 27

One-Year Gains on the Test of Science Reasoning
and Understanding, Form A, in a Junior College

Group Tested	N	Pre-Test		Post-Test		Adjusted Post-Test Mean
		Mean	S.D.	Mean	S.D.	
Biological Science 101*.....	86	22.6	6.4	27.1	6.6	29.7
Biological Science 111*.....	72	25.2	7.2	28.6	7.1	29.0
Physical Science 101†......	37	26.1	6.1	28.6	6.3	29.0
Chemistry 201............	50	25.5	6.1	28.8	6.1	28.7
Physical Science 101†......	31	25.2	6.1	28.6	6.4	27.8
Chemistry 201............	30	26.7	8.8	30.5	6.9	27.5
Biological Science 111†.....	32	27.1	5.7	28.1	7.2	26.9
Biological Science 101†.....	64	26.6	7.7	28.2	7.0	26.4

* A general education course with emphasis on scientific method.
† A general education course.

unusual attention to objectives of the Test of Science Reasoning and Understanding and a chemistry course produced gains comparing rather favorably with courses attempting special emphasis on the objectives of the Test of Science Reasoning and Understanding.

The techniques used by the teachers of the experimental sections reported on in these tables varied considerably. The teacher of the physical science course in Table 25 regularly used current science articles as part of the class work. These articles were read, analyzed in small groups, and issues resolved by experiment or by use of reference material. Extensive use was also made of exercises in which attention was focused on the abilities defined in the Guide for Construction of Evaluation Items (see pages 108–9).

In the course in biology in Table 26 the abilities in the guide were discussed with students; also illustrative exercises and reading passages were used to develop an awareness and understanding of them. In recitation and discussion students were continually pushed to relate their thinking to the problem recognition, information seeking, hypothesis formation, conclusion checking, and attitude awareness developed in the guide.

The extent of attention to the scientific method in other experimental work was not reported in detail, and it apparently varied considerably from instructor to instructor. The lack of control of the instructor variable in all of these comparisons is quite obviously a major weakness, but one over which the central office of the Study had no control.

In an entirely independent study, Perlman investigated the relative effectiveness of three different methods of teaching scientific thinking. His results, like some reported here, were rather inconclusive, although apparent differences seemed to favor the use of contemporary problem material in the laboratory. More to the point here, however, are some of Perlman's summary implications. After remarking that his results provide "Further indications here that scientific thinking and scientific approach to problems can be learned through direct classroom planning and procedures for the purpose," he points out that there are innumerable variations of the instructional approaches used. He further recommends the need for studies "in which not only the laboratory periods, but all class activities emphasize problem-solving processes." He also raises the question, "To what extent can a single course or section of a course with emphasis on scientific thinking and procedures among other things, overcome habits of many years of past school experience of students based upon processes that involve essentially memorization and recall?"[4] These remarks of Perlman are much to the point and emphasize issues raised by various experimental studies in this project.

CONCLUSIONS AND IMPLICATIONS

From the rather heterogeneous studies and data, even though only partially reported here, it would be rash to draw more than tentative conclusions. Such data as bear on the point confirm the committee judgment that the Test of Science Reasoning and Understanding measures more than reading skill or intelligence. Clearly those students who took science courses made greater gains than those who did not, and those who took more science tended to gain more than those who took but one course. In those cases where a valid comparison could be made between a general education science course and other science courses, the advantage lay with the general education course, although the differences were not large. Some results suggested that students with a combination of specialized and general education science made larger gains than

---

[4] James S. Perlman, "An Historical vs. Contemporary Problem Solving Use of the College Physical Science Laboratory Period of General Education," *The Journal of Experimental Education*, March 1953, pp. 251–57.

those taking either type exclusively. More striking, perhaps, is the marked variation in the gains found in different colleges with markedly different programs. In some colleges, even after allowance is made for the level of student ability, the gains made are relatively small compared with other colleges. It also seems reasonable to conclude that most science programs could achieve more in regard to these abilities than is currently the case. Observations in visiting science classes on some of the campuses and in talking with teachers, buttressed by the judgment of the Science Committee members, suggest that in most programs little more than lip service is paid to the objectives. Even in the classes where definite attempts were made to teach for scientific reasoning and understanding, the new instructional practices must be regarded as exploratory and sometimes rather superficial. It is quite conceivable, therefore, that the largest gain recorded in our findings is not indicative of the possible gain.

Mean gains of 5 to 10 points on the test may seem rather trivial and be taken either as an indication that the test is unsatisfactory or that little has been or can be done about such objectives. In rebuttal it should be noted that 5 to 10 points is 10 to 20 percent of the maximum test score of 50 points, which is a respectable gain even for broadly conceived achievement tests. Only in highly specific factual examinations based on materials actually covered are greater gains recorded, and usually there is a marked loss in such specific knowledge within a few months after completion of the course unless study is continued in that same area. The gains on such objectives as those studied here must be much more nearly those recorded in similar periods for improvement in reading and writing. Such abilities develop slowly under even the best of instruction.

The results of the testing and research side of the science venture are summarized in the following points: (1) Four forms of a promising new instrument for measuring certain general education outcomes have been made available; (2) such data as have been collected by use of this instrument in a number of general education programs indicate that some progress is made by students in regard to the abilities measured; (3) there is considerable variation in the kind of results obtained in the various programs and there is some indication that the amount of success is due to the attention given to the objectives.

The implications of the project on the instructional side may have more long-range value than the activity supposedly representing the major concern of the committee. In the handbook, *Science Reasoning and Understanding,* there are numerous indications of ways in which the three objectives studied by the committee can be made to be vital parts of the daily classroom experience of each student. The development of essay materials, partly for validation purposes and partly because of a growing concern that some teachers are all too likely to use objective techniques to the exclusion of the essay approach, has much merit. The consistent usage of structured essay exercises, as outlined in the handbook, for class work and discussion, for homework assignments, or for testing would give students more opportunity to develop the three abilities than any amount of textbook reading or instructor lecturing. Dr. Donald Decker, chairman of the Division of Sciences at the Colorado State College of Education, undertook to develop in a graduate seminar, composed of classroom teachers of science, essay ideas and materials similar to those developed in the Science Committee. He reported a great deal of enthusiasm on the part of the teachers, and summarized his reactions in the following paragraph:

I am also of the opinion that the amount of time and effort spent in a study such as the one in which the American Council on Education has been engaged should be of greatest value as those who have participated in the study use the knowledge and skills gained from that work to help other teachers at all levels improve science education. If these methods are workable and practical, then I believe they should be taught to those teachers who can use them. I find a great deal more significance in the study of evaluation in general education than the appraisal and improvement of current courses. To me there is the possibility of improved classroom techniques by the use of instruments for either testing or discussing the growth and development of students in relation to problem solving, attitudes, and the reading of current literature at all levels of science education.[5]

[5] Quoted from a personal letter to the Study Director, August 15, 1951.

6

OBJECTIVES IN THE HUMANITIES

Intercollege Committee on Humanities Objectives: PETER COFFIN, Wright Junior College; ROBERT F. DAVIDSON, University of Florida; HELEN E. ELCOCK, Kansas State College of Agriculture and Applied Science; JAMES FISHER, Boston University; JOHN KENDALL, Muskingum College; V. E. LEICHTY, Michigan State College; ROBERT MILLER, Florida State University; JAMES NARDIN, Colorado State College of Education; JOHN PLETZ, Wright Junior College; JAMES RICE, Stephens College; PAUL A. ROCHFORD, Colgate University; PAULA THIBAULT, Educational Testing Service

IT IS AGAINST a backdrop of confusion in regard to aims, methods, and content of humanities courses that the work of the Humanities Committee of the Co-operative Study of Evaluation in General Education must be examined. The teachers from participating colleges, who met regularly in the committee over a period of three years, represented almost every possible type of course organization in the area of the humanities. That these people could reconcile differences and maintain a lively interest in a prolonged project is evidence of a desire to find some unifying principle against which courses might be compared. It is further proof of a growing general concern about evaluation practices found on college campuses in respect to the humanities. The magnitude of the differences which at first divided the committee can best be illustrated by giving some attention to the way humanities courses have developed in American higher education.

Historically the content of the humanities consisted of the more human studies emphasized during the Renaissance in contrast to the theocentric curricula of the Middle Ages. However, in more recent interpretations, the humanities include any or all of literature, philosophy, music, architecture, drama, ballet, painting, and quite frequently religion and history. The precise combination of content, the manner in which it is treated, and the objectives sought differ widely from institution to institution, and apparently depend mainly on the interest and training of individuals to whom responsibility for the development of a course is assigned.

Perhaps the most frequently observed college course in the humanities is some variant of a survey of some one or several aspects of culture—in its earliest form a survey of the major literary developments of America or England. Of somewhat more recent vintage is the History of Civilization course (most generally defined with the adjective *Western*) in which students studied *about* the men and events which have shaped the Western European mind. Although still somewhat in vogue, these broad survey courses have quite frequently mutated into studies in greater depth of particular cultural epochs such as Greece in the Age of Pericles, the Middle Ages (usually the thirteenth century), the Renaissance and Reformation, the Age of Enlightenment, and modern times.

Combining elements of the survey of literature and the cultural epoch approach, some recent humanities courses have attempted to present each of a few major periods through a consideration of the major artistic and literary developments. Thus the sculpture, architecture, philosophy, and drama of Hellenic Greece are shown as interacting manifestations of the same spirit in contrast to similar phenomena of the Middle Ages or the twentieth century.

Representing a completely different approach to the humanities are those courses which use content as only a means to develop certain intellectual skills. Courses based upon Great Books, for example, are more designed to train students in a specific dialectical method of analysis than to provide information. Other courses seek, by means of analysis of a few selected documents in music or painting, to train students in the grammar of those subjects, not with any utilitarian view in mind, but because such intellectual training is good. Not infrequently such courses are arranged historically while emphasizing the disciplinary aspects.

Some people have objected to these courses on the ground that such rigor in the freshman or sophomore years tends to repel students from further contact with the humanities. They hold that a primary objective of humanities courses is to develop an appreciation of literature and the fine arts which will enrich the individual's total adult life. Students should be taught to like or appreciate such things before becoming critical and analytical. One course, organized but recently, merely introduces students to a variety of humanities experiences pretty much at a feeling level.

Other teachers have insisted that the essence of humanistic study is to be found only in creative work. They argue that an hour spent in the studio working with paints would be worth many hours studying about works of art or even studying works themselves. They contend that most education is too passive—that the lasting values are derived from active participation. Thus, they would provide studio courses of various sorts.

One can also detect other fundamental issues which serve to divide humanities courses and teachers. From one point of view humanities are regarded as means by which values are taught to college students. Proponents of this concept theorize that students are taught to be coldly rational in the solution of their problems in the sciences and social sciences. In the humanities they are shown that all ultimate solutions of the rational sciences rest upon value assumptions, and they are encouraged to examine some of those values. In place of relying upon the methods of science, the humanities utilize the methods of religion, philosophy, and esthetic insight.

Other divisiveness is found in respect to the kind of documents studied. Some teachers believe that students will probably never, in adult life, make much use of primary historical documents or certain esoteric paintings or musical selections. To compensate for this anticipated lack, but with the hope that students' level of taste will improve, unusual, difficult, and abstract documents are taught. Other teachers feel that a general course should provide experience with the materials students will be most likely to encounter as adults. To them, a study of television programs or motion pictures would be more appropriate than a study of Gregorian chants and Shakespeare's sonnets.

Such disparate conceptions of the nature of the humanities is reflected in the teaching techniques and evaluation practices. The survey-type course organization has placed a premium upon lecturing and testing for knowledge of facts. More analytical courses ostensibly rely to a greater extent on discussion, and conceive of evaluation as determining whether students can creatively organize a paper in which a specific document is criticized. The fine arts appreciation courses have perhaps the most difficult time with regard to teaching or testing. Since teachers do not want to dictate taste, they must expose students to a variety of selections without giving them much interpretive comment. Testing must be restricted to appraising knowledge of fact instead of the principal course objective of appreciation.

COMMON OBJECTIVES OF HUMANITIES COURSES

The interest and concern of the Humanities Committee in reconciling some of these differences and in finding appropriate evaluation techniques were directed to finding common aspects of humanities courses toward which an evaluation study could be oriented. The area selected was stated as an objective in which all courses should be interested: "To understand and enjoy literature, art, music and other cultural activities as expressions of personal and social experience, and to participate to some extent in some form of creative activity."[1] This objective seemed to represent the major common goals of survey courses, critical courses, appreciation courses, and studio offerings. The objective also appeared to be testable without demanding a common fund of knowledge on the part of students—an essential quality in a cooperative enterprise with such diverse points of view represented.

The affective elements of the objective seemed to consist of attitudes, interest, and participation. There was a feeling that students frequently rejected the values of humanities courses because of some deep-rooted dislike for the field of study. Such dislikes might have been conditioned by premature analytical study of works of literature, long hours of instrumental practice, or the cultural notion that practitioners of the humanities were not quite "pulling their share" of life's load. If these predilections existed and interfered with achievement of course objectives, they should be of concern to teachers. Appraisal of attitudes toward the

---

[1] *Higher Education for American Democracy, Vol. I—Establishing the Goals* (Washington: Government Printing Office; and New York: Harper & Bros., 1947), p. 54.

humanities might provide some indication of the degree to which students could accept the values of the humanities.

Participation in the humanities should indicate something about an individual's feeling toward art, music, literature, and the like on the ground that a choice between two possible activities would probably serve as an index of attitude or feeling. Increasing the quality of participation in these activities should be a legitimate concern of humanities teachers in general education courses. If some appropriate index could be obtained of the amount, kind, and degree of student participation in the arts, teachers could know to what extent they were affecting their students' behavior, and could adjust courses to better achieve this goal.

Humanities teachers, however, could not be concerned exclusively with changing students' likes or dislikes. They should also affect students' skill in understanding the arts as well as increasing their knowledge about them. Techniques were needed to measure students' ability to deal, at an intellectual level, with various documents in the humanities and to assess whatever common body of knowledge might be taught in the cooperating schools. The remainder of this discussion will be concerned with the way the Humanities Committee sought to evaluate student progress with respect to those aspects of participation, attitudes, analysis, and knowledge, which were of common interest to all its members.

THE HUMANITIES PARTICIPATION INVENTORY

There are many ways by which student participation in humanities activities might be assessed. Attendance checks at concerts, art displays, or lectures would be one method. A study of library call slips would be another, as also would be a survey of use made of listening rooms or studio facilities. Valuable as such means are, they have the disadvantage of being laborious to employ. A study of library call slips at one large institution, for example, required the full time of a research clerk for two entire weeks to enable teachers to obtain quickly the information with which to study student participation. An easy technique to accumulate data was needed.

One possibility involved the preparation of a rather complete list of humanities activities to be submitted to students with the request that they indicate how frequently they engaged in each activity. Such a list (which would run into many pages), however, might well defeat its purpose either by boring students or by discouraging them by showing the vast areas in which they had had no experience. A modification of this idea—consisting of a list of activities to which students were to respond three separate times: (1) in terms of the availability of each activity or experience, (2) how frequently they engaged in each activity, and (3) the intensity with which they participated—was developed and tried out with students. The lists of items, while not exhaustive, nonetheless contained too much to maintain student interest. Motivation lagged particularly the third time the students viewed the same list of activities.

Experiences with this inventory revealed that assessing participation was by no means as easy a task as had at first been anticipated. In addition to tiring of items seen three successive times, students found it impossible to respond to certain items because they were so far from their own experiences or because the alternative responses were unrealistic. For example, one of the series of responses provided for the list of activities was (1) not at all, (2) twice, (3) six times, (4) twelve times, (5) more than twelve times, during the first year. Most students found the item, "Directed or prepared choreography for dance groups," faintly amusing in terms of the key.

Finally a new conception of assessment of participation was evolved. A limited number of broad activities, representing the major fields of the humanities, were listed together with a means for students to give a rough estimate of the frequency, enjoyment, and seriousness with which they participated in each. This was done on the assumption that inferences about participation generally could be drawn from data about participation in carefully selected representative samples of activities.

The activities selected were reading short stories or novels; reading poetry; writing short stories, poems, or essays; attending movies, plays, operas, or ballets; listening to radio or TV programs; participating in plays; attending concerts or listening to classical music; singing; or playing an instrument; writing music; attending art exhibits or looking at prints; drawing, painting, or doing handicraft; reading philosophical or religious essays or books; and discussing such problems. Students were asked to indicate how frequently they participated, the degree of enjoyment they derived from the activity, and the seriousness with which they participated. A scoring device was prepared so that students could respond to the items on a standard five-choice IBM answer sheet, which permitted quick scoring and detailed analysis.

The items as printed in the final form of the Humanities Participation Inventory took the form:

> You read short stories or novels
> 1. 1. never. (If you choose this answer do not mark anything for items 2 or 3.)
>   2. occasionally.
>   3. frequently.
> 2. 1. with little or no enjoyment.
>   2. with a fair amount of enjoyment.
>   3. with great pleasure.
> 3. 1. just for the story.
>   2. paying some attention to plot and characterization.
>   3. making a detailed examination of the idea and structure of the work in its theatrical and literary contexts.

ATTITUDES TOWARD THE HUMANITIES

The second affective concern of the committee was with students' attitudes toward the humanities. There was some reason to believe that many students had unfavorable feelings about the humanities. The task, then, was to devise means by which these feelings or attitudes might be assessed, with a view to providing information for course planning on the basis of whatever sentiments were discovered. It should be pointed out that this was the least successful of all the committee's ventures.

In attempting to do this, a great number of issues had to be resolved some of which eventually proved beyond the resources available to the committee:

1. The first issue had to do with the nature of attitudes. The term *attitude* is used in such a variety of ways as to preclude easy general definition. Meanings range from fundamental life principles to vague feelings about certain objects. For its purpose the

committee accepted a technical definition that an attitude is an emotionalized tendency, organized through experience, to act for or against something. An attitude was thus conceived of as a feeling which had to be inferred from overt bevavior. It was thought of as only a tendency to act—not an act itself.

2. The second issue grew logically out of the first. An attitude is a tendency to act for or against something. What should be the nature of the something in which the committee members were interested? Was it possible to consider the humanities as a generalized object composed of many specific attitude objects? Or were attitudes toward certain objects so discretely organized in a person's experience that they conditioned but slightly, if at all, attitudes toward other similar objects? For example, could feelings of dislike toward modern artists be combined with feelings of distaste toward modern atonal music to yield a generalized attitude toward modern art forms which in turn combined with other antipathetic feelings about the entire area of the humanities? This issue was resolved by assuming that an inventory could be constructed which would yield a meaningful total index of a very general attitude but which could also be scored to obtain indexes of more specific objects. The final inventory developed provided for a general index and one for each of five major clusters of the arts.

3. Another fundamental issue involved the difference between attitudes and opinions, but was never successfully met. Some means had to be devised to observe relevant behavior from which inferences might be drawn. Questions or statements had to be prepared to which students could respond in such a way as to reveal the nature of their underlying attitude. Yet many of the statements which were written and in which the committee members were interested did not allow this sort of inference. For example, the statement, "Artists are inclined to be antisocial," was one in which art teachers were interested, yet which did not reveal an attitude but merely an opinion. One individual might hold this opinion and value the trait quite highly, while another person holding the same opinion might well disapprove of the trait. During the entire period of work on an attitude test this issue remained. Should a test elicit opinions about various aspects of the humanities which

could be considered separately, or should the instrument attempt only to measure attitude? One of the reasons that the resulting instrument was not successful was that these two conflicting points of view were never reconciled.

4. A fourth issue involved finding an appropriate technique to assess attitudes. While the field of attitude testing is relatively new, there have been developed a number of techniques, each having definite limitations. These might be classified in a variety of ways, but perhaps the most important involved the matter of disguise. The most clear-cut attitude statements are undisguised questions which reveal to the examinee the nature of the attitude being considered. The Army, for example, found in World War II that the best way of finding soldiers' attitudes toward service in the tropics was to ask them whether or not they liked hot weather. However, such direct questions may frequently result in dishonest answers if a socially acceptable response is clearly indicated. The quickest way to find out students' attitudes toward a teacher would be to ask them. However, the implied threat in an unfavorable response might prevent students from answering honestly. On the other hand, disguised questions may not allow reliable inferences. The committee resolved this difficulty by preparing a test of a number of items, most of which were undisguised but which, by means of a contrived method of response, were functionally disguised.[2] Apparently the solution was not successful, for students by and large gave socially acceptable answers even to questions about which their feelings were known to be different.

5. One last issue was in regard to the form items should take. Should items be entirely prescriptive, or could some indicative statements be used? There was some feeling that safe inferences concerning attitudes could only be made from prescriptive statements of the type, "All students should take courses in the humanities." However, the point of view prevailed that valid inferences could be drawn from some statements such as, "Modern art is rubbish."

The committee then proceeded to the development of its instrument. Students were asked to write themes on topics which

---

[2] See chap. 8 on the theory of this technique which was basic to the structure of the Inventory of Beliefs.

seemed likely to result in expressions of definite attitudinal statements. In all, about twenty-five hundred such statements were extracted from these papers and the most promising refined and fitted into a framework based on five major areas of the arts—music, literature, plastic arts, philosophy, and the combined arts. Most of the items included in the final 115 statements of the Attitudes Inventory were of a nature that teachers would want their students to disagree with them. A few, however, were of the opposite, although these were not to be counted in the student's score. Illustrations of each type of item are included below.

Disagree items (scored)
1. Most poetry seems like a meaningless jumble of words.
2. The reading of plays is boring.
3. The attempt to see any order or system in the arts is futile.
4. Art is a frill that society can do without.
5. Studying philosophy is useless.
6. Most philosophers are intellectual snobs.

Agree items (not scored)
1. Rational analysis can be helpful in judging a work of art.
2. The person who ignores modern painting is missing a rewarding experience.
3. The writings which help in understanding the meaning of the arts are useful to the student.

While the resulting instrument was not successful, the failure of the project is less important than the spirit which motivated it and the perspective with which those who worked on it came to regard their attempt. In the past many college teachers have been little concerned with the attitudes of students which they consciously or unconsciously were affecting. By making a concerted effort to evaluate changes in attitudes, the members of the Humanities Committee rejected this tradition. When the attempt failed, the committee went unanimously on record as upholding the validity of concern in their area. Better techniques should be developed and greater technical resources exploited in the future.

Interesting and provocative as the affective projects were, the major interests of the Humanities Committee members were in cognitive outcomes of general education. For the obvious reasons of disparity between the content of various courses, nothing could be done toward cooperatively testing for acquisition of knowledge. However, in two major areas there seemed to be possibility for cooperative inquiry. The first of these dealt with vocabulary.

HUMANITIES VOCABULARY TEST

Regardless of whether students study a history of Western civilization, a series of great books, or a sequence of important pictures and musical compositions, they are all expected to communicate freely with their peers as they meet them socially and at work. Such free communication presupposes a certain common vocabulary, regardless of where or how it was acquired. The Humanities Committee was interested in finding out the degree to which their several courses provided students with a common vocabulary in the humanities. Several approaches to such a project were possible:

1. A few terms might be selected which were common to all schools. Several levels of test items would then be prepared for each term, ranging from items demanding only simple recall of a definition to those demanding insight into a unique situation.

2. A thorough survey might be made of all terms common to courses represented in the committee. From these a representative sample might be selected according to the relative emphases accorded different phases of the humanities. Items testing for these concepts and terms might be at almost any or all levels of difficulty.

3. A third approach might involve coordination of a vocabulary test with some other instrument. Thus, if an objective-type test in critical thinking in the area of the humanities were developed, an instrument testing for knowledge of the terms that test required might be a worth-while enterprise.

Both the first and second approaches were attempted by the committee.

The first instrument constructed attempted to test knowledge of a relatively few vocabulary items at several different levels. However, the resultant pattern of items gave the impression of inadequate item distribution. The trial form, for example, contained clusters of items based upon Machiavellianism, Faust, and Oedipus. Twenty items out of sixty dealt with Darwinism, Marxism, and Freudianism. These topics, while highly interesting and rewarding, were certainly not representative of what was taught in humanities courses across the country.

When this attempt failed, the committee began an intensive study of terms and concepts in general use. Lists of important words taught in various courses were combined into a master list and teachers at all colleges asked to indicate whether each term was taught explicitly and to suggest the degree of importance attached to it. The seventy-five most frequently used and most important terms were then developed into objective test questions. The resulting test was tried out, the items revised, and a final form prepared.

The items on this test do not represent any radical departure from standard testing techniques. The greatest innovation of the test rests with the fidelity with which the instrument reflects current vocabulary found in most humanities courses. The items shown below are examples drawn from this final form of the test:

1. The essential difference between biography and autobiography lies in
    1. the action of the story.
    2. the relationship of the author to his subject.
    3. the style.
    4. the emphasis given to setting.
    5. the length.

2. A crescendo is *least* likely to occur in connection with a passage
    1. of increasing tension.
    2. of gradual relaxation.
    3. of mounting excitement.
    4. characterized by power and energy.
    5. which is building up to a climax.

3. The thrust of an arch is sometimes counterbalanced by
    1. an architrave.
    2. a buttress.
    3. a pendentive.
    4. a triforium.
    5. a pediment.

4. Which of the following objects most obviously violates the principles of functionalism?
    1. A sloped roof on a private dwelling.

2. A sail boat.
3. An electric lamp that looks like a candle.
4. An office desk made of metal.
5. A carving knife with a wooden handle.

CRITICAL ANALYSIS AND JUDGMENT IN THE HUMANITIES

By far the greatest interest of the Humanities Committee centered in a project designed to investigate a concept which was called "critical analysis and judgment." While not overtly taught for in many humanities courses, objectives of most courses claim skill in such an ability as a major goal. Thus, at a verbal level the stage was set for a detailed inquiry into the nature of critical analysis and judgment and the degree to which students developed facility in it as a result of general education course experience.

The concept of critical analysis and judgment is an attempt to reconcile two somewhat divergent theories regarding the nature of humanistic study. One point of view holds that humanistic works can and should be studied with the same methods and identical rigor with which the objects of scientific investigation are regarded. The only variable is the quality of the object of study. The botanist regards a leaf in its separate parts and in its unity. Based upon what he sees, he makes inferences and invents hypotheses which he tests in any of a variety of ways. In the same manner the social scientist regards a group as it functions, and from his observations he seeks to find explanations and laws. By similar application of the methodology of scientific investigation the various aspects of a work of art may be analyzed to obtain greater understanding of the laws which operated to bring it into existence. If a painting is the subject of investigation, the uses to which the primary raw material and artistic media are put can be noted and recorded. The subject matter or content of the picture, the technical proficiency of the rendition, the various uses of line, color, and shadow, indeed the total form of the work, can be made the basis for inference and generalization.

Viewed in this light, the skills necessary for the study of works of art are precisely those involved in critical thinking in the social or natural sciences. Indeed, at one stage in the work of the Humanities Committee the skills which its members believed essential for critical analysis were compared with those developed by the Critical Thinking Committee and were found to be almost identical.

However, most teachers of the humanities would reject this theory if it stopped there. They would contend that such a view violates the essential subjective quality of the humanities. Many teachers feel that critical analysis or the emotional feeling for a work of art are but means to the end of careful, mature assertions of subjective value judgments. It is this end which makes humanistic study unique, for the sciences or social sciences do not generate inquiry for the ends of pleasure, enjoyment, personal satisfaction, or esthetic appreciation. Some teachers, however, would even reject critical analysis whether or not judgment were made the consequence of analysis. They would feel that an individual's reaction to a work of art should be an emotional, aesthetic experience which is sacrificed if the work is approached on an intellectual level. In a sense the concept of critical analysis and judgment might be considered a middle ground between the pure objectivists and the pure subjectivists, for it attempts to emphasize neither sheer criticism nor sheer emotive response.

There were many ways open to the committee to define its meaning of critical analysis and judgment. Rejecting a completely a priori definition, it attempted to set the dimensions of the trait by studying test situations which seemed to demand abilities that might be subsumed under critical analysis and judgment. Test materials, whether of the objective or essay type, seemed for the most part to demand considerable knowledge of specific content, some demonstration of analytic ability, but virtually no judgmental skill. For example, one group of test items was prefaced by four short poems. Students were asked to make various comparisons of the thoughts of each poem, such as:

> The conception of life stated in *Invictus* is most nearly akin to that of
>
> 1. Housman
> 2. Herrick
> 3. Omar
> 4. Browning

Essay questions obtained were of the type:

> Compare the *Parthenon* and *Chartres Cathedral* as architectural expressions of the Greek and medieval attitudes.

Since the same sort of test materials were to be found in the various published tests examined, it became apparent that in spite of expressions to the contrary, representative teaching and evaluation in the humanities were restricted to knowledge of fact with some incidental attention paid to intellectual manipulation of that content. The implication was obvious that a test of critical analysis and judgment would be a somewhat new development requiring its own unique methodology.

Turning to the actual study of specific works of art, the committee attempted to specify what critical analysis and judgment involves by demonstrating the skills which each member would employ in a critique of a work of art. In a sense the group was attempting to develop a theory of criticism appropriate for freshman and sophomore college students. This system, after considerable experimentation and revision, was finally crystallized as a List of Abilities in Critical Judgment in the Humanities. It contained three major parts demanding (1) a subjective reaction, (2) analysis, and (3) critical judgment. Under each major heading are elements or abilities comprising it. Each ability is couched in sufficiently general terms as to be applicable to any of the major art media.

A LIST OF ABILITIES
IN CRITICAL JUDGMENT IN THE HUMANITIES
PART ONE: INFORMAL NOTES

Immediate (Pre-Analytical) Subjective Reaction

1. The subject matter and idea of the work, and its expressive, communicative, and evocative roles.
    a) Recognition of the subject matter or explicit recognition of the fact that there is no subject matter in the representational, imitative, or referential sense.
    b) Statement of personal thoughts and feelings of the student evoked by the work.
    c) Explicit recognition by the student of the subjectivity of personal thoughts and feelings evoked in him by the work.
    d) Comment on the probable ability of the work to arouse subjective reactions in people other than the student.

e) Description of ideas and feelings of the maker which seem to be expressed in the work.

Analysis

2. *Function and Context.*—The action and roles of the work of art in relationship to the various combinations of circumstances (contexts) within which it has had or does have meaning.

   a) Recognition of any political, religious, sociological, or economic functions of the work, or of the fact that it has none.

   b) Recognition of the esthetic function of the work, its role in bringing pleasure through perfection of form.

   c) Demonstration of the influence of various external factors, such as social context and environment, on the nature of the work.

   d) Speculation on the influence that the work might have upon society.

3. *Medium.*—The nature, use, and importance of medium in the work. On this section medium is used to mean language in literature, instruments or voice in music, as well as medium in painting.

   a) Recognition and description of the medium made use of in the work.

   b) Recognition and description of the general methods of expression (as defined in Section 3 of the Guide to Critical Analysis and Judgment in the Humanities)[3] made use of in the work. (Not applicable to music.)

   c) Recognition of the conventionality or unconventionality of the medium, use of language, use of instruments, or method of expression.

   d) Comment on the way that the limitations and possibilities of the medium influence the nature of the work.

   e) Comment on the way in which his esthetic problem influenced the maker in his choice of a particular medium.

   f) Ability to distinguish between performer and work performed, reproduction and original.

4. *Formal Elements and Organization.*—Consideration of separate major parts whose relationships to one another create the significance of the form of the work, and of things done to give unity, order, consistency, and intrinsic significance.

   a) Discovery and isolation of major or predominant elements ("devices" in literature) in the work.

   b) Objective description and characterization of the major elements ("devices" in literature).

   c) Comment on the expressive quality of separate elements ("devices" in literature).

[3] See pp. 157–58.

d) Comment on the independent function that separate elements ("devices" in literature) have in the total work, or recognition that there is no independent function.

e) Recognition of symbols or symbolic usages *together with* descriptions of their use and meaning in the work.

f) Recognition of the conventionality or unconventionality of the use of elements ("devices" in literature).

g) Recognition and description of a plan, scheme, or structure on which the work is based—a principle of organization governing the relationship of formal elements to each other in the total work.

h) Recognition of qualities or aspects of organization (without necessarily naming them as such) such as the following: dominance, subordination, unity, variety, balance, symmetry, proportion, continuity, consistency, emphasis, tension, rhythm, movement, repetition, distortion, etc.

i) Exemplification of qualities or aspects of organization found in the work by concrete references to the work.

j) Speculation as to whether external factors have influenced the nature of the organization of the work.

k) Comment on the use of organizational devices or over-all organization for expressive purposes.

5. *Style.*—Qualities of the work which are characteristic of the various forces which have affected its production.

a) Description of style characteristics generally typical of the historical period or era.

b) Description of style characteristics of the work typical of the particular school, trend, or movement within a historical period.

c) Description of style characteristics of the work typical of the maker of the work.

PART TWO: CRITICAL JUDGMENT

6. Part Two offers the student an opportunity to express a total reaction to or judgment of the work. Presumably he will make use of ideas or facts perceived during the analytic process on Part One, but he is free to select, reject, and add as he wishes. His statement should sum up to his concept of the general meaning or significance of the work. While this statement should be an over-all reaction, including the factors concerning the work that he thinks are most pertinent, it cannot be expected to cover and include all of the various kinds of significance which the work has within its total field.

a) Demonstration of *a* total, over-all coherent perception of the significance of the work.

b) Perception of the interrelations of form and content in the work.

c) Evidence that the student has attempted to respond to the work at its primary level of significance, verbal, visual, sonic, tactile, etc.

d) Effective use of factors noted in Part One, evidence of care in both inclusion and exclusion.

e) Evidence of an attempt to express reactions other than logical or rational.

f) Demonstration of the ability to separate personal, subjective judgments from judgments based on qualities intrinsic in the work.

g) Recognition of the various contexts within which value judgments can be assigned (comparison of this work with other works by the same artists, with works of art of all kinds and in all times, with important human endeavors in any field).

h) Recognition of the unique quality of the particular work and the unique nature of the student's experience in perceiving this particular work.

Having established a general mode of criticism and judgment, the next task was to prepare appropriate means to elicit student demonstration of the various abilities. Since whatever was developed had to be sufficiently flexible to allow for its use with any of a particular order of art works, and since a major element in the system was judgmental, objective-type techniques of measurement were considered inappropriate. Yet there had to be sufficient structure to ensure that students were given the opportunity to demonstrate the abilities. In completely unstructured situations students frequently fail to demonstrate these abilities merely because they do not know what is desired. The committee has found in this connection that questions or statements designed to elicit certain responses need to be carefully prepared. Students do not understand such an abstract statement as, "Give your reactions to ———." To obtain students' "reactions" questions need to be phrased in terms related to the experiences of students.

The device finally adopted—and called "Guides to Critical Analysis and Judgment in the Humanities"—was a series of fairly broad questions, each demanding analysis, at one level, of a work of art. For the sake of clarity, and in order to accommodate a few absolutely necessary technical terms, separate series of questions were prepared for painting, music, literature, and philosophy. Each series culminated in a broad requirement for a one-page critical essay expressing a judgment of the work of art. Each set of questions was printed on a form with space provided below each question for students to write their answers and a space on the back of the form for the essay. All forms are similar to the items for painting presented below.

GUIDE TO CRITICAL ANALYSIS AND JUDGMENT IN THE HUMANITIES

Part One: Informal Notes

In Part One you are asked to make notes in the spaces provided. Formal sentences are not necessary. There will probably be more things to note under some headings than others, but you should make your coverage as complete as possible. You will be told when the time allowed for Part One is up.

Subjective Reaction

1. Make notes on what the painting is about (subject matter), on how it affects you, on how it might affect other people, on what the feelings of the painter seem to have been, etc.

Analysis

2. What seem to be the creative and/or technical problems (matter of function, purpose, form, space limitations, etc.) with which he is dealing?
3. Describe the general method of expression (handling of space, distortion, use of light, interest in textures of the objects represented, etc.). Comment on any relationship you can detect between the results obtained and the medium used, and the appropriateness of the choice of medium. How did the artist's problems influence his choice of medium?
4. Describe the elements of the painting (things which can be considered separately, such as line; color, including hue; intensity and use of light and dark; shape; texture of paint; etc.). How are the elements used in the organization of the painting (specific devices or plans used to hold the elements together, or the lack of such plans).
5. Indicate the characteristics of the painting that lead you to believe that it belongs to some particular period, school, or artist.

Part Two: Synthesis: Expression of Over-all Judgment

6. In Part One you have made informal notes on the picture from various points of view suggested to you. In this part you are asked to write your over-all reaction to and judgment of the painting.

Organize your writing. Use only as many of the ideas jotted down in Part One as you think are pertinent, plus any additional ideas you may have. Your final judgment should represent much more than a compilation of the notes you have made. The important thing is to express in a good, well-rounded essay your judgment of the general significance and meaning of the painting.

Evaluating student performance on these Guides to Critical Analysis and Judgment in the Humanities involved comparing items from the List of Abilities with student responses. Credit was to be assigned for each ability demonstrated; thus considerably more reliability of scoring was ensured than could usually be attained with more conventional essay responses. However, evaluating responses proved much more difficult in practice than in theory. Careful reading of student papers in a search for previously determined responses is a most difficult, tedious, and time-consuming task. It is much easier, although much less reliable, to scan a paper and evaluate the performance impressionistically. Teachers who have used the scoring system have complained about the time and energy required, *but* their judgments with the Guides have frequently proven more reliable than their more subjective judgments of their own theme assignments.

Many teachers have also criticized the technique because the scoring system is essentially a quantitative one. They feel that such a system allows the same credit to be given for a naïve and for a sophisticated answer. There are two ways of responding to this criticism. One is to accept it as valid and to adapt the scoring so that student demonstration of each ability can be judged according to some numerical qualitative scale, as for example 0–3. To do this, however, makes more complex an already tortuously complicated system and also reduces the reliability of grading by increasing the subjective factor. The second response involves making the assumption that sophistication in an art area will usually be reflected in the number of abilities demonstrated as well as in the quality of such demonstration. Thus, the student who would be graded three on each of a number of abilities could be expected to maintain his rank with respect to other students if the quantitative rather than qualitative technique were used. Which of these solutions is better only further research can determine.

All of the projects of the Cooperative Study have demonstrated a curious attitude toward the objective test–essay issue. Projects begun with the creation of an objective test ended with an approach to the same ends by means of an essay test. On the other hand, projects initially concerned with essay responses have turned almost irresistibly to explore objective-test possibilities. The humanities project has been no exception. After a rationale of criticism was established, attempts were made to test for the same abilities by objective or short-answer tests. While these attempts were not notably successful, one technique is of sufficient importance to warrant attention.

At one institution a series of pictures has been prepared in a manila folder, one set for each student. Then, separate objective questions were prepared to sample the abilities from the List of Abilities in Critical Judgment. These questions may deal with from one to five of the pictures and the folder contains enough different prints to allow considerable flexibility. One form, for example, contains the following pictures:

Daumier, *The Washerwoman*
Lippi, *Madonna and Child*
Vermeer, *Lady with Lute*
Murillo, *Children of the Shell*
El Greco, *The Holy Family*
Matisse, *The Blue Window*
Rivera, *Mexican Child*

Typical questions are:

1. In which of these does the artist seem less interested in the subject than in formal problems?
2. Which of these seems to you more sentimental?
3. Which uses a subject which has a Biblical or mythological source?
4. Which picture uses most cool colors?
5. Which is more dramatic in its use of highlighting?
6. Which picture has the center of interest farthest to the left?
7. Considering the backgrounds of these paintings, which is the earliest in manner?

RESEARCH RESULTS

The several tests or inventories prepared by the Humanities Committee have been used in several kinds of research. The first kind consisted of studies made of the instruments themselves to appraise their reliability, internal consistency, and validity. The second sort has consisted of using the instruments as means of obtaining information about the humanities in general education.

As has been indicated earlier, the Attitudes Inventory did not prove successful. The items proved so easy that an inadequate range of scores was obtained to discriminate even between individuals possessing known differences of feelings concerning the humanities. The small range of scores, skewed toward one extreme, resulted in an excessively low estimate of test reliability.

The Humanities Participation Inventory, however, has proven to be an adequate measure of group tendencies. Estimates of test reliability ranged from .78 to .86, with one, for a somewhat atypical group, slightly over .90. The validity of the instrument was presumed on the basis of several corroborating data. In the first place, the inventory consists of simple questions of fact of concern to humanities teachers. Secondly, the inventory does reflect status and change with respect to humanities activities which were predictable by teachers on other bases. Further, the relationship between the Participation Inventory and other relevant measures is well within the normal range of expectancy. Lastly, the changes or growth which takes place in differing institutional groups conforms, in general, to expectations based upon knowledge of those institutions.

The Guides to Critical Analysis and Judgment in the Humanities, representing a somewhat unusual test technique, are not as amenable to statistical test analysis as were the two preceding instruments. However, whatever has been discovered has tended in the direction of supporting a claim for technical sufficiency. The guides were developed for a variety of reasons, a major one of which was to provide a more objective means for appraising subjective student responses. Experience with the instrument has revealed that while many teachers do not especially like the device, when they have taken the time to become familiar with it and have used the scoring possibilities, the results have been consistently quite reliable.

It should be mentioned in this connection that the guides have been used the least of all Study instruments. The approach to testing represented by the guides is considerably different from that commonly used. Further, teachers in the humanities have generally been suspicious of any kind of evaluation other than content-centered essay testing. It was therefore quite difficult, and at some institutions impossible, to interest humanities teachers, other than those actually on the committee, in the instrument. Many rejected it a priori as inadequate either because it did not, in their opinion, tap analytical abilities, or because it did not involve knowledge taught in a particular course. However, the guides were used extensively at a few schools. Our opinions of the instrument have been formed largely from their results.

Papers from these schools, dealing with the same art object, were pooled, reproduced, and scored by a number of raters. Tables 28, 29, and 30 present the coefficients of correlation between the ratings assigned by different raters. These figures are much higher than those usually obtained from several raters judging students' written work. They take on increased significance when it is realized that the raters came from different institutions approaching the humanities from several different points of view.

Estimates of the validity of an instrument such as this one are difficult to obtain. Indeed, the ability involved in the guides took

TABLE 28

COEFFICIENTS OF CORRELATION BETWEEN RATINGS OF DIFFERENT
TEACHERS ON PAPERS ON LITERATURE

	Rater 2	Rater 3	Rater 4	Rater 5	Rater 6	Rater 7	Rater 8
Rater 1........	.79	.82	.79	.70	.61	.80	.53
Rater 2........		.90	.88	.84	.82	.90	.84
Rater 3........			.78	.62	.54	.87	.67
Rater 4........				.89	.86	.77	.82
Rater 5........					.90	.68	.78
Rater 6........						.75	.78
Rater 7........							.68

TABLE 29

COEFFICIENTS OF CORRELATION BETWEEN RATINGS OF DIFFERENT
TEACHERS ON PAPERS ON MUSIC

	Rater 2	Rater 3	Rater 4	Rater 5
Rater 1................	.88	.89	.35	.89
Rater 2................		.88	.23	.83
Rater 3................			.42	.94
Rater 4................				.39

TABLE 30

COEFFICIENTS OF CORRELATION BETWEEN RATINGS OF DIFFERENT
TEACHERS ON PAPERS ON PAINTING

	Rater 2	Rater 3	Rater 4	Rater 5
Rater 1.................	.32	.24	.02	.53
Rater 2.................		.82	.66	.81
Rater 3.................			.73	.81
Rater 4.................				.56

reasonably precise definition only as work proceeded on its development. Nonetheless certain remarks can be made pointing toward a presumption of validity for the instrument.

The four guides were prepared by individuals actively engaged in teaching humanities courses. In their opinion the questions posed were of the order and nature to which they would like their students to be able to respond. They believed that the questions represented an important area of concern to their teaching. These facts justify a claim of logical or face validity for the instruments.

A second kind of evidence is obtained by comparing groups of students having had educational experience relevant to the purposes of the test. One such comparison was made between students having taken a general education course in the humanities, another having satisfied requirements by taking introductory courses from various areas of the humanities, and a third group having taken no formal humanities work. Table 31 below indicates the mean scores of each of these three groups on three of the forms of the guide (Painting, Music, and Literature).

These data suggest that students not having had experience in the area of the humanities do not achieve as well as do those who have had such courses. Although only the groups taking the

TABLE 31

MEAN SCORES OF EACH OF THREE GROUPS ON TESTS ON MUSIC,
LITERATURE, AND PAINTING

GROUP	MUSIC		LITERATURE		PAINTING	
	Mean	N	Mean	N	Mean	N
A general education humanities course....................	9.13	45	11.27	55	12.18	40
Various liberal arts humanities courses..................	10.50	24	12.00	20	12.86	14
No humanities courses.......	7.03	36	9.11	38	11.31	32

Music and Literature forms showed means which were statistically significant (1 percent level), the same direction of differences for painting reflects the main point—that the instrument distinguishes between these groups.

Since the Vocabulary Test was completed only toward the very end of the Cooperative Study, few data have been collected beyond item analysis data and estimates of reliability. Both kinds of evidence were satisfactory. Only three out of seventy-five items yielded low coefficients of discrimination. The reliability of the test was estimated at .83.

The Participation Inventory assesses a trait which it is quite logical to assume is but slightly related to academic aptitude or to tests requiring highly intellectual skills such as the Test of Critical Thinking. Evidence in support of this has been obtained from every study made. Both pre-test and post-test results have been compared with other pre-test and post-test scores for students from several colleges. The results of these comparisons, expressed as correlation coefficients, are given in Table 32 below.

The total participation scores of 100 students were correlated respectively with Art, Music, and Literature sections from the Kuder Preference Record—Vocational, with r's of .08, —.12, and .17 resulting. From these data it would appear that the trait being measured by the Participation Inventory is considerably different

TABLE 32

CORRELATION COEFFICIENTS BETWEEN THE HUMANITIES PARTICIPATION
INVENTORY AND OTHER TESTS

Test	Coefficient of Correlation			No. of Colleges	No. of Students
	Lowest r in Any College	Highest r in Any College	Average r*		
Pre-Test					
ACE Psychological Examination..	.12	.21	.17	3	220
Problems in Human Relations...	.02	.37	.21	3	220
Inventory of Beliefs...........	—.06	—.16	—.10	3	220
Post-Test					
ACE Psychological Examination..	.13	.14	.13	2	340
Problems in Human Relations...	.36	.27	.33	2	340
Inventory of Beliefs...........	.27	.17	.24	2	340

* Quinn McNemar, *Psychological Statistics* (New York: John Wiley & Sons, 1949), pp. 123–24.

from the preference ratings achieved by the use of the Kuder test.

The Participation Inventory scores correlated quite diversely with scores made on the various forms of the Guide to Critical Analysis and Judgment in the Humanities, as is demonstrated in Table 33.

Another series of correlations were made between scores on the Humanities Vocabulary Test and each of the three levels of participation—frequency, enjoyment, and seriousness—both on a pre-

TABLE 33

CORRELATION COEFFICIENTS BETWEEN THE HUMANITIES PARTICIPATION INVENTORY AND GUIDE TO CRITICAL ANALYSIS

Test	N	r
Pre-Test Critical Analysis and Judgment, Painting	100	.05
" " " " " " , Philosophy	100	.59
" " " " " " , Music	100	.48
" " " " " " , Literature	100	.32
" " " " " " , Music	33	.23
" " " " " " , Music	19	.64
" " " " " " , Philosophy	24	.50
" " " " " " , Literature	46	.53
" " " " " " , Literature	21	.34
" " " " " " , Painting	38	.02
" " " " " " , Painting	25	−.07
Post-Test " " " " , Literature	46	.49
" " " " " " , Music	40	−.13
" " " " " " , Painting	37	−.07

and on a post-test basis. The coefficients for the pre-test administration were .41 for frequency, .40 enjoyment, and .55 for seriousness. The post-test correlations demonstrated the same pattern; .30 for frequency, .39 enjoyment, and .42 for seriousness. These suggest that while there is scant relationship between academic aptitude and participation generally, command of vocabulary (which is an essential part of academic aptitude) is more related to serious participation than to the lower levels. Students, regardless of ability, may try, and actually enjoy, the attempt to engage in various humanities activities. The more able students, however, are the ones one would expect to approach their work seriously.

One major purpose intended for the Participation Inventory was to determine the participation experience of students at the time they enter college. Table 34 below represents, by percentages, students from four separate school groups who responded at each level of participation (frequency, enjoyment, and seriousness) to the five major areas of the arts. The letters to the left in the table indicate school, and the numbers on the same side of the table represent the degree indicated for each level of participation. For example, 15 percent of the students at School A indicated no participation in literature, 59 percent claimed some participation, and 24 percent indicated considerable participation in this area. In the Combined Arts, of those indicating some participation, 1 percent

TABLE 34

PARTICIPATION OF STUDENTS IN FOUR COLLEGES IN FIVE MAJOR
AREAS OF THE HUMANITIES

COLLEGE	DEGREE OF PARTICIPATION	LITERATURE			COMBINED ARTS			MUSIC			PLASTIC ARTS			PHILOSOPHY		
		F* %	E* %	S* %	F %	E %	S %	F %	E %	S %	F %	E %	S %	F %	E %	S %
A	1	15	7	39	14	1	8	38	2	23	36	4	20	20	6	6
	2	59	40	38	42	20	57	33	25	30	46	33	35	59	45	59
	3	24	36	8	41	62	18	26	40	7	14	24	6	17	25	11
	Omission	2	17	15	3	17	17	3	33	40	4	29	39	4	24	24
B	1	31	9	31	33	4	12	52	6	21	44	8	18	26	9	7
	2	54	44	32	36	27	39	31	23	19	44	32	29	55	44	44
	3	14	18	7	29	36	15	15	21	8	9	16	8	14	19	19
	Omission	1	29	30	2	33	34	2	50	52	3	44	45	5	28	30
C	1	27	8	35	34	2	11	51	4	22	51	7	17	34	11	5
	2	56	45	29	35	27	38	33	24	21	38	30	25	52	35	46
	3	16	20	8	29	37	16	15	21	7	9	13	7	11	18	12
	Omission	1	27	28	1	34	35	1	50	50	2	50	51	3	36	36
D	1	23	8	37	31	2	11	48	2	24	49	7	18	21	9	9
	2	54	40	32	43	30	43	33	26	19	43	31	26	63	45	53
	3	22	30	10	25	38	16	18	24	8	8	12	7	16	24	16
	Omission	1	22	21	1	30	31	1	48	49	0	50	49	0	22	22

* Key: F—Frequency
E—Enjoyment
S—Seriousness

did not particularly enjoy it, 20 percent enjoyed it fairly well, and 62 percent enjoyed it a great deal.

These data may be studied more effectively if combined into a shorter table. Table 35 presents averages of percentages of students who responded to the frequency, enjoyment, and seriousness categories at each of the three levels of intensity. Thus the first column, Literature, indicates the percentage of students who participate at each of the levels with the specific category of frequency, enjoyment, and seriousness. From this table several generalizations emerge.

(1) Students from each of the four schools participate at the lowest level in the areas of music and the plastic arts. (2) Students

TABLE 35

PARTICIPATION OF STUDENTS IN THE HUMANITIES AS TO FREQUENCY,
ENJOYMENT, AND SERIOUSNESS

College	Degree of Participation	Literature %	Combined Arts %	Music %	Plastic Arts %	Philosophy %
A	1	20	8	21	20	11
	2	46	30	29	38	54
	3	23	40	24	15	18
	Omission	11	12	25	24	17
B	1	24	16	26	23	14
	2	43	34	24	35	48
	3	13	27	15	8	17
	Omission	20	23	35	31	21
C	1	23	16	26	25	17
	2	43	33	26	31	44
	3	15	27	14	10	14
	Omission	19	23	34	34	25
D	1	33	15	25	25	13
	2	42	39	26	33	54
	3	21	26	17	9	19
	Omission	15	21	33	33	15

participate at a considerably higher level in the combined arts, literature, and philosophy. This is of course understandable, since the combined arts include the media of television and radio, and the philosophical section includes religious discussion.

Table 36 represents gains in participation made by students from four different schools. These gains were made with respect to the total score on the Participation Inventory. The population for each school has been divided into five approximately equal groups

TABLE 36

MEAN GAINS OF STUDENTS ON HUMANITIES PARTICIPATION INVENTORY
CLASSIFIED ACCORDING TO PRE-TEST STANDING

COLLEGE	INITIALLY LOW GROUP		INITIALLY LOW-MIDDLE GROUP		INITIALLY MIDDLE GROUP		INITIALLY HIGH-MIDDLE GROUP		INITIALLY HIGH GROUP		TOTAL GROUP		
	Gain	N	Gain	N	Gain	N	Gain	N	Gain	N	Mean Pre-Test	Mean Gain	N
Pre-Test Range	25–66		67–77		78–86		87–94		95–124				
1........	16.59	51	2.89	53	3.84	38	−0.30	47	−3.68	37	78.33	4.40	226
2........	28.08	13	1.57	7	−4.00	6	−12.33	3	−10.67	3	68.81	8.84	32
3........	8.67	6	7.22	9	2.00	6	7.12	8	−3.10	10	82.59	3.10	39
4........	17.88	24	8.46	35	7.24	49	3.51	35	0.04	45	83.85	6.41	188
Total 4 colleges..	18.00	94	5.05	104	4.94	99	1.39	93	−2.07	95	80.25	5.44	485

ranging from the one making the lowest initial score to the one making the highest initial score. Gains over a year's period are shown for each such school group.

From these data the fact emerges that, in general, the lower the pre-test score, the greater the gain made during the course of a year. One might explain this situation by arguing that the more interested students are not likely to increase the amount of participation—although it is hoped that the quality may be modified. On the other hand, those with low records of participation before coming to college might be expected to increase greatly the amount if for no other reason than the fact that so many activities are available on a modern college campus. The data seem to indicate this is so, and this is given considerable support by a study of changes in participation with respect to each activity made by students from one university over a period of a year. The following generalizations are based on data from that college.

1. More women apparently read novels and short stories before coming to college than did men (65 percent to 49 percent answered "frequently"). Both men and women read novels less frequently at the end of the year than at the beginning. Possibly the greater amount of nonfiction reading demanded by college courses is the explanation for this shift. However, precollege men read with considerably more seriousness than do women. The relative position of the two sexes was reversed at the end of the year in this regard.

2. Students read much less poetry than they do novels or short stories. Here again, however, the women have a better record than men. And again women develop greater seriousness in their reading of poetry than do men. Only a few students, however, regardless of sex, believe they read poetry at the highest level of seriousness.

3. Apparently college makes very little difference with respect to students' writing short stories, poems, and essays. Only a few, regardless of sex, claim to do so frequently. Men, however, gain in enjoyment in doing so over a year, whereas women remain about the same in this regard.

4. When students come to college and at the end of a year of college, they attend movies frequently and with great pleasure.

Their college experiences do not seem to result in any more serious approach to such participation.

5. Students do not attend plays frequently before or after a year of college. Nor do those who do attend do so with appreciably greater pleasure or seriousness. Men, however, drop in the frequency with which they do this activity.

6. No marked changes appear to take place with respect to attendance at operas and ballets. Students are about evenly divided between those who never attend and those who attend occasionally (which they define as once or twice a year).

7. As could be expected, students like to, and do, listen to the radio and television both before and after a year of college.

8. Students increase rather markedly the frequency with which they participate in plays, skits, and the like. The enjoyment which they derive and the seriousness with which they approach these activities do not seem to change.

9. No appreciable shifts occur with respect to attendance at concerts or recitals or in listening to classical music.

10. While there is a slight drop in the frequency with which students play musical instruments, there is a similarly slight increase in the seriousness with which those who do play their instruments.

11. Students do not attempt to write music, either before or after a year of college.

12. Students occasionally attend art exhibits or look at art prints, and they increase their tendency to do so over a period of a year—men more so than women. Their technical seriousness also increases, as might be expected in view of the orientation of the courses available to them.

13. Students apparently remain about the same with respect to painting from the beginning to the end of the school year. The same profile holds true with respect to handicraft. About half the students do and about half do not engage in such activities.

14. There is a slight increase in the frequency with which students read seriously and enjoy philosophical essays, but the gains are considerably less than humanities teachers might wish. The same sort of profile holds true with respect to serious discussion of philosophical and theological topics.

These data, drawn from one institution, do not indicate that much gain is being made in the amount or level of participation in the fields of the humanities. Nor could such gains reasonably be expected in view of the way college humanities courses are organized. As a matter of fact, one analysis of gains made by three groups of students—(1) those having had general education humanities courses, (2) those having had liberal arts courses in the humanities, and (3) those having had no course experience in the humanities—shows that the last category makes approximately the same order of scores in participation as students having general

TABLE 37

HUMANITIES PARTICIPATION SCORES FOR ONE INSTITUTION

Group	N	Mean	S.D.
General education humanities course....	61	74.98	14.05
Humanities courses other than general education..................	52	90.08	17.25
No humanities experience.............	25	74.44	20.80

education course experience. The markedly higher scores for the students taking non-general education humanities courses are very likely the result of selective factors such as including the scores of humanities majors. These data, indicated in Table 37, if characteristic of any appreciable number of colleges, suggest that some rethinking of the role of humanities courses is in order. If these data are valid, they would suggest that the objective of increasing participation either is inappropriate or that considerably more should be done to implement it.

It is unfortunate that the project upon which the Humanities Committee expended the greatest amount of time and effort should be supported by the least amount of empirical data. However, the very lack of such information is rather definite evidence about the activities and products of humanities courses.

The original research design called for students at the various colleges to view the same painting, read the same selection, or hear the same composition, both in a pre-test and in a post-test situation. The works of art selected were (1) El Greco, *View of Toledo*, (2) Shakespeare, Sonnet XXX ("When to the sessions of sweet silent thought. . . ."), and (3) Prokofiev, *Classical Sym-*

phony, First Movement. The test was administered in the fall of 1951, but the scoring of the test proved most difficult for staff members asked to participate in the project.

1. The idea of appraising quantitatively students' responses which they believed should only be appraised qualitatively was distasteful to many teachers in the humanities. Refusing to accept the assumption that quality of analysis and judgment could be inferred from quantity, such teachers rejected the rationale of the grading system, and thus invalidated results for research purposes.

2. The idea of restricting one's evaluation of students' papers to preconceived elements instead of evaluating in terms of subjective intuition also proved to be a barrier. Teachers of the humanities believe generally that estimates of student demonstration of critical analysis should be made by teachers unfettered by any particular set of categories on responses on which they can base a grade. In a sense they believe each student paper is as unique as a work of art and must be judged by criteria which appear to the initiated in the context of the paper. If this premise is accepted, then of course the entire rationale of the Guide to Critical Analysis and Judgment in the Humanities must be rejected. However, the rationale is accepted in theory. It is only the application of it that is rejected.

3. A third argument against the guides is ambiguous in nature and meaning. Teachers found that students did not achieve well on the guides, that they demonstrated a rather marked inability to see much meaning in a work of art. From this a number of teachers inferred that the guide was invalid because students who had been exposed to humanities courses could not be as bad as their responses would indicate.

It is possible, however, to accept the same evidence of nonperformance and to reach the conclusion that courses are to blame—not the instrument. Perhaps small gains are to be expected in view of the way a number of humanities courses are organized. Observations of classes and interviews with students suggest that students in typical humanities courses read assignments from textbooks, and then come to class either to listen passively to a teacher tell them *about* some work of art or to listen to or see a work *about* which they have studied. In either event they are acquiring knowledge but have little experience related to other objectives.

If the objectives of increased participation, analytical ability, or genuine appreciation are valid, then the way many humanities courses are conducted must be judged inadequate.

These are broad generalizations. Perhaps a few descriptions of actually observed class situations might underscore the differences between stated course objectives and classroom practice.

In one class, organized along cultural history lines, an hour was devoted to hearing three students read essays about artists from a particular period. The assignment, made several weeks earlier, was for each student to select an artist and do a research paper on him. These papers were then to be read in the class, which consisted of twenty-five students. At the rate of three or four a day, two weeks of class time were thus utilized in this activity. Unfortunately, the potentialities of student reporting were lost because no time was available for class discussion of the points raised in each paper. The reader was putting on a performance for one person—the teacher. The emphasis in each paper was on the facts of the painter's life—what analytical comments were included came obviously intact from some source book.

At another institution the humanities course was also of the cultural history type. Some two hundred and fifty students were gathered in a large lecture room to hear a professor *read* a paper on the beginnings of the Renaissance. The lecture was intended to provide a knowledge basis for a week's study in smaller classrooms. In the smaller sections, teachers gave other lectures covering in more detail the same ground broken by the speaker for the week. At no time were students encouraged to do anything other than respond to questions, the answers to which were to be found in a textbook or lecture.

In still another institution in which the course was of the critical-esthetic type, students were gathered in a small room while the teacher played selections from Bach and Beethoven and carried on a running commentary about them. The teacher's remarks were sound and he sought by a variety of ways to show many implications in other fields for the work of the composer. The teacher demonstrated a general education, but he was *giving* the students the results of his analyses rather than providing opportunity for them to arrive at their own judgments.

These teachers were all sincere, hard-working scholars who believed in general education, but one must nevertheless doubt whether by such procedures they could hope to change attitudes materially, increase the extent and seriousness of participation, or the critical facilities of students. Then why are such uninspired activities continued? A subjective judgment suggests the existence of three factors. First, a minority of teachers are convinced that out of broad knowledge will develop—for some students, at least—all the desired outcomes. A second factor is that the humanities, perhaps more than any other general education area, are beset with the complex problem of selection of the most significant contributions of all the ages to man's present cultural heritage. The vastness of the area and the often pronounced differences in viewpoint among the members of a humanities staff result in courses which are so crammed with important materials that mere coverage of them is a difficult achievement. Finally, instruction aimed at objectives such as critical judgment poses difficult and unsolved problems, as is clearly seen by a brief review of the experience of the Humanities Committee in developing the guides.

The Guides to Critical Analysis and Judgment in the Humanities, despite the devoted and continuing effort of a group of humanities teachers, are but rough first attempts to measure a skill which courses in the humanities have done but little to develop. In their present form they are difficult for students to use and perhaps even more difficult for teachers to grade. They also fall short of defining the task as the committee envisaged it. In part these difficulties are technical ones which could be overcome by continued effort. More complex, however, is the fact that some of the difficulties result from the unfamiliarity of teachers and students with genuinely active analysis and judgment. The tradition of giving and receiving information is so strong that other kinds of teaching or evaluation activities are greeted with some suspicion by both teachers and students. Only as larger numbers of teachers in the humanities find time to duplicate and carry even further fundamental thinking of the type reported in this chapter can much change be expected. In saying this, we do not suggest that others will arrive at the same conclusions or the same instruments, but if the work on the Guides to Critical Analysis and Judgment in the Humanities, for example, can provide leads for other kinds of evaluation and instructional activities, it will have been very worth while.

7

PERVASIVE OBJECTIVES 1: CRITICAL THINKING

Intercollege Committee on Critical Thinking: LILY DETCHEN, Pennsylvania College for Women; WESLEY DYKSTRA, Muskingum College; HARVEY GELDER, Western Washington College of Education; WALKER HILL, Michigan State College; KELLOGG W. HUNT, Florida State University; MORRIS T. KEETON, Antioch College; CECIL H. MILLER, Kansas State College of Agriculture and Applied Science; W. EDGAR MOORE, University of Florida; TROY ORGAN, Pennsylvania College for Women; CARL N. REXROAD, Stephens College; SYLVESTER R. TOUSSAINT, Colorado State College of Education

THE VERY EXISTENCE of the Intercollege Committee on Critical Thinking at once bears witness to the generally accepted importance of the objective and to the strong disagreements as to its nature and attainability. Despite the idealistic basing of the six committees on objectives, it is not unfair to say that, practically speaking, four of them arose primarily out of concern about the general education content areas usually designated as communications, social science, science, and the humanities. This was not true with regard to the remaining two objectives. Although concern about critical thinking had led to the organization of special courses in several of the colleges, this was atypical. The more usual practice was to consider it as an objective to be achieved through those courses based on some body of content. The issue was therefore raised not only as to the need of a separate committee but also as to whether there was any tangible task for it. Those convinced of the need and even of the primacy of such a committee had two major arguments: (1) that general education courses to

174

date had not emphasized critical thinking and that, accordingly, there was a strong possibility that other committees would ignore the objective; (2) that critical thinking stated as a general education objective is not limited to course content but rather is regarded as a behavior desirable in all the activities and problems in which the individual becomes involved.

Added to these arguments were the voices of one or two persons representing institutions with courses in philosophy, logic, or "clear thinking" which would otherwise not be represented. American—and particularly college faculty—mores dictated the formation of a committee as the logical way of quieting the disagreement.

Underlying this issue of the need for a separate committee on critical thinking are some basic differences in viewpoint about the nature of the learning process. Those opposing or at the least doubting the advisability of a separate committee feared that it betokened a faith in the discredited formal discipline or faculty psychology. In general, it has been found that no learning experience has any extensive mental disciplining power. Thorndike and others rather conclusively demonstrated that such transfer as does take place happens only when there are identical elements or components in the learning and the transfer situations. Arguing from this, it is plausible that the ability to think in science must be developed by studying science, and that the ability to think on social issues must be developed by a course dealing with social issues. Contributing to this viewpoint is the obvious principle that critical thinking about any issue must be based on the knowledge of relevant facts and generalizations.

An opposing viewpoint accepts the necessity of identical elements but points to some evidence that transfer does appear to take place to a greater extent and, in some cases, in a somewhat different way, than is expected according to this theory. Transfer is apparently promoted by the meaningful organization of knowledge, by habits of work, methods of attacking problems, and by a developed motivation to seek for the transfer of knowledge and abilities. Added to this is a suspicion on the part of many concerned with general education that the theory of identical elements and its reinforcement of the importance of specific knowledge have resulted in the use of a formal discipline approach in many general education courses. Knowing as a prerequisite to thinking is all too easily misinterpreted to mean that thinking follows naturally out of knowledge—or, at least, that it should. A logical extension of such reasoning is that critical thinking is a by-product of instruction rather than an immediate objective.

The preceding rationale of the differences in viewpoint about committee organization for attacking critical thinking was not explicit in the deliberations, but in retrospect it appears to have been the fundamental basis for disagreement. The Critical Thinking Committee itself was constantly concerned about the issue of the pervasiveness or specificity of the objective. It had high hopes that its work, coupled with that of other committees, might throw some light on the problem. Later evidence will show that this hope was achieved only if a sufficiently diminutive meaning is accorded to "some."

THE OBJECTIVE OF CRITICAL THINKING

A major aim of general education is for the student "to acquire and use the skills and habits involved in critical and constructive thinking."[1] One might—as many have—quibble over the choice of words in and the meaning of this statement. Seemingly the statement is already afflicted with unnecessary verbiage which adds little or nothing. Apparently "constructive" was added to ward off unjustified associations of critical with cynical or destructive. "Acquire and use" and "skills and habits" serve only to obfuscate the essence of the objective, which is that generally educated individuals ought "to think critically." Yet the reduction of the objective to this concise phrase does not mean that it embraces all of thinking, nor that the phrase has a clear and uniform meaning to all people. As a starting point in consideration of critical thinking, it perhaps can be accepted that students—as one result of their educational experience—should be able to carry on types of mental activity more complicated than simple recall and restatement of ideas, facts, principles, etc., given in the textbook or presented by

[1] *Higher Education for American Democracy, Vol. I—Establishing the Goals* (Washington: Government Printing Office; and New York: Harper & Bros., 1947), p. 57.

the instructor in his lectures, but this broad conception is useless for either evaluation or instruction.

One of the earliest points of agreement about critical thinking was that it did not include "imaginative thinking," but this negative approach was quickly abandoned for a positive approach involving a listing of critical thinking abilities. For this purpose "problem solving," which was regarded as embracing most of the aspects of critical thinking, was adopted as the ability to be particularized. This restriction was decided upon because of a feeling that problem solving is essential to effective living. A detailed list of problem-solving abilities follows.

A TENTATIVE LIST OF THE PROBLEM-SOLVING ASPECTS OF CRITICAL THINKING

1. *Ability To Recognize the Existence of a Problem*
   a) To recognize related conditions in a situation.
   b) To recognize conflicts and issues in a situation.
   c) To locate "missing links" in a series of ideas or incidents.
   d) To recognize problems which have no solution.

2. *Ability To Define the Problem*
   a) To identify the nature of the problem.
   b) To understand what is involved and required in the problem.
   c) To recognize ways in which the problem can be phrased.
   d) To define difficult and abstract elements of the problem in simple, concrete, and familiar terms.
   e) To break complex elements of the problem into workable parts.
   f) To identify the central elements of the problem.
   g) To place the elements of the problem into an order in which they can be handled.
   h) To eliminate extraneous elements from the problem.
   i) To place the problem in its context.

3. *Ability To Select Information Pertinent to the Solution of the Problem*
   a) To distinguish reliable and unreliable sources of information.
   b) To recognize bias upon which information is selected and rejected.
   c) To recognize information relevant to the solution of the problem.
   d) To select adequate and reliable samples of information.
   e) To systematize information.

f) To select information from personal experience relevant to the solution of the problem.

4. *Ability To Recognize Assumptions Bearing on the Problem*
   a) To identify unstated assumptions.
   b) To identify unsupported assumptions.
   c) To identify irrelevant assumptions.

5. *Ability To Make Relevant Hypotheses*
   a) To discover clues to the solution of the problem.
   b) To formulate various hypotheses on the basis of information and assumptions.
   c) To select the more promising hypotheses for first consideration.
   d) To check the consistency of the hypotheses with the information and assumptions.
   e) To make hypotheses concerning unknown and needed information.

6. *Ability To Draw Conclusions Validly from Assumptions, Hypotheses, and Pertinent Information*
   a) To detect logical relationships among terms and propositions.
   b) To recognize necessary and sufficient conditions.
   c) To identify cause and effect relationships.
   d) To identify and state the conclusion.

7. *Ability To Judge the Validity of the Processes Leading to the Conclusion*
   a) To distinguish validly drawn conclusions from others chosen, for example, because they are in accord with values, preferences, and biases.
   b) To distinguish a necessary inference from a probable one.
   c) To detect formal logical inconsistencies in the argument.

8. *Ability To Evaluate a Conclusion in Terms of Its Application*
   a) To recognize conditions which would be necessary to verify a conclusion.
   b) To recognize conditions which would make a conclusion inapplicable.
   c) To judge the adequacy of a conclusion as a solution of the problem.

The preceding list is only one of many possible. Critical thinking is a complicated mental activity, and an almost endless list of specifics could be produced, no two items of which would be completely interdependent. Equally clearly they would not be independent, particularly if an attempt is made to view them as they might be applied in solving a problem. Therefore, this or any other list must be regarded primarily as an aid in understanding the nature of critical thinking, and the specifics of the list must not be allowed to usurp attention to the point where their integration and augmentation by other unlisted abilities into the still undefined complex mental ability—critical thinking—is forgotten. The list of abilities above is not startlingly different from others that have been devised and no great claim for originality can be made for it. One bit of evidence on this point is that three other committees of the Study working independently produced lists which were essentially in one-to-one correspondence to the above. Evidence of the fallibility of the list is found in the extent to which it underwent revision and reduction.

A Brief List of Critical Thinking Abilities

The list of critical thinking skills utilized by the committee in its later deliberations involved only five points. These, accompanied by a brief rationale, follow:

1. *The ability to define a problem.*

    People frequently attempt to settle difficulties without even knowing what the difficulty is. Training in identifying and defining problems may relieve much of the frustration generated in such cases. The ability to define a problem is also important in listening and reading. The trick of good reading and listening often is simply a matter of identifying the problem dealt with so that the ideas fall into a pattern.

2. *The ability to select pertinent information for the solution of a problem.*

    Once a person has defined a problem and has thought about it sufficiently to be able to state the problem in his own words, he needs to decide what kinds of information might help him in solving the problem. This involves judging what kind of information is pertinent to the problem, and it involves estimating the reliability of information which might be pertinent. These abilities are necessary for the intelligent solution of problems, and interact with the ability to see what the problem really is.

3. *The ability to recognize stated and unstated assumptions.*

By an *assumption* is meant something that is a part of the argument but is taken for granted without any argument to justify it. It may be stated, or it may not be. If it is stated, it is simply *said* to be true, not *shown* to be true. Probably the speaker (or writer) expects it to be accepted without any question. Sometimes an argument rests on an assumption which is not stated at all; in fact, the person making the argument may not be aware that it is involved at all. But it must be believed if the argument is to be accepted.

This is not to say that we should never make any assumptions when we form conclusions on the basis of evidence. We can't avoid making assumptions. But we do need to be on the lookout for those assumptions (in our own arguments and in those of others) which are important because they make a difference in whether or not the conclusion ought to be accepted.

4. *The ability to formulate and select relevant and promising hypotheses.*

It is important to make a deliberate effort to think of as many possible solutions or hypotheses as possible and to develop the habit of doing this. Then we examine the possibilities to see where each of them would lead. We think them through to their probable consequences. Some of them may not require much thought; they can be quickly eliminated from further consideration. Others may need careful examination before we decide which hypothesis seems to be the best one.

5. *The ability to draw conclusions validly and to judge the validity of inferences.*

When we put pieces of evidence together and draw conclusions from them, it is important that we do it in such a way that the conclusion really follows from the evidence. This is what we usually call "correct reasoning" or "logical thinking." Granted that our evidence is pertinent and that it is true, we can still make mistakes in judging what conclusion it supports. When we avoid these mistakes, and reach a conclusion that does follow from the evidence, we have a "valid" conclusion.

We can learn to judge when we are confronted with a valid argument and when we are not. We particularly need to be able to judge those situations in which common beliefs and our own preconceptions might make us inclined to accept a conclusion that is not validly based on the evidence. Obviously, this is true both with respect to conclusions which we form for ourselves and with respect to conclusions which are formed by others and which we are asked to accept. Along with the ability to draw valid conclusions from evidence goes the ability to judge the validity of arguments which we hear or read.

The process of combination of abilities and the dropping of the subpoints under the major headings resulted from the committee members finding, first, that the more detailed list had served its purpose in bringing about a common understanding of the abilities and, second, that it was both unrealistic and impossible to find situations and develop test materials which clearly and unequivocally involved the separate abilities of the more disjunct list. The same difficulty applied but to a lesser degree to the abbreviated list.

REVIEW OF RELATED TESTS

It may be accepted as one of the maxims of evaluation that any individual or group undertaking an evaluation task will find all prior attempts unsatisfactory in some respect. Scientific objectivity dictates, however, that this be a conclusion arrived at after careful deliberation rather than an assumption made in advance. So it was with the committee.

A review of prior ventures in the area of critical thinking revealed the following instruments which appeared to merit detailed study:

1. General Educational Development Tests, College Level (Educational Testing Service)
2. American Council on Education Psychological Tests (Educational Testing Service)

3. Diagnostic Aptitude Tests (Psychological Corporation)
4. Primary Mental Abilities, Thurstone (Science Research Associates, Inc.)
5. Yale Aptitude Tests (Educational Records Bureau)
6. General Aptitude Test Battery, USES GATB (United States Employment Service)
7. Miller Analogies Test (Psychological Corporation)
8. Warren R. Baller, *The Case of Mickey Murphy,* A Case Study Instrument for Evaluating Teachers' Understanding of Child Growth and Development (University of Nebraska Press)
9. Watson-Glaser Test of Critical Thinking (World Book Company)
10. Tests on Critical Thinking of the Progressive Education Association Eight-Year Study: Interpretation of Data, Application of the Principles of Logical Reasoning, Nature of Proof (Educational Testing Service)
11. Reasoning tests such as those in Thouless' *How to Think Straight* (Simon & Schuster), and in various logic texts

One or more faculty members in the various cooperating institutions were requested to review and analyze one of these tests by (1) taking the test himself and rendering an introspective report of personal reactions and mental processes; and (2) arranging for students to take all or a part of the test and then report on their reactions to and mode of procedure with the test items. These reactions were then summarized by a written response to a number of questions. The following list of questions is typical of those used in the review of a test or section of a test.

1. Are the instructions for taking the test clear and understandable?
2. Are the items equitably spread among the various categories of skills which the test purports to measure?
3. Are the items equitably spread among the various divisions of knowledge or subject matter with which the test purports to be concerned?
4. Do you believe students could be expected to finish the test within the time specified for it?
5. Do the items seem to you to range from fairly easy to fairly difficult items?
6. Do the items represent sufficiently varied tasks so as to maintain student interest?
7. Do the test items reveal any discernible work or concept pattern?
8. Does the total test appear to be well suited for the educational level at which it will be used?
9. What is your general reaction to this test?

Utilizing such questions, extensive reviews of the instruments listed earlier were prepared. As expected, no instrument in its entirety was found to be satisfactory to evaluate critical thinking as construed by the committee, although particular items and testing techniques were found to be suggestive. While many particular criticisms were made of certain instruments, the major shortcomings were these: (1) use of problems or tasks devoid of realism, such as puzzles or abstract numerical or geometrical problems; (2) too limited coverage of critical thinking skills as listed by the committee; and (3) unsuitable content loading. The experience of reviewing these materials was productive in helping to crystallize the criteria to be met by any new instrument. The experience was also valuable in assuring the committee that what they envisaged as critical thinking was not identical with intelligence or academic aptitude as defined in tests of such abilities.

THE SPECIFICATIONS FOR A TEST OF CRITICAL THINKING

Coincidental with the review of existing instruments, attempts were made to collect accounts of situations illustrative of the critical or uncritical thinking of students in respect to the specific abilities agreed upon. These situations were culled from test experiences and classroom, campus, or other situations. In some cases, students were invited to contribute from their own experience or from observation. The faculty member collecting the situations was also invited to attempt to formulate them into a series of test items. Questions arising out of the attempts to fulfill this appeal forced the formulation of specifications for the types of problems or situations to be included in the contemplated test. The following criteria were arrived at:

1. The situations should be realistic in terms of student experience— not hypothetical, but recognizable as actual in their experience or in the experience of people known to them. The possibility of involvement of emotional reaction or of attitudes should not in itself be the basis for elimination of a situation.
2. The situations should be of such non-provincial nature as to be usable by all the institutions.
3. The situations should be so selected that the evaluation device may be used over a period of time without being invalidated through emphasis on matters of transitory importance.

4. The situations should be independent of particular courses and content so as to avoid overlapping with special area projects and to make some provision for evaluating the total growth of critical thinking resulting from all courses.
5. The situations should be so devised as to present all pertinent information or be so qualified that any information not so presented may be expected to have been attained by most students. The vocabulary should likewise be within the range of the majority of students.
6. Directions should be clear and less complicated than the thinking processes tested.
7. Items should be kept free of the terminology and conventions of formal logic.
8. For groups of items having a common set of responses, the elements of this "key" should be simple enough to be readily kept in mind.
9. Complicated problems or situations involving a large number of interrelated items should be avoided in favor of separate test situations involving only one or two items.
10. Words used should be found in some standard word list for the twelfth grade.
11. Warning should be given of the intent (if such exists) of using artificial or generally unfamiliar words.

Criteria 2 and 3 were regarded as necessary for a test for general usage, but it was recognized that issues of timely and local interest might often be better for instructional purposes than problems lacking these qualities. It was also considered desirable to make some specification of the sources from which the problems or situations might be drawn. The following analysis of problem sources was accepted for this purpose. The subpoints are illustrative rather than exhaustive.

1. Problems in reference to self.
   a) Faced with problems involving his own intellectual and physical capabilities and limitations, how does the individual go about solving them?

2. Problems in reference to other people.
   a) Given certain facts involving the motives of others, how does the student proceed to analyze them? Is he able to form some hypotheses about the motives of others after observing their demonstrated behavior? Does he see the limitations of such hypotheses? Given certain motives, does he try to decide why such motives are present?

b) Presented with the facts of other persons' values or individual points of view, how does the student proceed to interpret them? Is he able to see assumptions upon which such points of view are based? Can he predict inferences or implications which might be drawn from such points of view?

c) Presented with the existence of inconsistent behavior on the part of individuals, is the student able to analyze the different roles in which they are acting?

3. Problems in reference to the physical and natural universe.

a) How does the student go about explaining the changing and unchanging elements of the universe? Does he attempt to bring what he knows about the universe to bear in solving his problems? Is he, for example, aware of the implications for himself, as a man, of accepting Einstein's theory of relativity?

4. Problems in reference to society.

a) How does the student think about differing cultural values? Does he engage in rationalization or does he seek to find explanations?

b) Faced with various historical facts indicating social change, is the student able to see the implications of those facts? For example, can he accept the fact that the traditional family might be changing and might possibly disappear? How does he explain the changes which have taken place in Western civilization since 1800?

5. Problems in reference to values and ethical standards.

a) Can the individual think clearly and objectively about concepts of democracy? Can he see the implications of those concepts? Can he detect upon what assumptions those concepts are based?

b) To what sort of critical analysis is the student willing and able to subject various systems of ethics and morality? At what point in the process of his thinking does he rely upon faith to sustain his point of view?

These five areas were regarded as defining the "content" axis for a two-way chart describing the dimensions of possible evaluation instruments. Figure 6 illustrates the relationship between the two elements. The cells of the chart show the relative emphasis placed on a particular ability in reference to a particular content. The non-content column 6 was introduced to cover the possibility of using materials such as puzzles or of employing syllogisms using undefined or manufactured words or phrases. It was agreed that such materials should be used only if they seemed to be the best way to get at certain critical thinking skills.

Since there was no rational basis for deciding exactly what percentage of items should be allocated to each cell, the chart was regarded more as a convenient scheme for classifying items to avoid imbalance in the test. The aim was to fill as many cells as possible, although ultimately a decision as to the weighting of the abilities was agreed upon.

These steps involving the definition of the objective of critical thinking and the development of a set of specifications for a test paralleled, rather than preceded, the writing and tryout of items. In fact, some of the test specifications already noted were arrived at only after use and analysis of the earlier test forms.

CONTENT AXIS — CRITICAL THINKING ABILITIES	1 Self	2 Others	3 Society	4 Natural & Physical Universe	5 Values & Ethical Standards	6 Non-Content Problems
1. Ability to define a problem		1	1		3	
2. Ability to select pertinent information		1		6		
3. Ability to recognize assumptions		12	1		3	
4. Ability to formulate relevant hypotheses	9	6				
5. Ability to draw conclusions validly		2	3	4		

FIG. 6.—Chart exhibiting the specifications for the Test of Critical Thinking

THE DEVELOPMENT OF A TEST OF CRITICAL THINKING

The variety of procedures utilized in obtaining test materials, trying them out, and revising them would take too much time to report in detail. Assignments were made to committee members to write a certain number of items fitting certain specifications or cells in the chart given above, and these assignments were in turn passed on to other faculty members. Tests and test fragments composed of such items were given to students. For some problems students were asked to write out a response as a basis for selection of distracters for an objective test item. Tape recordings were made of students' oral responses to objective test items. In other cases written analyses or defenses by students of their chosen answer were collected. All items with information on student reactions were extensively reviewed by committee members as well as by other faculty members. These procedures were as extensively employed in validation as in test development, and will be reported in more detail under that heading. Trial forms of tests were developed and given extensively to students, so that data on the difficulty and the discrimination of items could be computed. From all of this effort two forms—A and B—of A Test of Critical Thinking were prepared for use with entering freshmen in the fall of 1951.

The two forms of the Test of Critical Thinking were originally developed with the hope that they might be equivalent forms. Form A, however, was given the best of the material based on tryouts, and Form B was then made up of similar residual material revised in an effort to make it equally satisfactory. In tryouts with random or matched groups, B was much inferior to A, and its use was discontinued. Form A was used in post-testing freshmen in the spring of 1952 and a few sophomores in the spring of 1953. Even Form A was not altogether satisfactory, for it was found to be somewhat too easy, and it contained a number of nondiscriminating items. Hence, still another form, Form G, was prepared. Form G consists of the best of the items of all earlier forms. The items retained were those which attained the best coefficients of discrimination in the year's testing, but attention was also given to maintaining a proper balance in respect to the objectives of the test, and to the selection of somewhat more difficult items. Form G was used with entering freshmen in the fall of 1952 and again in the spring of 1953. Some of the results of these testings and associated studies will be presented in later sections.

The specifications for Form G of the test with illustrative items will be helpful to those who do not have at hand a copy of the test or manual. The illustrative items are similar to those in Form G but they are selected from some of the less satisfactory materials rejected for the final form of the test.

1. *Ability To Define Problems*

A recently married couple decide that they will give $200 of their annual income to charity. Their problem is:

1. What charity-supported works are most deserving and in

need of the money they can give, and what distribution of their $200 best balances these demands?

2. How shall they deal with those making the appeals, with the least time and bother and with the most congenial response to their requests?

3. Which of the appeals that come to them is most worthy?

4. Whether this amount ($200) is too much or too little for the cause they want to aid.

5. Whether concentration of their gift in one agency would do more ultimate good than distribution of it among several users.

2. *Ability To Select Pertinent Information*

The head physician at Cowlick College wishes a reasonably accurate estimate of the number of cases of chicken pox treated at the infirmary during the past five years, but his time is limited. A total of 10,000 cases of all kinds of sickness were treated during the period. A study of which of the following samples from his records would probably be adequate and still conserve his time?

1. Every odd-numbered case from the 10,000.

2. Every twentieth case from the 10,000.

3. 400 cases selected to represent proportionately each age group.

4. The last 400 cases treated.

5. The last 200 cases treated.

3. *Ability To Recognize Assumptions*

Items 34 through 47 refer to the following newspaper advertisement:

"Wanna buy a duct? If you're planning to install a warm air heating system, ask your contractor about the advantages of Blake Aluminum for ductwork. Many have already found it saves money because it's easier for workmen to handle, gives more long-run satisfaction because it never rusts, never needs painting, is always neat. Aluminum's natural insulation prevents excessive heat loss; sound is deadened, too. Approved for FHA financing."

In this advertisement the writer makes a number of claims for his product. He also takes for granted a number of ideas about it, about prospective buyers of heating systems, etc. Mark each of the statements 34 through 47 according to this scale:

1. The writer states this, although maybe not in just these words.

2. The writer does not state this, but he does state something which shows that he must have taken it for granted.
3. The writer does not state this, nor does it have any relation to his argument.
4. The writer does not state this, and it would weaken his argument if he did state it.

35. Ordinary ducts are harder to handle than aluminum ducts.
38. Durability as well as initial expense should be considered in buying heating equipment.

4. *Ability To Formulate and Select Relevant Hypotheses*

Two hundred Negro school children and their parents filed suit in Atlanta Federal District Court, demanding an end to racial segregation in the schools. The suit asked that the separation of schools for those of different races be declared unconstitutional and be ordered to cease forthwith. The *Atlanta Constitution*, the city's largest newspaper, editorialized, in effect:

EITHER THE SUIT WILL BE WITHDRAWN OR MANY
WHO HAVE WORKED FOR EQUAL OPPORTUNITIES
WILL BE ALIENATED

A group of people, discussing the suit and the editorial, made the comments given in Problems 252–257. Mark each of these comments according to the following scale:

1. That means just the same thing the editorial said.
2. You disagree with the editorial then.
3. You can't tell from what the editorial said whether that is true or not.

252. The suit won't be withdrawn, but not many who worked for equal opportunities will be alienated.
253. If the suit is withdrawn, not many who have worked for equal opportunities will be alienated.
256. Failure to withdraw this suit will be a matter of alienating many who have worked for equal opportunities.

5. *Ability To Draw Conclusions Validly and To Judge the Validity of Inferences*

In Items 14 through 17 you are to accept as true that *all window-washers are poorly paid*, and *some window-washers have large families*. Mark each of the conclusions, *14* through *17* according to the following scale:

1. *Must be true* on the basis of the given statements.

2. *Might be true* on the basis of the given statements.
3. *Must be false* on the basis of the given statements.

14. Some people who have large families are not poorly paid.
15. Some people who are poorly paid have large families.
17. No people who are poorly paid have large families.

RESEARCH ASPECTS OF THE PROJECT

Reliability of the Test

The reliability of a test is a function of many factors—the test, the time allowed, the conditions of administration, and the characteristics of the individuals tested. Students respond rather consistently to factual tests because responding to such tests is a familiar role. Tests which are novel in instructions and type of exercise involve a somewhat more random response with consequent lowering of reliability. Experience also indicates that the critical thinking type of item requires more time so that fewer items can be covered in a specified time interval, and results in a further reduction of reliability.

Another factor to be wrestled with is the length of the test. A test of two hours' working time—other things being equal—will be more reliable than one of one-hour working time. Against this must be balanced the convenience of using the test. The committee—like the others in the Study—decided that the use of such a test would be sharply curtailed unless it could be given in the usual fifty-minute period. Reliability was deliberately sacrificed to expediency. This is less serious than it might have been if individual scores were a matter of major concern or if reliable subscores were demanded. The decision was that the test was for use in studying group changes rather than individual, and that a single score was to be used on the test. The original plan called for two equivalent forms of the test so that if greater reliability were desired both could be administered; thus, in effect, the test would be of double length. Otherwise, alternate forms might be used for pre- and post-testing. Poor results with Form B led to its abandonment and the decision to develop a single form, Form G.

One estimate of the reliability of Form G was obtained by computing an adjusted split-halves coefficient from a sample comprised of the first 10 percent of the sample from four institutions. The resulting coefficient was .84 for the 97 cases. Later, Kuder-Richardson formula No. 20 was employed on a 20 percent sample with the following results:

$$N = 231 \qquad \text{Mean} = 29.09 \qquad \text{S.D.} = 7.21 \qquad r = .79$$

Several institutions reported reliabilities in the range .80–.85 computed for their own student groups. Such results—while lower than might be desired—must be considered satisfactory for the purposes for which the test is proposed. Experience indicates that it is somewhat more difficult to obtain high reliability for tests of this type than for content-loaded achievement tests.

Related to reliability is the performance of the items in terms of difficulty and discrimination. Evidence on both of these points is presented in the test manual and need not be reproduced here. However, the statistical evidence of this sort on the final Form G was excellent, showing all items making a contribution to the total test score.

Intercorrelations of the Critical Thinking Abilities

Related to the reliability and to the decision to avoid part scores is evidence on the interrelation of the groups of items classified under the five major abilities. One such set of intercorrelations is given in Table 38. This is based on only one institution but indicates the general order of magnitude of the correlations as verified for other colleges.

Form C, made up of all items from Forms A and B and other

TABLE 38

INTERCORRELATION OF ABILITIES TESTED ON TEST OF CRITICAL THINKING

(N=224 freshmen and sophomores)

PARTS	NO. OF ITEMS	CORRELATION COEFFICIENTS				
		Definition	Selecting Information	Recognizing Assumptions	Selecting Hypotheses	Drawing Conclusions
Definitions.............	6	x				
Selecting Information.....	12	.15	x			
Recognizing Assumptions..	14	.19	.23	x		
Selecting Hypotheses.....	10	.08	.20	.18	x	
Drawing Conclusions.....	15	.28	.28	.42	.26	x
Total.................	57	.40	.51	.67	.64	.73

items employed in the tryout forms, was developed solely for research purposes. This form was divided into four sections dealing respectively with the abilities 2, 3, 4, and 5. Information based upon these longer tests of the major abilities incorporated in Form C suggests that perfectly reliable tests of these abilities would intercorrelate to the extent of about .65 to .85; such intercorrelations point to the fact that the abilities are somewhat distinctive and that longer subtests might have some diagnostic significance not available in the present short form (see Table 39).

TABLE 39

INTERCORRELATION OF SCORES ON THE PARTS OF THE TEST OF CRITICAL THINKING, FORM C

SUBTESTS	ESTIMATE OF RELIABILITY	CORRELATION COEFFICIENT		
		C-1	C-2	C-3
C-1	.66			
C-2	.83	.48		
C-3	.72	.41	.57	
C-4	.76	.48	.63	.55

Validity of the Test

Validity was a particularly perplexing problem for the Critical Thinking Committee. Indeed, validity is not an intrinsic characteristic of a test but a characteristic jointly of the test and the situation in which the test is used. For schools wherein or for students to whom little experience is provided in the development of critical thinking skills, no test of critical thinking can have much validity as a measure of attainment of that educational objective. It is much as though a test in mathematics were employed to assess the development of an art class. No matter how valid and reliable the mathematics test for some purposes, it would not be valid in that situation.

The natural way to check test validity is to compare that test with some direct criterion of the ability tested. If there were adequate means available to measure critical thinking or if teacher judgments were thoroughly satisfactory, there would have been no need to construct a test. These arguments are not presented to avoid the responsibility of offering some evidence of validity; rather, they are meant to show that the task is not a simple one. As with other of the tests of the Study, our case for validity, then, must rest on the cumulative significance of a large number of both positive and non-negative findings and on the steps taken in writing the tests in the first place. Unfortunately, most of the evidence discussed in this and following sections is based on Form A rather than on Form G, but there is evidence which suggests that Form G (which is, after all, only a slight revision of Form A) is more satisfactory than Form A.

The first measures to ensure validity were those involved in the process of the development of the tests. The judgment of the faculty members that the tasks involved in the items were meaningful and educationally significant is not to be taken lightly, but no one could be more skeptical of this judgment than the committee itself. Hence this judgment was buttressed by: (1) Recordings were obtained where students verbalized (with prodding, if necessary) their responses to critical thinking questions in front of a tape recorder. Their thought process was then compared with the one hypothesized, and flaws in the items were also uncovered. (2) Test items were restructured so that the stem only could be presented to students for an essay response. This provided a check on the thinking involved and suggested responses suitable for the objective form. (3) Test items with answers were presented with the instruction that the answer should be selected and then a paragraph written to justify or defend the choice.

These checks ensured, for most of the retained and revised items, that correct thinking would result in selection of the correct answer, and that the wrong answers corresponded to incorrect thinking or to guessing. This evidence, combined with the judgments of the committee, also helped in selecting items which can and do evoke the mental processes originally accepted as descriptive of some aspects of critical thinking.

Another approach to the investigation of validity involved the use of two criterion groups made up of students classified by teachers, residence hall counselors, or other students as evidencing critical thinking or lack of it. Several such studies were carried out independently at many institutions.

Dr. Lily Detchen requested twenty-two instructors at the Pennsylvania College for Women to rate on critical thinking all the seniors well known to them. The ability was discussed with the instructors to the point where they understood the qualities involved, and they then rated students as superior, average, or inferior. An item analysis (of Form A) was then made on the basis of the teacher ratings and compared with the item analysis based on the total test score, with the results shown in Table 40.

TABLE 40

ITEM ANALYSIS OF A TEST OF CRITICAL THINKING

Analysis	No. of Items
Found acceptable by teacher rating but not by test score criterion	4
Found acceptable by test score criterion but not by teacher rating	9
Found acceptable by both methods	34
Found unacceptable by both methods	10
Total number of items in test	57

A majority of the test items were found to make discriminations corresponding to the teachers' judgments. When the teacher ratings were compared directly with test scores, the results given in Table 41 were found:

TABLE 41

COMPARISON OF TEACHER RATING AND SCORES ON THE TEST OF CRITICAL THINKING

PERFORMANCE ON THE TEST	TEACHER RATING		TOTAL NO. OF STUDENTS
	Clearly Superior	Clearly Inferior	
Above median	19	1	20
Below median	2	10	12
Total	21	11	32

Dr. Carl Rexroad obtained rather extensive data at Stephens College on a group of girls who had taken the Test of Critical Thinking. All were enrolled in psychology. Psychology instructors, advisers, residence hall personnel, and students cooperated in providing ratings of critical thinking utilizing the forms shown in

Figures 7 and 8. Although not all these ratings could be obtained for all cases, the volume of evidence was still impressive. The results are shown in Table 42.

TABLE 42

CORRELATION BETWEEN STUDENTS ON RATINGS OF CRITICAL THINKING AND
THEIR SCORES ON A TEST OF CRITICAL THINKING

RATINGS BY	N	RATINGS		TEST SCORES*		CORRELA-TION
		Mean	S.D.	Mean	S.D.	
Psychology teacher....	322	3.22	1.29	118.40	21.54	.66
Adviser.............	236	3.33	1.07	118.78	21.25	.50
Hall counselor........	266	3.40	1.00	119.30	21.12	.42
Self.................	244	3.09	.72	119.90	21.90	.50
Peers (at least three raters).............	169	3.59	.67	120.00	21.08	.62

* Composite of several forms of the test.

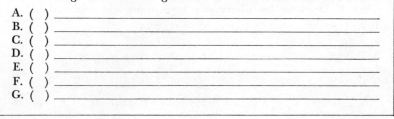

Developing a good test is a very complicated business, and so we are asking your further help in determining how good the experimental Test of Critical Thinking is.

1. Your name _____

2. How well do you think you did? Don't be modest and don't brag.

Circle
one
number

5—as well as the highest fifth of all students
4—as well as the high fifth
3—as well as the middle fifth
2—only as well as the low fifth
1—only as well as the lowest fifth

3. How well do you think others you know did?

3.1 List below the names of students taking psychology whom you know well enough to make a guess as to how well they did.

3.2 Make your guess by comparing them with yourself, and then deciding on and writing in the chosen number from 2 above.

A. ( ) _____
B. ( ) _____
C. ( ) _____
D. ( ) _____
E. ( ) _____
F. ( ) _____
G. ( ) _____

FIG. 7.—Form for recording student judgment of the Test of Critical Thinking

HOW ABOUT A GOOD SCOUT DEED?

Stephens is a participant in the Cooperative Study of Evaluation in General Education. One instrument being developed is a Test of Critical Thinking.

This CT test is designed to measure how skillful the student is in

   a) defining and analyzing problems.
   b) recognizing unstated assumptions in an argument.
   c) determining the relevancy of data.
   d) drawing valid conclusions or inferences from data given.
   e) formulating and testing hypotheses.

The items of the test were chosen so that as nearly as possible

   a) arrival at the correct answer would depend upon seeing and judging relationships rather than on a background of knowledge.
   b) the item would be close enough to a possible life situation to make it challenging.
   c) the item would be emotionally neutral.

You are being asked to judge (or guess) how well the students listed below should do on the test. Your cooperation will definitely help to determine how good the test is.

In making your judgments remember that you are judging only how able the student is in doing the kind of thinking described above,
   not how able he is in any and all kinds of thinking.
   not how wide his store of information.
   not how much his emotions interfere with his doing straight thinking about some matters.

In recording your judgments use the appropriate number from the following:

   5—should score in the highest fifth
   4—should score in the high fifth
   3—should score in the middle fifth
   2—should score in the low fifth
   1—should score in the lowest fifth

Make a judgment on any student whom you have observed sufficiently to have even a vague impression as to her ability to think critically. Mark X for those for whom you have insufficient observation.

1. ( ) _____   6. ( ) _____
2. ( ) _____   7. ( ) _____
3. ( ) _____   8. ( ) _____
4. ( ) _____   9. ( ) _____
5. ( ) _____   10. ( ) _____

Return to Psychology Department

FIG. 8.—Form for recording faculty judgments of the Test of Critical Thinking

The mean ratings in Table 42 compare reasonably well with the test scores. It is worth noting that the psychology teachers who knew the test reasonably well and the students who had taken the test both made ratings which correlated more highly than those of other groups. Students tended to rate themselves lower than did the staff or peers. This is easily seen in Figure 9 wherein are plotted the mean ratings and test scores for the five different ratings.

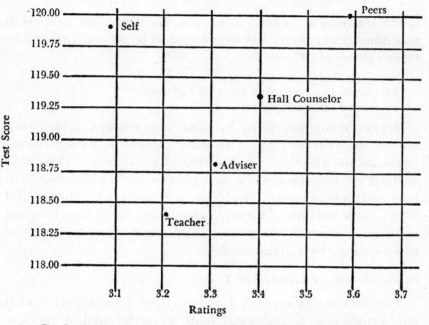

FIG. 9.—Relation between ratings and Critical Thinking Test Scores.

At Kansas State College four instructors provided critical thinking ratings for seven classes which were compared with the test scores. The reader for one of the instructors also provided ratings. The pooled ratings compared with the test scores are shown in Table 43.

Chi-square, a measure of association, is found to be 23.67, which is well beyond the .01 level (chi-square equals 13.28 for 4 degrees of freedom). Analysis of the separate ratings, however, shows significant association at or beyond the .01 level in only two classes.

Another bit of evidence relevant to the issue of validity is found

TABLE 43

TEACHERS' RATING ON CRITICAL THINKING

CRITICAL THINKING TEST SCORE	TEACHER RATING			NO. OF STUDENTS
	Low	Medium	High	
Low....................	15	16	4	35
Medium.................	14	39	13	66
High...................	1	21	17	39
No. of items.............	30	76	34	140

in the reactions of students to the test. Such reactions were taken in a number of colleges and were found to be generally favorable. Of one group of 207 students:

    120 reported enjoying the test;
    54 reported indifference or mingled reactions;
    33 reported dislike of the test.

Reasons commonly given by those who enjoyed it used such phrases as: "challenging," "increases power to evaluate facts," "good mental exercise," "had to think for a change." Those who disliked the test reported in such phrases as: "ambiguous," "too long and monotonous," "problems over my head," "felt as if I didn't know anything." Clearly, all students found it to be a test requiring a somewhat different type of mental activity than those to which they were accustomed.

Intercorrelations with Other Tests

The intercorrelation of A Test of Critical Thinking with other tests provides some additional basis for understanding the test. Such data are also rather tenuous evidence of validity which can be at best non-negative rather than positive. For example, if critical thinking is not identical with intelligence, then a test of critical thinking should not correlate very highly with an academic aptitude or intelligence test. On the other hand, a low correlation with intelligence would be equally suspect. Tables 44–47 exhibit data of this type.

The correlations reported in Table 44 are selected from many computed at various colleges. These were chosen either because of the size of the group involved or because they represented unique evidence even though based on small groups. Correlations reported here and with the various tests of intelligence and aptitude range from .38 to .71. Although there are exceptions, the Test of Critical Thinking, as expected, shows somewhat higher correlations with verbally loaded over quantitatively loaded tests.

TABLE 44

CORRELATIONS OF A TEST OF CRITICAL THINKING WITH INTELLIGENCE
OR ACADEMIC APTITUDE TESTS

Name of Test	Group	N	r
ACE Psychological Examination			
Total Score............................	Freshmen	336	.38
Total Score............................	Freshmen	300	.69
Total Score............................	Freshman Women	208	.40
Linguistic Score........................	Freshman Men	239	.42
Linguistic Score........................	Freshman Women	208	.55
Ohio State Psychological Examination........	Freshmen	165	.65
CEEB Scholastic Aptitude Test..............	Freshman Men	318	.60
Yale Aptitude, Verbal Reasoning.............	Freshmen	166	.52
Yale Aptitude, Quantitative Reasoning........	Freshmen	166	.52
Otis Self-Administering Tests of Mental Ability.	Freshman Women	65	.71

TABLE 45

CORRELATION OF CRITICAL THINKING TEST WITH VARIOUS ACHIEVEMENT TESTS

Name of Test	Source of Data	Group	N	r
Cooperative General Culture (History of Social Study)...	Antioch College	Freshmen	165	.50
Nelson-Denny Reading, Form A Vocabulary..............	Pennsylvania College for Women	Freshman women	150	.37
Paragraph Comprehension..		″ ″	150	.50
Total...................		″ ″	150	.56
MSC Reading Test..........	Michigan State College	Freshman men	164	.49
MSC Reading Test..........		Freshman women	134	.53
MSC Reading Test..........		Grad. students	19	.80
GED College Level Social Studies, Form B..........	Pennsylvania College for Women	Freshman women	150	.56
GED College Level Correctness and Effectiveness of Expression, Form B..		″ ″	150	.47
Cooperative Reading (C2) Vocabulary..............	Stephens College	College women	641	.57
Speed...................		″ ″	641	.60
Level...................		″ ″	641	.55
Total...................		″ ″	641	.65
Iowa High School Content English.................	Pennsylvania College for Women	Scholarship applicants (85% of them above median on Iowa High School Content Total Score)	80	.39
Mathematics..............			80	.68
Science.................			80	.38
History and Social Studies..			80	.47
Total...................			80	.67

There being no planned program for relating the Test of Critical Thinking to subject-matter achievement tests, the correlations reported in Table 45 are the result of local investigations. Except for the correlation of .68 with the Mathematics section of the Iowa High School Content Examination, the correlations are not surprising. Despite the generally high level of the scholarship applicants at the Pennsylvania College for Women, the Test of Critical Thinking was found to have a good range and was used along with the Iowa High School Content Examination scores in making decisions about scholarships.

TABLE 46

CORRELATION OF THE TEST OF CRITICAL THINKING WITH
COURSE EXAMINATIONS AND GRADES

Course or Examination	Institution	Group	N	r
First-year average/Critical Thinking pre-test..........	Pennsylvania College for Women	Freshman women	144	.58
First-year average/Critical Thinking post-test.........		Freshman women	144	.69
Four-year point average......		Senior women	101	.32
History of Western Civilization......................		Freshman women	50	.52
Biology.....................		Freshman women	50	.60
Freshman English...........		Freshman women	50	.49
Human Development*.......		Freshman women	50	.70
Grade-point average.........	Stephens College	College women	641	.49
Grade-point average in general education courses......	Michigan State College	Juniors and seniors	67	.62
Grade-point average in all other courses.............		Juniors and seniors	67	.15
Practical logic comprehensive examination..............	University of Florida	Freshmen	288	.59

* The examination in Human Development included some experimental critical thinking items.

The data from Table 46, like those from Table 45, were reported as phases of voluntary local studies. Correlations between the Test of Critical Thinking scores and grades commonly equaled or exceeded the correlations of academic aptitude tests such as the ACE Psychological Examination with grades. The surprising difference in correlations with general education course grades and with other courses found at Michigan State College is thought to result from the emphasis on critical thinking in the general education courses. This emphasis is reflected in examinations which require this ability in considerable measure and which determine 50 percent of the grade.

In general, the correlations shown in the preceding tables are in the expected range. While correlating reasonably well with tests of intellectual ability, there is no reason to classify the test as a test of intelligence. The correlation is almost equally good with

TABLE 47

TYPICAL CORRELATIONS OF THE TEST OF CRITICAL THINKING WITH
OTHER TESTS OF CRITICAL THINKING

Test	Institution	Group	N	r
Science Reasoning and Under-standing, Form A	Pennsylvania College for Women........ Antioch College......	Freshman women Freshmen	150 40	.39 .50
Critical Analysis in Reading and Writing	Pennsylvania College for Women........ Michigan State College Michigan State College	Freshman women Freshman women Freshman men	150	.53 .51 .32
Critical Thinking in Social Science	Pennsylvania College for Women........ Antioch College...... University of Florida..	Freshman women Freshmen Freshmen	150 86 300	.69 .66 .67
Critical Judgment in the Hu-manities (Literature)	Western Washington College of Education	Freshmen and sophomores.....	98	.38
Watson-Glaser Critical Think-ing Appraisal	Michigan State College Michigan State College	Freshman women Freshman men	164 134	.61 .53

various achievement tests and with grades. In fact, as already remarked, most of the colleges computing such correlations found the Test of Critical Thinking slightly higher in correlation with grades than their usual academic aptitude test. Higher correlations were found with grades in certain courses where a priori considerations indicated greater emphasis on critical thinking. One of the most outstanding of these is the correlation reported from one college of .62 with general education course grades against .15 for other courses. On the other hand, a course in practical logic supposedly specifically aimed at this objective yielded a correlation of .59, no higher than that found for other courses or combinations of courses. Correlations with the Test of Critical Thinking in the Social Sciences ran rather consistently above .60, showing that these two have much in common despite difference in the content and problems utilized. It was the judgment of all directly concerned that the results were consistent with expectation.

Measurement of Change in Critical Thinking Test Scores

A major concern throughout the work of the Critical Thinking Committee was the accumulation of evidence on the extent to which critical thinking ability is or can be improved by education. Still more specific is the question of the differences in development induced by varying patterns of general education courses or by general education courses as against more traditional departmental offerings. The issue of the relative effectiveness of a concentrated course in logic or critical thinking as against the more diffuse emphases in a number of courses is a pertinent one. Although something more can and will be said about some of these matters in chapter 10, it may as well be stated that no answers are available here for such questions as those just posed. A variety of types of evidence, however, will be presented indicating that A Test of Critical Thinking does show evidence of differences in student groups and that this evidence bears some relation to the educational experience.

For such comparisons, pre- and post-test data from a number of institutions and data from groups of students matched in terms of ability are available. In general, students do make higher scores after one and two years of college, and student groups of successive years show continued but decreasing increments in tested ability. Before examining such data, two prior questions need to be considered. First, since Form B was discontinued, all repetitions utilized the same form. Therefore, there is some concern attached to knowing the practice effect. Investigation of this in two institutions wherein the same form (Form A) was repeated at intervals of a few days up to two months (embracing very little class work, however, because of the intervening Christmas holidays) revealed mean differences of about one raw score point. The practice effect, then, is small and probably even less significant for longer intervals of time when recall of specific items or techniques of analysis would presumably be less.

The second question involves the extent to which differences in gains might be simply due to differences in the original groups.

TABLE 48

PRE-TEST MEANS AND STANDARD DEVIATIONS ON A TEST OF
CRITICAL THINKING, FORM A

Institution	N	Range of Scores	Mean	S.D.
A............	336	48–11	30.24	7.01
B............	124	46–15	31.23	7.02
C............	271	48– 5	26.96	7.44
D............	250	46– 8	27.51	7.41

Four of the colleges making most extensive use of the test had the pre-test results shown in Table 48. The means were found to differ significantly, but the ACE Psychological Examination means were likewise found to differ significantly. Adjusted for differences in ability, the means for A Test of Critical Thinking were as follows:

Institution A 29.51
            B 28.84
            C 29.48
            D 28.76

Differences are no longer significant. This may be taken as an indication that, allowing for ability, the students entering various colleges (the four above were very different in their programs and in the type of students attracted) do not differ in critical thinking ability.

Table 49 shows combined data for a number of colleges on the pre-test and post-test results over the freshman year. The difference between means computed from Table 49 might be inflated because of selection involved in the post-test. Still another factor involved in dealing with gains is the negative correlation of gains with pre-test. These negative correlations are generally small, the largest in absolute value being .31 over a period of four months. Over longer

TABLE 49

DATA DERIVED FROM PRE- AND POST-TESTING FRESHMEN,
TEST OF CRITICAL THINKING, FORM A

Test	Mean Scores			No. of Students	No. of Colleges
	Lowest Reported by a College	Highest Reported by a College	All Students		
Pre-test............	26.96	37.85	32.15	2,171	12
Post-test...........	33.00	42.99	36.98	743	5

intervals the correlations were in the neighborhood of $-.15$. Since this phenomenon is a rather familiar one and not unique to this test, further comments and possible explanations will be reserved until later. The implication is, however, that gains are meaningful only as they are related to pre-test status. A school or individual with high initial performance cannot be expected to do as well in gains over one or two years as a school or individual with low initial performance.

In order to arrive at Table 50, all pre-test scores in colleges contributing 45 or more pre- and post-test scores for the same students

TABLE 50

Mean Gains of Students on A Test of Critical Thinking, Form A, Classified According to Pre-Test Standing

College	Initially Low Group		Initially Low-Middle Group		Initially Middle Group		Initially High-Middle Group		Initially High Group		Total Group		
	Gain	N	Gain	N	Gain	N	Gain	N	Gain	N	Mean Pre-Test	Mean Gain	N
Pre-Test Range	11–27		28–31		32–34		35–39		40–53				
1.........	5.00	2	5.67	3	5.00	6	5.82	11	1.40	30	40.06	3.13	52
2.........	7.58	12	3.09	11	3.90	10	−0.50	8	0.83	12	33.04	3.02	53
3.........	5.52	46	5.34	32	4.54	26	3.18	39	1.31	32	32.33	4.05	75
4.........	10.80	50	7.54	50	5.55	47	5.00	60	2.26	47	33.42	6.24	254
5.........	4.68	75	3.00	70	1.63	51	−1.11	47	0.83	18	30.65	2.33	261
6.........	6.78	23	4.09	22	4.38	21	3.23	39	1.40	25	33.87	3.84	130
7.........	6.05	19	2.86	14	−1.45	11	1.29	21	2.50	12	32.95	2.55	77
Total 7 colleges..	6.68	227	4.65	202	3.47	172	2.60	225	1.59	176	32.85	3.91	1,002

were thrown into a single distribution which was then divided as nearly as possible into five equal groups. The students for each college were then sorted into these groups, so that a college such as No. 1, with a generally very able group of students, may have only a few cases in certain cells. The general pattern of decreasing gain with higher pre-test scores is apparent.

These data may be used as a basis for inference relative to gains or growth of the individuals concerned and, similarly, may be used as growth norms against which to compare other groups.

None of the gains recorded by the initially high group in any college was very large. For scores above 40 on a 57-item test, it is quite possible that gains are very difficult to make, although the gains of 2.50 and 2.26 registered by some institutions exceed gains made for lower pre-test groups in other colleges. From Table 50 several significant facts emerge: (1) Students in different colleges vary considerably in gains made in critical thinking. (2) Because of the differential gains due to pre-test status, total group gains are not the best index of program effectiveness. For example, College No. 1 achieves excellent results for the four lower groups but has so many students in the top group that the total group gain is relatively small. (3) The colleges showing the larger gains have quite different educational programs so that no simple explanations are available. (4) The college with the largest gain places considerable emphasis on a comprehensive examination program which heavily emphasizes thought-type items rather than simple recall.

The numbers in Table 50 make risky any conclusions, however tentative. Nevertheless, the general picture presented is confirmed by more extensive data involving students unmatched from pre- to post-test. The test does point to the differences in the growth of students in critical thinking and is suggestive, therefore, of the generalization that the set of abilities included in the test can be developed if sufficient thought is given to providing an appropriate educational experience.

Table 51 shows the gains when students are classified both by ability and pre-test status. The tendency is for students whose ability level is relatively better than their pre-test level to make the larger gains.

Numerous small investigations were made comparing the critical

TABLE 51

MEAN GAINS OF STUDENTS ON TEST OF CRITICAL THINKING, FORM A, POST-TEST, CLASSIFIED ACCORDING TO QUARTILE RANK ON THE ACE PSYCHOLOGICAL EXAMINATION AND THE TEST OF CRITICAL THINKING, FORM A, PRE-TEST

ACE PSYCHOLOGICAL EXAMINATION QUARTILE RANK	QUARTILE RANK ON TEST OF CRITICAL THINKING, FORM A								TOTAL	
	First (low)		Second		Third		Fourth			
	Gain	N	Gain	N	Gain	N	Gain	N	Gain	N
First (low)....	11.58	36	7.73	22	5.40	15	....	....	9.15	73
Second.......	11.16	19	5.67	18	5.20	20	.95	16	5.89	73
Third........	13.58	12	9.81	21	2.76	17	3.26	23	6.73	73
Fourth.......	18.00	6	9.58	12	8.00	21	2.85	34	6.68	73
Total........	12.33	73	8.12	73	5.48	73	2.52	73	7.11	292

thinking scores of matched groups and the gains made by matched groups. In these cases the matching was done in terms of ability. Out of these such generalizations as the following emerge: (1) Greatest gains are made in the freshman year, a typical picture being a four-point gain the first year. (2) Older freshmen and upperclassmen show less progress than freshmen of average or below average age.

RELATION TO INSTRUCTION AND COURSES

There was no direct relationship between the work of the Critical Thinking Committee and any particular type of course. It is not to be expected, therefore, that many direct implications can be drawn about modifications in classroom procedure. In fact, the task defined by the committee involved a concept of critical thinking as a set of problem-solving abilities transcending particular courses and course content.

Such evidence—and it was unsystematic in nature—as became available gave no advantage to those institutions having a special course dealing with critical thinking. In one particular investigation, pre- and post-testing in a course in logic—done by Dr. Charles F. Virtue, University of Maine—no marked improvement was noted on the Test of Critical Thinking. Dr. Virtue remarked that the objectives of such a course probably do not coincide with those of the test. Logic—in his analysis—aims at development of a critical appraisal of thinking but not necessarily developing better thinkers.

Likewise, it is unclear whether general education course experience has resulted in any greater development of critical thinking in students than results from other courses. Consistently the largest gains were recorded in the freshman year, and subjective appraisal of the three or four programs showing the largest gain would indicate that these involve some of the better organized general education experiences for the freshman year. Pre- and post-test results on a one-year basis for advanced students reveal gains much smaller than those of freshmen. What the results might be over a year for individuals not enrolled in college or in any educational program, we do not know. Several groups that were contacted on this point lacked interest in cooperating.

SUMMARY

The Test of Critical Thinking provides a way of studying the growth in certain aspects of critical thinking of single groups, or the relative performance of several classes. Data presently available provide some basis for noting whether gains are as great as have been found elsewhere. The nature of the program which will produce greater gain remains unspecified, but it may be significant that those colleges recording the largest gains were ones with courses specifically organized for general education purposes and with definite requirements for all students involving the completion of all or a major portion of these courses.

The marked interest shown by students taking the test and their reactions to it suggest that the test does require a type of mental activity different from that found in many courses. Judgments by residence hall personnel, instructors, and peers suggest that the ability measured by the test has some carry-over to behavior. There is also reason to believe that it is not synonymous with intelligence. Experiences of some of the other committees concerned with critical thinking suggest that more appropriate course experience can be developed to make a heavier contribution to these abilities.

8

PERVASIVE OBJECTIVES 2: ATTITUDES

Intercollege Committee on Attitudes, Values, and Personal Adjustment: GLADYS BELLINGER, Kansas State College of Agriculture and Applied Science; DAVID BURKHART, Boston University; RUTH CHURCHILL, Antioch College; WILLIAM DAVISON, Stephens College; MAURICE FREEHILL, Western Washington College of Education; LEO A. HAAK, Michigan State College; DARRELL HOLMES, Muskingum College; ARNO LUKER, Colorado State College of Education; J. L. McCREIGHT, Muskingum College; MILO MILANOVICH, Muskingum College; SAMUEL NEEL, Florida State University; C. ROBERT PACE, Syracuse University; MARY KATHERINE SMITH, Muskingum College; GEORGE STERN, University of Chicago; CORNELIA WILLIAMS, University of Minnesota

THE NINETEENTH-CENTURY emphasis on positivism, on scientific rigor, and on knowing and teaching historical facts *wie es eigentlich gewesen war* led teachers in early twentieth-century American colleges and universities to attempt the impossible, of trying to affect the intellect of students without reference to their non-cognitive being. Students in colleges and universities were expected to acquire whatever knowledge to which they were exposed. The assumed concomitant, the acquisition of skill in reasoning ability, was accepted without question. Beyond the acquisition of knowledge and the development of intellectual adroitness, college teaching assumed no responsibilities.

The impact on educational thinking of John Dewey, Thorndike, the Gestalt school of psychology, and progressive education has resulted in a rejection of such a restricted concept of education. Students are now presumed to enter school complete with bodies, good and bad habits, attitudes, and principles of behavior, all interacting to form the entity which is to be educated. It is true that this concern for all aspects of the human organism has been more manifest in the kindergarten and elementary schools than in higher education. The unbracketing of chairs for the convenience of wiggle-worm children, the providing of milk at recess to stoke their perpetually mobile engines, and the provision of subjects to appeal to their ever-changing interests, are all exemplary. High schools and colleges have been much slower in realizing that the organisms inhabiting their classrooms are not bodiless intellects to be molded in the images of their mentors.

Of recent years, however, higher education, particularly at the policy-making level, has verbalized a concern for some of the noncognitive aspects of learning. The Report of the President's Commission on Higher Education lists eleven goals or objectives for a general education designed to meet the needs of an ever-expanding number of American youth. Each one of these major goals recognizes to some degree the importance of an affective domain among educational objectives. Thus, students are expected to develop a code of behavior based on ethical *principles*. They are to *participate* as responsible citizens. They should recognize *personal responsibility* for fostering international understanding. In addition to learning facts about their physical environment, they should *appreciate* the implications of scientific discovery for human welfare. They should attain a *satisfactory emotional* and *social adjustment*. They are to *enjoy* literature, art, and music, and should acquire *attitudes* basic to a satisfying family life. Their selection of a vocation should be socially useful and *personally satisfying,* and should allow an individual to make full use of his *interests*. Even the most intellectually oriented of these objectives have their affective concomitant. Thus, under the major goal of acquiring and using the skills and habits involved in critical and constructive thinking, students are expected to develop a stimulating *intellectual curiosity*.[1]

Even more significant than such statements of objectives have been the concrete developments of college administration and cur-

---

[1] *Higher Education for American Democracy, Vol. I—Establishing the Goals* (Washington: Government Printing Office; and New York: Harper & Bros., 1947), pp. 50–57.

ricular practice emphasizing the same concern. The emergence of university-supported groups of trained counselors on college campuses to advise with students about the many problems, intellectual or emotional, with which students are faced, the provision of well-staffed health centers, the increased emphasis on dormitory living for male as well as for female students, and the evolution of courses variously labeled Effective Living, Human Growth and Development, Human Understanding, or Human Relationships, all attest to the growing importance attached to education for the whole individual.

In view of such interest and concern, it was logical for the Co-operative Study of Evaluation in General Education to demonstrate an active interest in affective as well as in cognitive areas. From its inception there was no doubt that one of the major operating groups of the Study should concern itself with some non-intellectual outcomes of education. The vehicle selected for this purpose was an intercollege committee dealing with how general education affected attitudes, values, and personal adjustment.

The title of this committee, which was composed of counselors, professional evaluators, and teachers in courses dealing with human relations, furnished such a broad field of possible operations that considerable self-restriction had to be imposed before the group could make its efforts effective. The first modification consisted of removing the concept of personal adjustment from active consideration by the committee. There was never any thought that personal adjustment was unimportant. There was the belief, however, that personal adjustment varied so from individual to individual, from time to time, and from place to place, that any study not making elaborate use of the tools of psychotherapy would be unable to obtain any meaningful evidence. Thus, the committee concentrated its attention on attitudes and values.

Even the discarding of personal adjustment left many further issues to be considered and many technical difficulties to be overcome. The term "attitudes" has many and varied meanings which may range anywhere from an ethical principle of doing unto others as we would have them do unto us, to a pronounced feeling of being for or against something. The definitions of attitudes which technical workers in this field have advanced furnish almost as much variety. Most, however, involve elements reflected in the definition, "An attitude is an emotionalized tendency to act for or against something." This underscores the hypothetical aspect; that is, an attitude is like intelligence—one will never see it, one must only infer it from certain overt behavior. It further links attitudes clearly to the affective or emotional domain. Some individuals contend that attitudes which are not intellectually informed are unimportant. The definition advanced rejects this contention. An attitude, that is, a feeling for or against something, may be of crucial importance and still be completely uninformed. It may be based solely on an emotional feeling. This conception of attitudes, accepted by the Attitudes Committee, carried as concomitants many vexatious problems. Clearly there could be as many attitudes as there are objects or orders of objects toward which individuals could be for or against. Even in the restricted area of general education there are literally thousands of objects which could reasonably be of concern to a committee investigating in this area. Attitudes toward general education, toward specific courses, toward teachers, toward certain principles, toward theories, even toward historical figures, were possible, and each of these would be of some interest to certain schools, teachers, or students. Obviously, attitudes toward a variety of discrete objects could not be appraised by a relatively small committee operating for a short period of time.

The committee developed an hierarchical conception of attitudes which hypothesized that attitudes toward discrete objects —for example, particular persons, particular books, or specific events—condition attitudes toward more generic forms of the same objects. Thus, attitudes toward *Das Kapital, Mein Kampf,* and Mother Goose rhymes, condition attitudes toward books. Attitudes toward Joe, the Negro janitor, condition attitudes toward Negroes. Attitudes toward these general categories condition one's feeling of for or against even higher levels of abstraction. Thus, attitudes toward Negroes, Jews, Chinese, and white American Protestants condition one's feeling toward human beings generally. As attitudes increase in their degree of abstraction, they can be conceived of as ethical principles or values which interact with other ethical principles of values. This entire hierarchy of attitudes rests upon and in turn affects the biological and psychic aspects of personality. Thus, the committee hypothesized that attitudes toward various specific objects were conditioned by certain personality configurations which resulted from a particular course of development of some individuals' physical, mental, and emotional traits. This conception allowed selection of areas of investigation at a fairly high level of abstraction. Information about these abstract attitudes would then permit inferences to be made concerning more specific manifestations of the same attitudes.

Before making final selection of the precise nature of its inquiry, the committee developed a series of four assumptions of general working principles which were to govern its activities.

1. Measurement is a process of making inferences and judgments from observed samples of behavior. An attitude test is a collection of behavior (including verbal behavior) samples. The validity of measurment will depend upon the adequacy with which behavior is sampled.
2. Attitudes have several dimensions—direction, range, intensity, and consistency. Techniques of measurement must be designed to observe or test specific attitudes in enough different situations to include all dimensions.
3. The committee is primarily interested in attitudes as outcomes of general education as a whole. Whenever possible, attitudes with which the committee concerns itself should be those to the development of which all course areas, as well as co-curricular activities, should contribute.
4. The committee felt it important to caution itself and others against too much enthusiasm for measuring instruments of the "verbal statement" type. Such instruments are the easiest to construct but are also easiest for sophisticated students to falsify. It has been found that such instruments have a discouragingly low correlation with actual behavior.

Using these principles as criteria for selection, the committee then had to select the specific attitudes with which to work and to find or develop appropriate appraisal techniques. As a preliminary to the selection of specific attitudes, a number of possible values, traits, attitudes, or points of view were listed to be used as the basis for discussion with local institutional staff members and with students. Out of such discussions it was hoped that interest toward some particular complex of these would crystallize to guide the committee in its further work. It will be noted that the rubrics under which these statements were subsumed corresponded almost exactly to the rubrics of behavior developed by the Critical Thinking Committee.

ATTITUDES OF CONCERN TO GENERAL EDUCATION

A. Attitudes toward self such as:
   1. Conscious personal development.
   2. Respect for others coupled with humility for self—seeing the individual in the perspective of the group.
   3. Understanding and acceptance of a bi-sexual world.
   4. Willingness to look honestly at one's self.
   5. Willingness to gain self-knowledge through inventories and other objective sources of information.
   6. Moderate elation or disappointment in terms of the long view.
   7. Favoring goal-setting consistent with ability to achieve.
   8. "Emotional maturity."
   9. Giving and receiving affection freely.
   10. Self-evaluation (inadequacy *vs.* overestimation).
   11. Self-assertion (demanding *vs.* complete yielding to demands of others).
   12. Aggressions (hostile *vs.* guilt-submissive).
   13. Undemanded creative effort—joy in one's work.
   14. Appraisal of achievement in terms of one's possibilities rather than in terms of the performance of competitors.
   15. Focus on areas of greatest interest—willingness to let some things go.
   16. Recognition that daily life is something to be enjoyed.

B. Attitudes toward others such as:
   1. Trust in the basic good will of individuals—prior to the examination of motives.
   2. Reacting to others in terms of understanding rather than stereotypes.
   3. Willingness to accept personal responsibility for making social groups work.
   4. Identification of individual or family with the community.
   5. Desire to establish empathy with individuals who hold opposing points of view.
   6. Desire to find agreements by compromise on nonessentials.
   7. Willingness to let others take precedence at times for the good

of the group, to allow them to play roles for which they are specially qualified.

8. Tolerance for the other person's point of view (esthetic, political, moral, etc.).

C. Attitudes toward society such as:

1. Recognition that social change is inevitable but not necessarily desirable.
2. Belief in the right of all men to life, liberty, and the pursuit of happiness.
3. Tolerance for ways of life other than our own.
4. Respect for the dignity and worth of the individual.
5. Constructive discontent with social ills.
6. Pride in achievements of the United States along with recognition of its weaknesses.
7. Cooperation with others in group action through democratic processes.
8. Balanced attitude toward values of the new, the old, and the *status quo.*
9. Reliance upon persuasion rather than force to achieve social ends.

D. Attitudes toward intellectual, rational, and scientific thought processes such as:

1. Systematic reflection accepted as preferable to snap judgment.
2. Disposition to regard most problems as problems that can be solved, but that some are insoluble.
3. Recognition of the limitations of knowledge and appreciation of the functions of faith.
4. Recognition that learning is a continuous, lifelong process.
5. Respect for expert judgments combined with the desire to validate these judgments against experience.
6. Willingness to reserve judgment but also to act when action is required.
7. Responsibility of the student to take initiative in the learning process.
8. Making practical applications of what is learned.
9. Intellectual curiosity and honesty.
10. Faith in the possibility of communication with others and a recognition of the limitations of language.
11. Desire to relate all of knowledge into a systematic and coherent pattern as over against compartmentalizing knowledge in discrete areas.
12. Disposition to regard the solution of problems as relative to the

particular cultural context in which the problems arise rather than constituting a solution which is of absolute validity for all cultures and epochs.

E. Attitudes toward ethical standards and values of our culture.
    (No topics were listed under this heading.)

During its first long meeting in the summer of 1950 the Attitudes Committee was faced with a plethora of possibilities for activity. Attempting a study with respect to any one of the attitudes originally listed could prove a challenging task for the group. However, consideration of any single attitude or even several might skew the work of the committee in such a way that the central relationship between its work and the tasks of the other intercollege committees might be lost. Was it possible to evolve a study which, although demanding relatively few measuring instruments, would clearly impinge on a majority of the attitudes of interest to the committee? Was it possible to prepare instruments dealing with traits so broad as to be of concern to the other intercollege committees?

In answering these questions affirmatively, the committee pursued two parallel lines of investigation which resulted in two discrete, but interacting, instruments. The two instruments were used in two independent clusters of research studies which, although serving to illuminate each other, are sufficiently unique as to warrant separate treatment.

THE DEVELOPMENT OF THE INVENTORY OF BELIEFS

The opinions which people hold may be regarded as reflections of their attitudes, values, and adjustment. From one point of view they are responses and feelings, the relationship among which helps to define personality—that is, the mode of reaction to self, to others, to institutions, and to ideas. From another point of view, many statements of opinion may be regarded as generalizations based on facts, principles, or concepts which are widely shared by educators (and may be regarded as objectives of education) but which at the same time are still regarded as matters of belief and individual interpretation by the layman or person who possesses less breadth of understanding and insight.

The studies of many psychologists over the past ten years have provided an encouraging demonstration of how opinions can be used as indicators of basic personality structure. Many useful relationships and concepts have been put to empirical test. The volume on *The Authoritarian Personality*[2] is especially fruitful.

It appeared promising to attempt some kind of merger of the insights of psychologists regarding personality patterns and the insights of educators regarding the behavior (broadly viewed) which should characterize the product of general education. Such a merger would attempt to express the relationship between these psychological and educational interests. Instruments resulting would be concerned with the differentiation between the mature, independent, reality-minded, flexible, adaptive, secure, and comfortable individual who is seen as the potential base and anticipated outcome of a program of general education in a free society, and the childish, self-centered, threatened, aggressive, rigid, compulsive, insecure, and uncomfortable individual whose concomitant attitudes and values are seen as essentially antidemocratic and in opposition to the objectives of general education.

The fundamental assumption underlying such a scale is that the objectives of general education can serve as a base from which may be inferred the model organization characterizing the personalities of those most adaptable to the purposes of general education. An attempt should be made to explore the manifestations of the antidemocratic–democratic continuum as relevant to the problems of general education in terms of the individual's relations to (1) ideas and intellectual abstractions, (2) social groups and identifications, (3) interpersonal relations, and (4) the self.

These four levels of personal involvements are seen as indexes of the kind of psychological maturity which are significant for general education. By investigating these four levels in the light of underlying psychological variables or dimensions, information may be obtained concerning the basic personality structure of the individual. Re-examining these four levels in terms of the expressed contents of each provides information on the attitudinal orientation and level of attainment specific to each content area. In addi-

[2] T. W. Adorno, *et al.*, *The Authoritarian Personality* (New York: Harper & Bros., 1950).

tion, there might also be the possibility of collecting data relevant to such matters as logical thinking, consistency, evasiveness, and possibly others.

The formal structure of such a scale was expressed tentatively as follows:

Level	*Content*	*Variables or Dimensions*
1. Ideas and institutions (ideocentrism)	1.1 Philosophy	1.11 Materialistic, manipulative, power, cynical
	1.2 Religion	1.21 Mystical, ritualistic, nonpersonal
	1.3 Arts	1.31 Romantic, antisensual, anti-intellectual, anticultural
	1.4 Sciences	1.41 Application, limitation, antirational
	1.5 Politics, economics	1.51 Dependence, adherence to outmoded ideas, distrust, denial of conflicts
2. Social groups (ethnocentrism)	2.1 Out-groups (Negroes, Jews, other minorities, foreigners)	2.11 Personal characteristics (offensive, immature, threatening, intrusive, seclusive)
		2.12 Solutions (pseudodemocratic: segregation, limited participation; antidemocratic: elimination, exclusion; insoluble: fatalism, despair, cynicism.
	2.2 In-groups (Americanism)	2.21 Uncritical acceptance of values, exclusive pride in memberships, blindness to or dismissal of shortcomings
3. Individuals, interpersonal relations (sociocentrism)	3.1 Family (parents) 3.2 School (teachers) 3.3 Church (ministers) 3.4 State (public officials) 3.5 Business and consumer relations (tradesmen) 3.6 Friends, peers, siblings	3.11 to 3.16 Irrational acceptance of external authority, unwillingness to assume personal responsibility, shift of responsibility to others, blaming others for failure (extra-punitive), resistance to departure from tradition, depersonalization of relationships, sentimentality (momism, etc.)

Level	Content	Variables or Dimensions
4. Self (egocentrism)	4.1 Self-concept, self-evaluation	4.11 Perception of external world as threatening, as manipulatable, submission and aggression, rigidity and compulsion, superstition and stereotype, destructiveness and cynicism, free-floating anxiety, preoccupation with health and sex; over-spiritualization, denial, and fear (self, others), depersonalized sexuality

To implement this conception in the form of a test a number (some three thousand) of clichés, pseudo-rational statements, or inappropriate generalizations were collected. From these were selected statements to comprise a trial test form. Each statement included was judged to be revelatory of some of the four personality dimensions listed above. Insofar as possible each statement was also to be capable of being judged as a point of fact if sufficient information were available. For example, the statement, "Sending letters to congressmen is a waste of time," is at once an indication of a cynical evaluation of authority and a statement which can be examined factually by recourse to appropriate evidence. Similarly the item, "The predictions of economists about the future of business are no better than guesses," is at the same time an expression of irrationality or anti-intellectualism and a statement contrary to known fact.

On the basis of expert judgment and statistical test performance data, 120 such statements were finally selected for inclusion in a final form of the Inventory of Beliefs. These statements were to be presented to students to be judged by a four-element key: (1) Strongly agree, (2) Agree, (3) Disagree, and (4) Strongly disagree.

All of the statements included were intended by the committee to be items with which students *should* disagree. This limitation was based upon a number of considerations. First, disagree items were much easier to find than were "agree" items. Our everyday speech, newspapers, and light literature are replete with glib generalizations which have just enough truth about them to make them appear plausible, yet which would be rejected on close analysis unless some inner compulsion required their acceptance. Statements such as, "If you want a thing done right, you have to do it yourself," or "Man has an inherent guide to right and wrong—his conscience," are part of our culture. It is much more difficult to find short statements, capable of eliciting the same order of response which are not either banal or hopelessly complicated.

Second, the fundamental purposes of the Inventory of Beliefs could best be served by posing items with which mature individuals should disagree. Particularly as research was carried on with trial forms of the inventory, it became apparent that the inventory had its greatest utility in isolating a homogeneous group of individuals representing the antithesis of the mature, adaptive individual desired as a product of general education. It seemed that the identification could best be obtained by presenting only those statements to which but a limited number of persons would agree. Items which could be accepted by a number of less rigid individuals were therefore not employed.

Still a further reason for including only disagree items involves the way in which individuals perceive a given cluster of objects. If individuals, to use an analogy, are given certain objects of black and of white color, they have little difficulty in discriminating between the two, even though the blacks and the whites may respectively range in tone. The black-white dichotomy, however, serves to preclude discrimination of tone within either of the two principal colors. However, students presented only the black objects without being given the white ones for reference are more easily led to discriminate among the various tones represented. This phenomenon appears to be operative on a test such as the Inventory of Beliefs. Students presented with only disagree items have no "white" reference point, hence tend to discriminate between the various disagree items which they might accept and those which they might reject. If some agree items are intermixed with the disagree items, the disagree items stand exposed as black and the individuals tend to subscribe to only the culturally acceptable ones. Since the committee was interested in the concepts best exemplified by the disagree items, it seemed best not to give students the reference point of even a few agree ones.

Another testing technique involved the four-element key rather than an odd-numbered one. In the final analysis, the committee was interested only in whether or not individuals accepted or rejected items. However, some examinees find themselves frustrated by simple dichotomized response keys of agree-disagree. To accommodate their feelings, and in view of the fact that no ambivalent response was provided, gradations of agree and of disagree were employed. The use of such a key has considerable support from experiences of researchers using forced choice techniques. It further has the support of Sanford and his associates,[3] who used a six-element key, still avoiding the neutral position on their F-scale which is, in a sense, a prototype for the present instrument.

The final form of the Inventory of Beliefs consisted of 120 statements distributed among the four dimensions of ideas and institutions, social groups, individuals, and interpersonal relations, and self. These four qualities were represented by items of concern to the content of the several general education areas. Those items dealing with ideas and institutions would have relevance for general education courses in the humanities, sciences, and some social sciences. The social groups items and the individuals and interpersonal relations items would have primary relevance for the social sciences. Items dealing with the self would have particular relevance for some aspects of the usual social science offering and a great deal of relevance for courses such as Effective Living or Human Growth and Development. Each of the subject-matter orientations of specific items had a counterpart in some psychological variable or dimension of personality. Those items of the ideas and institutions category which dealt with philosophy would represent a materialistic, manipulative, power-centered, or cynical orientation.

The total responses to all of the items were conceived to have meaning as an index of personality structure. The individual scoring low on the test, that is, accepting a large number of statements, was conceived of as being immature, rigid in his outlook, authoritarian in his relationships with others, and compulsive in many

[3] In Adorno, *et al., ibid.,* p. 59.

of his actions. The person scoring high on the test, that is, rejecting a goodly number of statements, was conceived of as being adaptive, flexible, mature, and democratic in his relations with other people.

In addition to the total score, individual items were considered to have significance as discrete expressions of opinions and to reflect level of achievement in specific general education courses. Teachers of humanities, for example, might be interested in knowing the proportion of a student body who believe that "Reviewers and critics of art, music, and literature decide what they like and then force their tastes on the public." Science teachers might be interested in the opinions of students on the statement, "Science is infringing upon religion when it attempts to delve into the origin of life itself." All teachers might find it not only interesting but profitable to know how students feel about the statement, "A lot of teachers these days have radical ideas which need to be carefully watched." On the subject-matter side, one point which social scientists probably emphasize to the eclipse of all others is the interdependence of individuals and society. Students' responses to the statement, "Each man is on his own in life and must determine his own destiny," could reveal how successful teachers have been in getting their point of view across. The human adjustment teachers who constantly emphasize the practical and therapeutic values of conversation might like to know if students believe, "We would be better off if people would talk less and would work more."

While this particular form of the Inventory of Beliefs represents the final development of the test by the Attitudes Committee, many of the insights concerning it and leads to further research with it have stemmed from modifications of the basic inventory by George G. Stern and his associates at the University of Chicago. Stern has constructed two other forms of the inventory, Form S and Form T, each of which used a large nucleus of items from the original inventory plus other items either to be agreed with or items involving another dimension to be used in explaining some of the responses obtained to the items used from the original test.

The 120-item form of the test has the disadvantage of requiring between 30 and 45 minutes of class time to administer. It became apparent that all of the 120 items were highly interrelated; this interrelationship suggested that the test might be divided in half by some rational means so that two comparable 60-item inventories would result without appreciably lessening the reliability of the technique. Such a split was made on the basis of item analysis data and original item affiliation to the various dimensions. Sufficient experimental work has been completed to warrant the conclusion that individuals wanting a shorter form of the test could use either group of 60 items with impunity. The precise assignment of items to these two forms is indicated in an instructor's manual for the Inventory of Beliefs.[4]

INVENTORY OF BELIEFS RESEARCH STUDIES

The Inventory of Beliefs has been subjected to considerable research as to its technical effectiveness. Form I of the inventory has proven to be sufficiently reliable for purposes of group or individual measurement. Some thirty-odd reliability studies have been made resulting in coefficients ranging from .68 to .95 with a median coefficient of .86. Even the two shorter forms of the test have proven almost as reliable as the original, although they should not be used for individual diagnosis or prediction.

The validity of the Inventory of Beliefs has been studied in several different ways. Its validity as a list of statements of concern to general education was presumed on the basis of the expert opinion of the persons who prepared it and of the sources from which the item raw material was derived. This was corroborated by submitting the inventory to two groups of faculty members, asking one group to judge each item in terms of how it would want "ideal" products of general education to respond. The other group was asked to judge whether or not expert opinion in the relevant field would tend to support or to deny the statement. The results from these two studies revealed that a large majority of the faculty judges could accept 100 out of the 120 items as relevant to the objectives of general education and that three-fourths of the entire list consisted of statements the truth or falsity of which could be established by fact and expert opinion.

The validity of the test as providing an index of personality

[4] Princeton, N.J.: Educational Testing Service.

structure was assessed in two principal ways: studying various intertest correlations and studying characteristics of persons whose scores fell at the two extremities of the range. Table 52 presents some intertest correlations with other measures used in the Cooperative Study.

TABLE 52

COEFFICIENTS OF CORRELATION OF THE INVENTORY OF BELIEFS WITH OTHER TESTS

TEST	COEFFICIENT OF CORRELATION			No. OF COLLEGES	No. OF STUDENTS
	Lowest r in Any College	Highest r in Any College	Average r*		
	Pre-Test				
ACE Psychological Examination..	.05	.47	.25	12	2,171
Critical Thinking, Form A.......	.12	.43	.25	12	2,171
Critical Thinking in Social Science	−.10	.46	.30	12	2,171
Problems in Human Relations...	−.08	.49	.38	11	1,853
Critical Thinking, Form B.......	.14	.37	.29	5	641
Critical Analysis in Reading and Writing....................	.07	.37	.24	8	1,397
Science Reasoning and Understanding, Form A............	.16	.46	.31	8	1,010
Science Reasoning and Understanding, Form B............	.07	.38	.21	5	639
Humanities Participation Inventory.....................	−.06	.16	.10	3	220
	Post-Test				
ACE Psychological Examination..	.12	.43	.21	5	743
Critical Thinking, Form A.......	.05	.39	.22	5	743
Critical Thinking in Social Science	.24	.63	.35	5	743
Problems in Human Relations...	.36	.47	.45	4	505
Critical Thinking, Form B.......	.12	.28	.19	4	452
Humanities Participation Inventory.....................	.17	.27	.24	2	340
Critical Analysis in Reading and Writing....................	.04	.31	.21	6	994
Science Reasoning and Understanding, Form A............	.25	.61	.32	5	864
Science Reasoning and Understanding, Form B............	.24	.40	.35	2	156

* Quinn McNemar, *Psychological Statistics* (New York: John Wiley & Sons, Inc., 1949), pp. 123–24.

These data emphasize the affective quality of the instruments. The correlation coefficients between the inventory and the tests requiring critical thinking are generally quite low as compared with similar statistics showing the relationship between tests of critical thinking ability.[5] The highest coefficients obtained were

[5] See chap. 7.

between the Inventory of Beliefs and the Problems in Human Relations Test—both products of the Attitudes Committee and both possessing considerable overlap in respect to the traits involved. The coefficients between the Inventory of Beliefs and the American Council on Education Psychological Examination were generally quite low.

Low scores on the Inventory of Beliefs might be presumed to represent an atypical segment of a college population. This presumption led to inquiry with respect to possible differences between very low and very high scorers. As a result of such inquiry a considerable body of data has been accumulated which either directly supports, or does not contradict, the conclusion that the inventory does measure certain types of personality structure. Because of limitations in space these data cannot be presented in detail, but they have been presented elsewhere.[6]

The data and the generalizations which follow have been substantiated by roughly parallel studies in two institutions, as well as by a confirmatory replication undertaken by one of them. They are supported, therefore, by three independent samplings of students from populations of 200 to 500. The samples upon which the generalizations are based represent students from these populations who scored at the extremes of the inventory distributions and were *also equated for intelligence*. These matched groups range in size from 29 to 61 for each extreme.

Two facts should be noted: first, these data are based on populations characterized by their wide score range on the inventory; comparisons of groups less widely separated do not reveal such differences. Second, many of these data have been obtained through the use of experimental forms of the inventory (Forms

[6] 1. George Stern, *et al.*, "Assessment of Personality II . . . [etc.] (Dittoed; Chicago, Ill.: University of Chicago, 1952).

2. S. Goldberg and G. Stern, "The Authoritarian Personality and General Education," paper presented at 60th Annual Convention of American Psychological Association, September 1952, Washington, D.C., abstracted.

3. G. Stern, "New Techniques in Testing," *College Faculty Bulletin, University of Chicago,* January 1953.

4. G. Stern, "Studies in Personality Typologies: The N, R, and S Syndromes," paper presented to the Midwestern Psychological Association, May 1953, Chicago, Ill.

5. G. Stern, "Personality-Centered Research and Psychological Unification," paper presented at 61st Annual Convention, American Psychological Association, September 1953, Cleveland, Ohio, abstracted.

S and T). These forms provide indexes which offer greater diagnostic precision insofar as personality dimensions are concerned, but otherwise do not appear to differ from the published form of the inventory. All three forms contain 60 common items; S and T were developed by the addition of 40 new items to make a total of 100 in each test. These new items provide a basis for a differential key (both agree and disagree responses) in contrast to the unidirectional scoring of the parent form (all disagree responses). The reliabilities of all three forms are uniformly high, as previously noted.

Placement data:

Significant differences (level generally .001 or less) are found favoring the high scorers with respect to matriculation in the area of humanities, social sciences, and English, that is, more high scorers enter these fields than do low scorers. In the natural sciences, however, neither group is distinguishable from the general populations from which they were drawn.

Achievement data:

Test performance.—Although differences in over-all grade averages are negligible, significant differences favoring the high scorers are found in comprehensive examinations in the areas of the social sciences and humanities.

Withdrawals.—A significantly larger number of low scorers are found to have withdrawn from school by the end of the first year.

Interests and attitudes:

High scorers were found significantly higher than low scorers in their scores for artistic, musical, and social science; significantly lower for computational and clerical (Kuder Preference Record).

Significant differences in vocational choices were found. The high scorers prefer occupations involving interpersonal, expressive, or abstract activity, such as psychology, music, or theoretical physics. The low scorers prefer more impersonal, concrete, or status-oriented vocations such as engineering, medicine, or law.

Significant differences in religious affiliation were found, the low scorers being more likely to be associated with orthodox or fundamentalist groups than are the high scorers.

Analyses of data from an activities inventory indicates high scorers seem to prefer activities which reflect autonomous or independent behavior, abstract and analytical intellectual interests, and esthetic experiences. Low scorers reject such activities, their preferences reflecting orientation toward the achievement of financial status, security, compulsive orderliness, and submissive or dependent behavior.

Consistent with these findings are the results from several other studies. At one institution teachers and students were solicited for estimates of students possessing the greatest degree of leadership. These "leaders" made significantly higher Inventory of Beliefs scores than the student population at large. In another study the populations from a large Northern and a large Southern university were compared. The students from the Northern university achieved better on the Inventory of Beliefs than did their Southern counterparts. However, when Southern students of high academic aptitude were compared with similarly qualified Northern students the reverse obtained. Southern students of this category appeared less authoritarian than did Northern students. Perhaps an explanation of this lies in the possibility that intelligent Southerners, in a college environment, overcompensate for those aspects of the Southern social climate which are restrictive for some minority groups.

It must be emphasized that the Inventory of Beliefs yields a range of scores, only a segment of which shows critical relationship to other factors. Early experimental work with the instrument proved quite disappointing, since these studies were based on the entire range of scores. The inventory may be conceived of, by analogy, as similar to various medical tests which identify only a selected group demonstrating definite pathology. The chest X-ray does nothing more than discriminate between the small percentage of the population who may have lung pathology and the large majority who are negative *for that test alone*. The inventory differentiates between the low scorers and all others. These low scorers are the individuals who present a somewhat homogeneous common complex of traits.

Pre- and Post-Testing Results

The Inventory of Beliefs has been administered on a pre-test and a post-test basis to students from a number of colleges. The gains on the test made over a year's time are recorded in Table 53 for each of these institutions.

The two schools whose students made the greatest gains (1 and 2) are schools whose student bodies are highly selected and whose programs of general education are carefully integrated. Classes are conducted with considerable emphasis placed on small discussion sections in which the teacher is considered as only a moderator. Whether such factors are operative we cannot tell. They do, however, take on added significance in this regard when the gains of other schools are examined. Students from School 3, for example, have approximately the same pre-test score as School 2, yet there

TABLE 53

MEAN GAINS OF STUDENTS ON INVENTORY OF BELIEFS POST-TEST, CLASSIFIED ACCORDING TO PRE-TEST STANDING

COLLEGE	INITIALLY LOW GROUP		INITIALLY LOW-MIDDLE GROUP		INITIALLY MIDDLE GROUP		INITIALLY HIGH-MIDDLE GROUP		INITIALLY HIGH GROUP		TOTAL GROUP		
	Gain	N	Gain	N	Gain	N	Gain	N	Gain	N	Mean Pre-Test	Mean Gain	N
Pre-Test Range	14–48		49–55		56–63		64–72		73–113				
1.......	21.00	6	24.00	5	14.08	13	15.44	16	6.39	74	77.08	10.08	114
2.......	17.41	32	7.65	26	10.41	29	7.08	25	7.45	29	59.74	10.29	141
3.......	6.65	51	3.85	40	3.31	39	0.77	44	−1.32	47	59.90	2.69	221
4.......	7.92	101	6.04	95	5.46	95	4.59	79	−0.35	80	58.65	4.95	450
5.......	7.77	73	5.66	65	4.60	75	0.08	62	−2.07	43	58.31	3.76	318
6.......	0.80	10	5.70	10	−0.22	9	−4.29	7	−8.50	4	57.22	−0.03	40
7.......	10.62	156	6.92	110	4.62	133	5.18	100	1.60	72	57.34	6.42	571
8.......	4.51	43	−1.03	64	−1.06	52	0.50	48	−4.76	54	60.58	−0.61	261
9.......	9.37	19	3.40	10	4.47	17	−0.69	16	−0.73	11	58.26	3.68	73
10.......	7.08	13	6.25	12	5.43	14	5.36	14	2.75	12	60.45	5.40	65
11.......	13.86	21	6.37	19	6.88	26	6.44	25	6.64	33	61.62	7.83	124
12.......	8.00	4	11.83	6	7.75	16	0.38	21	−0.80	44	71.97	2.20	91
13.......	6.50	12	2.80	5	0.70	20	0.58	19	−0.67	21	63.90	1.34	77
Total 13 colleges.	9.09	541	5.31	467	4.65	538	3.32	476	1.01	524	60.30	4.72	2,546

is a marked difference in gains. School 3 is a private institution whose students may or may not take the general education courses which are organized into fairly large lecture sections with little attention paid to articulation of the course content or conduct with the rest of the campus life.

Schools 5 and 7 demonstrate other possibilities. Both are state-supported, land-grant colleges appealing to approximately the same kind of student. School 5 has had a limited program of general education, whereas School 7 has had a program well developed and required of all students in the institution, regardless of their eventual field of specialization.

Students at several institutions were tested with the inventory

TABLE 54

MEAN GAINS OF STUDENTS TESTED BY THE INVENTORY OF BELIEFS
THREE TIMES OVER A TWO-YEAR PERIOD

TESTING DATE	COLLEGE A			COLLEGE B		
	N	Mean	S.D.	N	Mean	S.D.
Fall 1951	....	56.53	....	24	63.08	11.29
Spring 1952	....	61.65	....	24	70.25	14.41
Spring 1953	....	62.11	....	24	72.33	11.88

three different times—at the beginning and end of the freshman
year and at the end of the sophomore year. These data, illustrated
in Table 54, reveal the pattern found elsewhere of a markedly
lower gain for the second year.

TABLE 55

SOME ITEMS SHOWING CHANGES IN STUDENTS' BELIEFS ON
PRE-TEST AND POST-TEST OF INVENTORY OF BELIEFS

Item No.	Item	% Dis-agreeing, Pre-Test	% Dis-agreeing, Post-Test
	Items dealing with philosophy and religion		
59	Most intellectuals would be lost if they had to make a living in the realistic world of business	58	92
97	There is a source of knowledge that is not dependent upon observation	34	29
	Items dealing with psychology		
79	A sexual pervert is an insult to humanity and should be punished severely	49	67
101	Parents know as much about how to teach children as public school teachers	84	82
	Items dealing with ethics and interpersonal relations		
21	Nobody can make a million dollars without hurting other people	64	54
34	Each man is on his own in life and must determine his own destiny	18	34
	Items dealing with humanities		
5	Reviewers and critics of art, music, and literature decide what they like and then force their tastes on the public	66	51
29	Books and movies should start dealing with entertaining or uplifting themes instead of the present unpleasant, immoral, or tragic ones	36	63
	Items dealing with natural science		
80	A lot of science is just using big words to describe things which many people already know through common sense	62	74
92	The scientist who really counts is the one who turns theories into practical use	10	25
	Items dealing with social science		
68	Most Negroes would become overbearing and disagreeable if not kept in their place	73	90
83	Public officials may try to be honest but they are caught in a web of influence which tends to corrupt them	37	23

The influence of maturity has been suggested by a number of comparisons between matched groups of freshmen and seniors and between varying age groups of a freshman population. In general, all such studies show that older students make significantly higher scores than do younger ones. None of these, however, is of such magnitude as to discredit the fact of differential gains by institutions indicated above.

It may be of some interest to note the nature of the items on the Inventory of Beliefs and how students shift over a period of time with respect to some of them. Table 55 presents some of the items from the inventory together with a percentage of students from one large population who rejected the item in the fall 1951 and the percentage of the same group rejecting the same the following spring.

THE DEVELOPMENT OF THE PROBLEMS IN HUMAN RELATIONS TEST

The Inventory of Beliefs was designed primarily to reveal something of underlying personality structure. This personality structure, it was suspected, would manifest itself in a number of different ways, a major one of which would be the degree to which individuals demonstrated respect for the worth and dignity of human beings. However, so fundamental to a democracy is this concern or regard for the worth of others that the committee believed a separate evaluation project was warranted to assess its presence or absence in students.

Consistent with the general rationale of attitudes, this project for the worth and dignity of others appeared to involve several more specific attitudes, which might be classified:

1. Those directed toward persons
   a) Toward the views and vocations of others
   b) Toward special privilege for oneself and others (involving acceptance or rejection)
   c) Toward the equality of various racial and socioeconomic groups
   d) Toward the rise of minority groups (including the concept of protection for their rights)
2. Those directed toward processes
   a) Toward the concept of cooperation

b) Toward acceptance or rejection of evidence

c) Toward the values of free discussion

The committee believed that student feeling for or against these objects could be assessed by means of situational-type objective test questions and that student responses to such questions would provide an index of respect or disrespect toward human personality possessed by individual students. The situations included a variety of conflicts which arise in everyday living, resolvable in any of several different ways. The committee hypothesized that the way students met such conflicts would be based upon their attitude toward the parties included in the controversy.

To ensure that situations appeared plausible and natural, students in classes of the participating colleges were asked to describe incidents which they had witnessed within the past week exemplary of either respect or lack of respect for human beings. Student responses varied from reflecting only a superficial concern for mores of etiquette to those demonstrating insight into the kinds of issues which fundamentally divide people. The more promising responses were stated as open-end problems which were then submitted to other groups of students who were asked how they, as individuals, would resolve each one. For example:

> It was customary for the X Department to grant an award to the senior with the highest grades. Because of her intense desire to win this award, Betty B cheated in examinations. What should be done about Betty?

Responses to such situations provided the raw material out of which foils for objective-type questions could be constructed. These responses appeared to reflect in general five fairly definite points of view from which individuals approached the solutions to interpersonal situations. These five were assigned descriptive titles and described as follows:

1. *Hard-boiled Autocrat.*—The hard-boiled autocrat believes that he must constantly check up on everything to keep things going. He gives the orders and others carry them out. He believes that the only way to get conscientious performance is to expect and secure discipline and immediate acceptance of all orders. He is careful not to spoil his employees, his wife, his children, his students, or others by too much praise. He pays his employees and that is all they need. He supports

his wife and children. It is their place to carry out directives, not to question or always understand them. He is very conscious of his position and authority and believes that others cannot be trusted very long on their initiative.

2. *Benevolent Autocrat.*—The benevolent autocrat would be startled to realize that his techniques are autocratic. In contrast to the hard-boiled autocrat, he is interested in his employees, students, family, etc. He wants to see them happy, praises them as much as he criticizes them, is seldom harsh or severe, and likes to think that he is developing a happy family group. He urges them to bring their problems to him and is interested in all of the details of their work. Actually he trades benevolence for loyalty. The crux of his autocracy lies in the technique by which he secures dependence upon himself. He says, with a pat on the back, "That's the way I like it. . . . I am glad you did it that way. . . . That's the way I want it done," or "That isn't the way I told you to do it." In this way he dominates them by making himself the source of all standards. Any failure to live up to these standards he receives with hurt surprise and intense anger as personal disloyalty to him. He is also very protecting and makes them further indebted to him thereby.

3. *Laissez Faire.*—The *laissez-faire* personality may be one who has no confidence in his ability to handle an interpersonal relationship or play the role of leader. As a supervisor, he may bury himself in paper work and stay away from those he is supervising. He may also be the one who believes that to be a "good fellow" means license. He is not able to destroy the cordiality of any interpersonal relation and thus is unable to be aggressive in any interpersonal relation. He leaves too much responsibility with others; sets no clear goals toward which they may work; is incapable of making decisions or helping the group arrive at decisions; and tends to let things drift.

4. *Democratic.*—The democratic personality is one who endeavors whenever possible to share with his group (students, employees, family, committee, etc.) the decision-making about work planning, assignment, and scheduling. Where a decision must be made by him, he helps the group to understand clearly the basis of his decision. He is careful to develop as much participation, opinion-giving, and decision-making as possible, and a feeling of responsibility for the success of the work on the part of everyone. He is concerned that each person clearly understands his role and has opportunities for success in it. His praises and criticisms are always delivered objectively in terms of work results and never personally in terms of what he may or may not like. He encourages worth-while suggestions and the development of new procedures.

5. *Resort to "Experts" or Other Authority Figures.*—Some of the responses classified in this category are the kind which might be ex-

pected of an authoritarian personality; some are what might be expected of the *laissez-faire* personality; others are what might be expected of the democratic personality who has respect for the knowledge, opinions, and skills of the expert. It might also be expected that the overdependent and immature individual will choose a large number of responses in this category. Experience may eliminate this as a category or further refine it.

Sixty situations were selected and prepared in the form of five-choice multiple response questions, with each response being designed to parallel some one of the five personality types. Thus, persons judging each of the sixty test items would classify themselves as either hard-boiled autocrats, benevolent autocrats, *laissez-faire* personalities, democratic individuals, or one making frequent resort to expert authority. From these sixty items, administered to large groups of students, the committee selected thirty items for inclusion in the final form of the Problems in Human Relations Test. Each item contained responses representative of several of the five categories. However, the category in which the committee was chiefly interested was the democratic one. The other classifications were included as rational foils for the objective test situations, and as providing means for explaining why individuals did not subscribe to the democratic point of view. The committee was unwilling merely to dichotomize the trait with which it was concerned, but felt that further elaboration of the nondemocratic point of view was appropriate.

In preparing the responses to the situations, the committee encountered an obstacle in the nature of the democratic responses. To write alternatives clearly reflecting respect for human beings, but not automatically revealing themselves as socially approved was a most difficult task. The fact that disguise of the crucial responses was so difficult has probably made the test less effective than it might otherwise have been. The difficulty of the committee in this regard may be contrasted with the relative ease with which it prepared the Inventory of Beliefs, which by its nature was a disguised test and proved considerably more effective, probably, because of it. In this same connection democratic responses frequently appeared in their undisguised form as being banal or highly unsophisticated. This further served to weaken the instrument.

Illustrative of the items included in the final form of the test are the following:

1. Tom and Bob who know each other only slightly were double-dating two girls who were roommates. A sudden storm made it impossible to go to the beach as planned. Tom suggested going to a movie. After making the suggestion, he realized Bob was without funds.

    As Tom, what would you do?
    1. Pay for the party.
    2. Lend Bob money.
    3. Leave it up to the girls.
    4. Get Bob to suggest something.
    5. Apologize to Bob for making the suggestion.

2. Your social organization has pledged a student who is not liked by some of the members. One of your friends threatens to leave the social organization if this person is initiated. What would you do?
    1. Talk to your friend.
    2. Do not initiate the prospective member.
    3. Get more members to support the prospective member.
    4. Vote on the prospective member.
    5. Postpone the vote until the matter works itself out.

While most of the situations deal explicitly with conflicts with which college students might be familiar, an attempt was made to involve various kinds of minority groups toward which undemocratic attitudes might be manifest. There are items dealing with Negroes, very young children, criminals, Jews and Chinese, drunkards, neurotics, and the insane. These are the persons against whom prejudices are frequently directed and are the individuals most resented by the extra-punitive authoritarian persons of concern both in the Problems in Human Relations Test and in the Inventory of Beliefs.

The scoring key for the Problems in Human Relations Test was prepared a priori on the basis of the face validity of the situations and the alternative responses. The reliability of the Problems in Human Relations Test using such a key proved to be inadequate. Other data, however, accumulated during the early phases of research activity, suggested that the test had possibilities for the purposes for which it was intended. With this in mind, the committee searched for another method of keying the instrument which might result in greater reliability. Since the best judgment of the committee members had been expended in preparing the original key, empirical means appeared to be the only solution.

Rejecting for a time the entire original key, the committee reviewed each item of the test and selected only those situations which possessed one very clear-cut response indicative of the democratic category. These few responses were combined into a key and papers scored. The upper and lower 27 percent of the papers based on this short key were selected and item analyses made of every single item in the test. Those items showing high coefficients of discrimination were selected for inclusion in another key. The reliability of the test was then computed on the basis of this second key and was found to be slightly increased. The process was repeated and new coefficients of discrimination computed for every item. Again the items possessing the highest correlation coefficients were selected for inclusion in still a third key, and again reliability coefficients were computed, revealing still more increase. This process was repeated until two conditions became apparent: (1) a drop in reliability, and (2) a change in complexion of the items included in a key from homogeneity, as judged by inspection, to heterogeneity.

In addition to such analysis of the democratic category, similar inquiries were made for the other dimensions of the test. These studies revealed that the benevolent autocrat category was, statistically, at least, nonexistent in the instrument. The same was found with respect to the resort to authority category. These analyses of the nondemocratic aspects were done, it should be clearly emphasized, not with the intention of developing a series of subscores, but with the sole purpose of clarifying the meaning of the major or democratic scale.

The Problems in Human Relations Test has been subjected to various kinds of analyses to determine its effectiveness as a measuring instrument, and has also been used to study certain groups of students in general education courses to determine their status and the changes which occur with respect to the basic trait. As has been indicated, the reliability of the test using the initially defined key was slightly lower than might have been desired, ranging from .64 to .73. However, the reliability, estimated by means of the Kuder-Richardson approach, of the final, statistically developed key was .82, which suggested the feasibility of using the instrument for purposes of group measurement.

Item analyses of the test indicated that the coefficients of discrimination were generally quite high, much higher, in fact, than one normally would expect. Part of the magnitude of these coefficients is explainable by the fact that the test was a relatively short one, giving each item greater weight in determining the final score. The difficulty of the items was also satisfactory, but exhibited, however, a slight tendency for the items to be a little too easy. This evidence underscores the point previously made, that the correct or democratic responses were, for the most part, fairly obvious.

The validity of the instrument was studied from several different points of view. Face validity, of course, is the basic consideration. In addition, various groups of students possessing relevant traits as judged by other means were compared with respect to scores on the Problems in Human Relations Test. In one study students were judged by teachers as to their possession or lack of possession of respect for the dignity and worth of human personality. A presumption of validity was supported by the generally higher scores on the Problems in Human Relations Test made by persons judged to possess the trait than those made by persons judged as lacking the trait. In another study, student leaders were shown to possess the trait to a much greater extent than the student population at large. Still a third study revealed that in general older individuals made higher scores on the test.

One major concern of those who built the test was with the relationship between scores on the Problems in Human Relations Test and other measures. Tables 56 and 57 indicate some of the relationships discovered, expressed as correlation coefficients. The four groups treated in the tables represent populations who were each administered one distinct battery of Study tests of which one was the Problems in Human Relations Test.

One could expect to find positive correlations between the Problems in Human Relations Test and other verbal measures. However, since the responses on the Problems in Human Relations Test were opinions rather than the solutions to intellectual problems, relationships with tests demanding greater cognition should be fairly low. The evidence in Tables 56 and 57 verifies these ex-

TABLE 56

COEFFICIENTS OF CORRELATION BETWEEN PROBLEMS IN HUMAN RELATIONS PRE-TEST AND CERTAIN OTHER TESTS, 1951

Test	Group I			Group II			Group III			Group IV		
	Lr*	Hr*	Ar*	Lr	Hr	Ar	Lr	Hr	Ar	Lr	Hr	Ar
ACE Psychological Examination	.10	.37	.24	.13	.31	.23	.13	.39	.27	.13	.41	.25
Critical Thinking, Form A	.14	.39	.26				.11	.39	.27	.11	.40	.21
Critical Thinking in Social Science	.16	.41	.27									
Inventory of Beliefs	.08	.49	.38	.27	.35	.31	.27	.45	.36	.25	.62	.38
Humanities Participation Inventory				.02	.37	.21						
Critical Analysis in Reading and Writing							.16	.37	.26	.16	.41	.26
Science Reasoning and Understanding, Form A										.21	.42	.24

TABLE 57

COEFFICIENTS OF CORRELATION BETWEEN PROBLEMS IN HUMAN RELATIONS POST-TEST AND CERTAIN OTHER TESTS, 1952

Test	Group I			Group II			Group III			Group IV		
	Lr*	Hr*	Ar*	Lr	Hr	Ar	Lr	Hr	Ar	Lr	Hr	Ar
ACE Psychological Examination	.21	.38	.26	.19	.32	.24	.18	.30	.24	.18	.52	.27
Critical Thinking, Form A	.20	.36	.25				.16	.26	.23	.20	.34	.23
Critical Thinking in Social Science	.27	.42	.33									
Inventory of Beliefs	.36	.47		.41	.40	.41	.34	.44	.39	.13	.54	.42
Humanities Participation Inventory				.36	.27	.33						
Critical Analysis in Reading and Writing							.22	.38	.30			.23
Science Reasoning and Understanding, Form A										.30	.38	.31

* Key: L=lowest relationship in any college;
H=the highest relationship;
A=indicates the average of relationships found in all colleges administering the test.
These averages were computed by means of the Z transformation; see Quinn McNemar, *Psychological Statistics* (New York: Wiley & Sons, 1949), pp. 123–24.

pectations. The generally higher correlations found between the Inventory of Beliefs and the Problems in Human Relations Test suggest some overlap with respect to the traits being appraised. This is, of course, in keeping with the rationale of the two instruments, which conceives of the Problems in Human Relations Test as assessing directly one of the basic traits appraised indirectly by the Inventory of Beliefs.

Regardless of their institution, female students generally made higher democratic scores than did male students, and male students made appreciably higher scores in the more authoritarian aspects of the test. These differences can probably be accounted for by the fact that in our culture, at least at a superficial level, females are generally conceived to be the more considerate, adaptive sex. Thus, females would be more readily attracted by the obviously democratic solutions to the problems than would males who, by cultural definition, are supposed to be more hard-boiled, power-centered, and egocentric. Whether these differences exist in basic personality or in the subconscious of individuals needs to be explored by further research.

Pre- and Post-Test Results

Students from a number of institutions were tested in the fall of 1951 and again in the spring of 1952. The results of this testing are indicated in Table 58, showing how students from each school,

TABLE 58

MEAN GAINS OF STUDENTS ON PROBLEMS IN HUMAN RELATIONS TEST, CLASSIFIED ACCORDING TO PRE-TEST STANDING

COLLEGE	INITIALLY LOW GROUP		INITIALLY LOW-MIDDLE GROUP		INITIALLY MIDDLE GROUP		INITIALLY HIGH-MIDDLE GROUP		INITIALLY HIGH GROUP		TOTAL GROUP		
	Gain	N	Gain	N	Gain	N	Gain	N	Gain	N	Mean Pre-Test	Mean Gain	N
Pre-Test Range	2–12		13–15		16–17		18–20		21–28				
1........	6.00	2	3.14	14	2.55	11	0.89	35	0.84	50	19.89	1.40	112
2........	2.52	56	1.24	45	0.58	38	1.33	49	−1.47	32	15.89	1.08	220
3........	3.99	87	2.07	107	1.18	83	0.40	103	−0.52	81	16.38	1.44	461
4........	3.29	76	1.10	62	1.21	38	0.58	55	−0.93	30	14.93	1.41	261
5........	2.30	20	1.61	18	0.93	14	1.13	24	−0.05	21	16.69	1.18	97
6........	1.29	14	−0.25	20	−0.50	24	−1.12	33	−0.31	26	17.46	−0.38	117
7........	4.55	11	3.72	18	4.60	25	1.34	32	−0.28	39	18.14	2.11	125
8........	4.27	15	2.00	32	1.57	14	0.16	19	−0.75	12	15.78	1.57	92
9........	1.39	18	0.23	13	0.50	10	−0.37	19	−0.47	17	16.47	0.23	77
Total 9 colleges.	3.19	299	1.67	329	1.31	257	1.51	369	−0.36	308	16.53	1.23	1,562

divided according to their pre-test status, changed over the period of a year.

From these data certain suggestions emerge. The first is a replication of the tendency found with all of the Cooperative Study tests, that the lower the student's pre-test score, the greater the gain made over the period of a year. Again we must underscore the point that we have no way of knowing whether this is primarily statistical regression or whether it has deeper significance. The second is the generally slight gain made by students from each one of the schools represented. There are, it is true, some major differences as between the loss of -0.38 for School 6 and the gain of 2.11 made by students in School 7. However, such gains and losses do not fit into any meaningful pattern with respect to real institutional differences.

RELATIONSHIP OF THE ATTITUDES COMMITTEE TO OTHER INTERCOLLEGE COMMITTEES

The work of the Attitudes Committee, while partly successful and partly unsuccessful, must be judged as having had considerable impact on the entire Cooperative Study, and avenues have at least been opened for future research and educational practice. Each of the six Study committees came sooner or later to a concern with the affective area of their respective disciplines. They were interested in the degree to which attitudes furthered or retarded critical thinking and the other cognitive traits being investigated. The existence of a separate Attitudes Committee, devoting intensive energy to the affective domain, allowed them to rely on it for techniques of measurement, and thus the other committees were provided with greater time for investigation of other objectives of general education. The Attitudes Committee responded to this implied assignment by developing two instruments, each of which could be considered as relevant for any one or all of the five cognitive-oriented committees. The sort of person identified by the Inventory of Beliefs at the low end of the scale was considered as of just as much concern for the science teacher as for the humanities teacher. The trait of respecting individual human personality is an important outcome of all courses in general education.

SIGNIFICANCE OF THE ATTITUDES PROJECTS

If the work of the Attitudes Committee, particularly with respect to the Inventory of Beliefs, is substantiated by subsequent research, a major new conception of education may well have evolved. This conception assigns much greater importance to the role of personality and to the affective aspects of learning than has traditionally been the case. The traditional means of predicting academic success has been through such things as aptitude tests (either psychological or subject) and high school grades or patterns of courses taken. While some of these means have been fairly satisfactory in indicating which students might expect and which might not expect to profit from college, there has always been a large number of students whose subsequent achievement belied predictions made about them. Evidence obtained from the Inventory of Beliefs suggests that perhaps identification of students can be made on some basis other than intellectual prowess. In three institutions, albeit somewhat atypical ones, the Inventory of Beliefs or an adaptation of it identified approximately 17 percent of the student body who could be expected to have difficulty accommodating to a general education program. This group of individuals was not an inept one. As a matter of fact, their psychological aptitude test scores were equal to those of the rest of the student body. However, with the exception of this common academic aptitude, the group represented a collection of individuals different from their peers. This group apparently could not profit from general education courses organized as they were at the three institutions in which they had matriculated. Individuals of this group either dropped out of school before the first year was up, or else led a very frustrating existence trying to reconcile their notions of what college education is all about with the ideas reflected in the classes they attended.

The existence of this group of students poses the serious problem for teachers and administrators of what should be done with this fairly large segment of the student population. One solution is to assume that the personality traits characteristic of the group are so deep-seated and all-pervasive that education cannot change them appreciably. If this assumption is warranted, colleges must either prepare special curricula applicable to the group, find curricula such as certain technical ones for which they may be suited, or else accept a high mortality rate among these individuals. The second possible solution is to assume that while the personality structure is deeply imbedded in the physical and emotional structure of the individual, it still may be altered if appropriate techniques are brought to bear. While such persons probably react negatively to typical classroom situations, there is the possibility of reordering some classroom work, emphasizing student counseling, and exercising judgment in providing student living accommodations, so that these persons may be gradually brought closer to the norms for the entire student body. Both of these possibilities need to be explored, for resources of this nation are insufficient to permit the luxury of wasting the talents of any able subgroup of the student body.

The Inventory of Beliefs has tentatively identified, and further work has described, one portion of a population for whom certain special considerations are suggested. It might be possible that there are other similar elements of the population different in characteristics who might need other kinds of special treatment. The research incident to the development of the Inventory of Beliefs suggests approaches which may be appropriate to defining such groups.

With the concern for the affective domain as relevant to higher education have come major concomitant problems ranging from ethical matters to merely items of technique.

One major question which must arise and which has certainly not been answered is whether or not teachers are ethically justified in trying to affect student attitudes. If teachers answer this in the affirmative—that is, that they are entitled to try to affect attitudes—they may come perilously close to the kind of indoctrination found in totalitarian nations. If we accept the definition of attitudes which was postulated at the beginning of this chapter, then an attitude in the final analysis is a matter of individual conscience. Are teachers entitled to inculcate favorable attitudes toward tolerance, toward intellectual curiosity, toward the academic life, and toward certain principles commonly accepted by teachers? Those teachers who answer yes will have a difficult time specifying precisely at what level they will try positively to affect attitudes and at what level they will leave such matters to the individual. Teachers denying their right to affect these emotional aspects may very well be accused of negativism in not wanting to take a stand, and of outright prevarication in denying that they do affect student attitudes.

If teachers elect to try to affect attitudes overtly, the question as to how this may be done arises. Some people contend that attitudes may be affected best through providing knowledge. They would argue that the more we teach students about the world in which we live, the more favorable will be the attitudes of these students about those aspects of life which really count. Unfortunately, research in the affective domain denies that this happens. The generally low correlations between attitudes tests and more cognitive ones suggest that attitudes toward and knowledge or thinking about the same matters can develop quite independently of each other. While students gain generally over the period of a year with respect to the two attitudes tests this committee developed, those gains do not seem to be associated with gains made in what might appear to be relevant areas of knowledge.

If attitudes seem to be unaffected by course work in general education, are there ways open to college teachers which can yield positive results? In developing democratic sentiments on the part of their students, the implications of practices in the classroom or professor's office might do much more toward affecting student feeling than any number of lectures about the subject. In spite of claims that democracy is cultivated on college campuses, the atmosphere at most institutions must be judged quite authoritarian, particularly as directed toward students. In the few colleges in the Study where greater attention is paid to student opinion, where students are allowed a responsible voice in the conduct of the institution, gains on tests revealing democratic attitudes were larger than elsewhere. While considerably more research is needed, it is reasonable to suggest that example and opportunity to participate may be better techniques for changing attitudes than those traditionally associated with collegiate instruction.

9

IMPLICATIONS AND UNRESOLVED ISSUES

IN PREVIOUS chapters the activities of the Cooperative Study of Evaluation in General Education have been reported in a reasonably objective manner, although the commentary and the interpretations must inevitably reflect something of the preconceptions of the writers. In this chapter, we shall attempt to summarize the more obvious implications of the Study and to point to several hypotheses needing further investigation. We shall also attempt to make a personal and subjective appraisal of the Study and of general education as viewed through the Study by the directors. If justification for the latter is needed, it lies primarily in the obligation which we—as participants in all committee and workshop sessions, as visitors to the various cooperating colleges, and as consultants at other colleges interested in the activities of the Study—feel to organize our experiences in the various phases of the Study and relate them to the total general education movement.

Although the Study developed out of a concern for the collection of evidence on the effectiveness of general education or, more particularly, of the various types of general education in achieving its commonly accepted goals, the unique freedom allowed the directors and the intercollege committees resulted in a shift in emphasis. The committees' interpretation of their functions accorded to the problem of instruction as important a role as was inevitably assigned to the development of evaluation instruments and to the collection and analysis of data. The operations of the committees themselves and of the total project provide also a significant case study in the value of cooperative endeavor among educational institutions. Thus, the complex nature of the project results in a variety of implications and in a situation in which no one but the directors have quite the overview necessary for an appraisal of the Study. This is a further justification for the subjective nature of sections of this chapter.

The views or opinions expressed in this chapter are the responsibility of the directors alone and are not to be imputed as views shared by the intercollege members, the cooperating colleges, the Committee on Measurement and Evaluation, or its parent body, the American Council on Education. This does not mean that originality is claimed for these views, but rather re-emphasizes the personal nature of this particular statement of those views, many of which are not firmly based on objective evidence.

THE FOUR AREAS OF CONTRIBUTION OF THE STUDY

The achievements and implications of the Study may be examined under four major headings. First and most tangible are the tests or evaluation instruments and the instructional materials developed. Ignoring preliminary forms or discarded instruments, eighteen different tests and forms of tests were developed. Although some of these, particularly the instruments dealing with critical analysis and judgment in the humanities, have instructional implications, the three major contributions to instructional techniques are to be found in the handbooks developed for theme analysis, for teaching critical thinking in the social sciences, and for teaching science reasoning and understanding. All of these, with information about their availability, are listed in Appendix I. An additional handbook for the teaching of critical analysis and judgment in the humanities has been outlined and probably this will become available at some later date.

The second area of achievement is in the collection of data on gains made by students as determined by pre- and post-testing. These gains have been discussed only in reference to the individual tests. Institutional patterns of gain and attempts to rationalize these patterns provide an even more interesting and challenging result of the project.

A third contribution growing directly out of the previous one is to be found in the formulation of several hypotheses which merit further investigation. These involve the nature of integration, a possible way of measuring it, and a series of suggestions as to some of the factors involved in gains.

The fourth contribution of the Study is to be found in the extent to which experience in it promoted changes in the participants and, through them, changes in the various cooperating colleges.

Since all the tests and instructional materials have been adequately discussed in preceding chapters, only the contributions in the second, third, and fourth areas will be discussed here.

RE-EXAMINING THE TEST RESULTS

The statistical evidence on gains already presented suggests that (1) students do make some progress in regard to general education goals; (2) the amount of progress is apparently dependent on the nature of the educational experience provided and varies in ways which correspond reasonably well to identifiable elements in that experience; and (3) general education outcomes measured by the Study instruments are interrelated, and the degree of interrelation varies among the colleges. These generalizations are based on pre- and post-testing of freshmen in the cooperating colleges, the data on longer periods being too limited for any significant analysis.

The variation in the size of the one-year gains among colleges raises the question as to whether there may be identifiable elements accounting for these differences. The most obvious possibility is that the objectives measured may receive more attention in some courses or colleges than in others. There is reason to believe that the gains are in some cases largely a matter of maturation rather than of a significant general education experience. In fact, in many of the cooperating colleges gains in intelligence or in college aptitude have been found over a one-year period which compare favorably with the gains made in the Study tests.

To obtain further insight into the variation in gains, it is of interest to see whether certain schools consistently register the larger gains on all tests or whether there is a tendency for different types of institutions to show differing patterns of gain on the various tests. If a few institutions tend to make the largest gains on all tests, then the characteristics of these institutions as compared with a similar group making the smallest gains become of interest in an attempt to explain their apparent effectiveness.

There are, of course, many reasons why the statistical results of the Study need to be interpreted with great caution. The data on gains from the various colleges are incomplete, partly because of the difficulties in obtaining post-test data, partly because some of the test forms used—for example, Form B of the Test of Critical Thinking—turned out to be unsatisfactory, and partly because some of the committee members had little interest in the collection of statistical data. The length of the Study forced pre- and post-testing a year earlier than was desirable, with the result that some aspects of the testing were not well coordinated because the com-

TABLE 59

RANKS OF FOUR COLLEGES IN GAINS MADE ON EVALUATION
STUDY TESTS OVER ONE YEAR

College	Science Form A	Critical Thinking Form A	Critical Thinking in Social Science	Inventory of Beliefs	Human Relations
A		2	3	1	2
B	2			2	
C	1	1	1	4	
D	3	3		3	1

mittees had not been brought to the stage of thinking about such matters. Another difficulty in interpreting test results is the lack of adequate objective indication of the characteristics of particular programs. Visits on the various campuses, and the close contact with committee members during the period of the Study increased the bases for understanding of programs but left that understanding heavily subjective.

In compiling the gains made by colleges (making allowance for the ability level of the students involved), four institutions were found consistently to rank one, two, or three in the size of gain made. For example, using only results from a single and commonly used form of each test, Table 59 shows the rank of these four in five different tests. Other colleges involved in each tabulation have been dropped in order to emphasize this particular comparison.

These four colleges superficially, at least, have little in common. One is a large publicly supported state institution; three are privately supported liberal arts colleges. Two are coeducational; one is a college for women, and the other a college for men. Three are selective to various degrees on admissions; the state institution requires standing in the upper 50 percent of the high school graduating class. It would be easy to elaborate on differences among these four institutions, but the really crucial question is whether they have anything in common which differentiates them from another group of four colleges registering low gains on the tests. Four such low-gain institutions were found, and at this point we shall attempt to set up in double columns the contrasting characteristics of the two groups of colleges. These characteristics are the more obvious ones known to us. There may be others more subtle which have escaped our observation.

Characteristics of *Institutions with Large Gains*	*Characteristics of* *Institutions with Small Gains*
1. Most students reside on the campus.	1. Large percentage of students commute.
2. Admission involves more than high school graduation.	2. High school graduation sufficient for admission.
3. A core program of general education required of all students.	3. No set program required of all students, possibly one or two common courses.
4. Program of exemption or credit by examinations.	4. No exemption or credit program by examinations.
5. Staff of general education courses strongly general education oriented.	5. Staff of general education courses oriented to specialized offerings and teach a general education course as a sideline.
6. Broadly conceived evaluation activity a continuing part of the program.	6. Little evaluation other than regular examinations made by individual teachers.
7. General education experiences not confined to courses.	7. General education experience largely limited to that provided by general education courses.
8. General education courses not waived for major in related field.	8. General education courses commonly not taken by one majoring in related field.
9. Strong administrative interest and active coordination of general education as a unit.	9. General education is provided through largely independent, uncoordinated courses.

These contrasting characteristics are not always characteristic of every one of the four low- and four high-gain colleges. The first four characteristics, in our judgment, are associated with every institution of the respective groups. The fifth characteristic involving the orientation of staff is a matter of judgment. One of the low-gain group has a staff strongly dedicated to general education, but we believe the staffs in the remaining three low-gain institutions are not general education oriented. Likewise, on the part of the low-gain group there would appear to be a single exception to each of the characteristics 6, 7, 8, and 9. In the high-gain group, there is one exception to characteristic 8 and a great deal of variation in the applicability of characteristic 7. The smaller liberal arts type of private college accords students very active educational planning, and student contacts with faculty are very close and by no means limited to the classroom. The large state school has extensive extra services for individualization but attempts to accomplish most of its general education objectives through formal instruction. Perhaps the results of this situation are revealed by Table 59, which shows the ranks of high-gain institutions. On the tests of Science Reasoning and Understanding, and Critical Thinking in Social Science, Institution C, the large publicly supported college, ranked first. On the Inventory of Beliefs—an area much more difficult to affect—C came fourth, behind the three smaller colleges with highly integrated programs.

The preceding characterizations must be viewed with caution, but to the extent that our data and judgments are valid it appears that general education, if successful in its objectives, cannot be left to chance either in the courses offered and the teachers offering them, nor can it be regarded as something achievable entirely from a program of formal instruction.

Hypotheses for Further Research

Regarding gains.—The recurring pattern of association of large gains with low pre-test scores and small gains with high pre-test scores has been provocative of much speculation despite the fact that similar results have been reported from like studies. Several possible explanations have been voiced, with the true situation very likely being that a complex of several factors is involved. Among these explanations are the following:

1. *A "ceiling" effect,* by which is meant that initially high scorers simply have a reduced possibility for gain. The importance of this was to some extent refuted by the fact that the same pattern was

found even with certain tests for which even the highest pre-test score was far from a perfect performance. Even so, something of these effects must be present.

2. *A regression effect,* or tendency on retesting to move toward the population mean. On a chance basis there is more possibility for low scores to be higher than to go lower and for high scores to drop rather than to gain. Unquestionably this factor is involved.

3. *A focus of instruction effect,* that is, that instruction may be aimed at the average or below-average student rather than at the able individual. One study in the science area in which the largest gain found was for a special section composed of the most able students is consistent with this possibility. Comments from students interviewed on a number of campuses and classroom observations also give credence to this as a contributing factor.

4. *Familiarity or unfamiliarity with terminology and concepts.* Students with low scores may be unfamiliar with the vocabulary or concepts used in a test even though a definite attempt was made to minimize this factor. The gain for low pre-test students may then be more a gain in knowledge than in the ability supposedly measured by the test, whereas the high pre-test student must make his gain almost entirely in the ability itself. Content-oriented instruction would then favor the low pre-test group.

5. *Differential motivation.* This factor is conceived of as operating in two somewhat different ways. Able students, being somewhat more conscientious, may apply themselves when tested at the beginning of the year to a greater extent than the less able student. If the test at the end of the year is not used for grading, the more sophisticated near-sophomore may take it less seriously and refuse to spend much time on the more difficult questions which would serve to increase the score of the more able students. This motivation was also seen as operating to magnify institutional differences since some student groups are more habituated to and appreciative of attempts to evaluate the effects of education.

These five factors are not entirely independent and there may be still others not yet envisaged. It is apparent, however, that any attempt to explain the negative correlation between pre-test scores and gains is fraught with difficulties. All of these factors may be involved, but even then they may be involved in different proportions depending on the particular college, course, instructor, student, or test.

Another difficulty is that any of three hypotheses as to the relation of gains and initial status is plausible. It might be argued with some reason that general education is a leveling agent so that the differences between students should decrease. In this case the smaller gain for the initially more able student is to be expected. It might be argued that all students should improve equally if the program is properly adjusted to individual differences, in which case gains should be equal over the entire range of pre-tested ability. Finally, some teachers might take the view that the best-prepared student has the greatest possibility for further development and should make a greater gain than the less well-prepared student. Evidence accumulated here seems to favor the first of these three hypotheses, but it is quite probable that careful planning of instruction and selection of appropriate test materials might result in evidence favoring either of the other two hypotheses. This is one of the unsolved—perhaps unsolvable—problems raised in the study.

Regarding intercorrelations and integration.—Intercorrelations among the various tests of the Study have been exhibited in earlier chapters. From these it is evident, as was expected, that the various evaluation devices of the Study are mildly intercorrelated and they are likewise correlated with other tests in about the manner to be expected. The hypothesis concerning correlations which we were most interested in investigating was that intercorrelations among tests involving general education objectives should increase as a result of a significant program of general education experience. The rationale for this is simply an extension into the statistical area of the concept of an integrated personality as one who has developed all his abilities and who can and does bring to bear all his resources upon any task confronting him. If this means, as it seems to, that such an individual is able to think critically in regard to a variety of problems and has overcome or at least is aware of his bias and prejudice, then a program contributing to this kind of development should result in an individual who performs more consistently over a wide range of tasks. It follows that tests sampling these tasks and abilities should be more highly correlated than before.

TABLE 60

COMPARISON OF PRE- AND POST-TEST CORRELATIONS ON EVALUATION STUDY TESTS FOR TWO COLLEGES

COLLEGE	CRITICAL THINKING IN SOCIAL SCIENCE WITH:						SCIENCE REASONING AND UNDERSTANDING WITH:						CRITICAL THINKING WITH:				INVENTORY OF BELIEFS		NO. OF CASES INVOLVED IN ANY CORRELATION
	Critical Thinking		Inventory of Beliefs		Problems in Human Relations		Critical Thinking		Inventory of Beliefs		Problems in Human Relations		Inventory of Beliefs		Problems in Human Relations				
	Pre	Post	Pre	Post	Pre	Post	Pre	Post	Pre	Post	Pre	Post	Pre	Post	Pre	Post	Pre	Post	
A.....	.66	.67	.46	.63	.30	.42	.56	.70	.29	.61	.12	.30	.42	.43	.24	.29	.31	.47	45–113
E.....	.50	.63	.24	.29	.16	.30	.48	.52	.23	.33	.20	.30	.13	.21	.22	.20	.45	.46	91–364

Table 60 exhibits a pattern of pre- and post-test intercorrelations for two colleges. One of these is College A of the high-gain group and College E is one of the four in the low-gain group discussed earlier.

For College A the intercorrelations increased from pre-test to post-test in all nine pairs and for College E in eight out of the nine pairs. The exception for College E involves only a slight decrease. The magnitude of the increments in College A is considerably greater than for College E. Tests of the significance of the difference of the pairs of correlations have been applied, and many pairs are found not to differ at a statistically significant level. Since statistical significance depends on the number of cases, smaller differences for College E may be significant. However, significance here does not depend on individual pairs but on the consistency of the pattern, for a random relationship would result in some increases and some decreases in correlation. The two institutions were the only ones for which post-test intercorrelations were consistently higher. On the assumption that gains or losses are equally likely, there are about two chances in 1,000 that a gain would occur in all nine pairs of correlations. The chance of gains in all but one case is about two in 100. On these grounds the results here are significant and in accord with our hypothesis that intercorrelations should increase as a result of general education. Furthermore, the increases in correlations for Institution A, already shown to have large gains, are found to be larger than for College E, which registered small gains on the tests. These results correspond to subjective estimates of the extent to which the educational experience at the two institutions affords opportunity for integration and with the apparent fact that the amount of integration possible in a program must depend on the extent of changes in the students.

In Table 61 is shown another comparison of pre- and post-test correlations. As indicated by the letters, the colleges involved are A and C of Table 59 in which it was indicated that College C made the largest gains recorded on several of the tests. Since College C did not use the Problems in Human Relations Test, the correlations compared are fewer in number than before.

College A shows an increment from pre- to post-test in all pairs, the data here being identical with those given earlier. College C

TABLE 61

COMPARISON OF PRE- AND POST-TEST CORRELATIONS ON EVALUATION
STUDY TESTS FOR TWO COLLEGES

COLLEGE	CRITICAL THINKING IN SOCIAL SCIENCE WITH:				SCIENCE REASONING & UNDERSTANDING WITH:				CRITICAL THINKING WITH:		NO. ON WHICH CORRELATIONS ARE BASED
	Critical Thinking		Inventory of Beliefs		Critical Thinking		Inventory of Beliefs		Inventory of Beliefs		
	Pre	Post	Pre	Post	Pre	Post	Pre	Post	Pre	Post	
A............	.66	.67	.46	.63	.56	.70	.29	.61	.42	.43	45– 88
C............	.63	.55	.29	.24	.58	.41	.19	.27	.21	.17	238–447

shows a decrease in all but one of the pairs. The general trend clearly suggests that integration, to the extent that it is defined by our correlation hypothesis, is not obtainable through good courses unless definite steps are taken to interrelate them in or out of the classroom. In College A each student is a member of the community government, made up of students, faculty, and members of the college administration, which is responsible for policy decisions in both the administration of the college itself and in campus community living. There is no phase of the college operations—faculty selection, curriculm planning, college maintenance, or planning the budget—in which students do not have a direct and substantial voice. Nothing comparable to this experience can be found in College C, where the only planned general education experience is to be found in the courses which are themselves highly independent.

A particular aspect of the contrast between College A and College C that seems relevant to the matter of integration is the correlation of the Inventory of Beliefs with other tests. Whereas the correlation of this inventory with other tests for College C is distinctly lower than the intercorrelations of these other tests, for College A these correlations are of about the same order. This implies that there is no artificial distinction between the affective and cognitive outcomes in the educational experience provided in College A.

Such results suggest that the answer to some of the issues raised earlier about the generality or pervasiveness of critical thinking depends upon the nature of the educational program. Certainly the contrasts pointed out in preceding paragraphs indicate the possibility that the magnitude of test intercorrelations is influenced by the school's program. There is much room for experimentation on this matter. Meanwhile our results permit a suggestion that the availability of uncoordinated courses taught as an extra responsibility by a group of part-time specialists is not the route to the best results on general education objectives. There is also an indication that although a group of well-organized but independent courses taught by a full-time faculty may produce excellent results on cognitive outcomes, it may not do much in producing development of students in the affective area. The fact that the four colleges making the largest gains have shown concern for improved testing and comprehensive evaluation procedures is also suggestive. Curriculum construction for general education, if our evidence and our hypothesis based upon it have any validity, is much more than the matter of assigning separate groups of teachers to develop a number of discrete courses.

Effect on Participating Individuals and Colleges

Opinions differ as to the extent to which a subsidized cooperative educational project should be justified on the basis of its effect on the individuals and colleges directly involved. There is a natural desire on the part of those who support the project that it affect in some significant way the total pattern of development in education by producing results which cannot be ignored. A more realistic conception of the nature of educational research and of its potential consumers—the teachers—points to the possibility that any research evidence will be so qualified by the variable human elements of teachers and students that the immediate effect of any research results will be slight. Belief in the results and the acceptance and basing of practice on them by several teachers or colleges will be more effective than wide dissemination of the findings. The prestige of personalities and of programs outweighs research data—irritating as this may be to the researcher. On this basis it is appropriate to examine the effect of the Evaluation Study on the participants.

Naturally, the changes were most marked in individuals. It would be possible to point to three or four members in each of the committees who developed through their experiences in the Study an entirely different viewpoint about the nature and purposes of general education and the means of accomplishing these purposes. The changes in viewpoint were evident both to others and to the individuals themselves. There were several cases in which course testing programs were almost completely revised because of the interest aroused in improved testing. There were several cases in which the contacts of several faculty members from a college became the means for developing increased local cooperation between general education course staffs. Individuals in at least three of the cooperating colleges found that ideas developed in the Study were of interest to teachers and to graduate student groups. An objective survey of the reaction of committee members was made at the final workshop of the Study. Dean Horace Morse, who was associated with the Study as liaison officer for the General College at Minnesota and as consultant to the Social Science Committee, summarized the results.[1] There was a nearly unanimous opinion rendered by the participants that the experience was very interesting, very stimulating, and very valuable to them as individuals. They were somewhat less sure that it was having great effect on other faculty members in their own institutions, and they wisely assigned to the directors in writing their final report the responsibility for conveying the significance of the Study to other colleges.

The effect of the project on colleges is less easy to discern than the effect on individuals. In some cases where there were committees organized at a college whose activities paralleled the committees of the Study, a number of individuals were influenced to the point where a somewhat different orientation toward general education developed. In other colleges the lack of any definite Study-related organization on the campus gave no opportunity for committee participants to communicate what they were doing. Two colleges involved in the Study would seem to have received nothing significant from their membership in it. In one case the loss from the faculty of all those working on Study committees resulted in almost complete lack of contact during the last year; in the other the membership was purely nominal from the beginning of the project.

[1] Horace T. Morse, "What Do Participants Think about the ACE Evaluation Study?" *Journal of Higher Education*, December 1953, pp. 469–77, 501.

The full extent of the effectiveness of the Study on individuals and colleges is impossible to assess because it is frequently too subtle or too confounded with other happenings even to identify. As with general education itself, it may be that there are long-term results which are even more significant than the immediate and obvious ones.

Instructional Deficiencies in General Education

The average instructor of a general education course has little familiarity with the extensive general education literature. Administrators find money to attend meetings and to purchase books and periodicals dealing with broad educational issues. The average faculty member is trained as a specialist and his affiliation with his own professional societies and his own professional journals and books consume any money he may reasonably be expected to assign to his professional advancement. This is particularly true in those cases where general education teaching is a part-time function, but it is still true for the full-time general education staff member who, unsure of the future of general education, must keep a hand, foot, and head in the door opening to his specialty. The result is that the high aims and ideals of the general education movement are more apparent in the literature than in the typical general education classroom.

Visits to sixty-four general education classes on six different campuses during the winter and spring of 1953 provide the basis for the preceding comment. The following two generalizations are not applicable to all teachers and classes observed but would hold for a clear majority: (1) there is more concern about the unique contribution of a particular course than there is about the combined effects of a set of general education courses or experiences; (2) integration is viewed more as a problem of organizing materials drawn from various disciplines through identification of a logical set of principles and concepts than as a characteristic of a generally educated person.

In part the views implied by these generalizations are actual convictions of teachers. There are many cases, however, where teachers with a broad student-oriented general education point of view simply find it impossible to break away from practices hallowed by tradition. In fact, instruction aimed at general education objectives requires the development of new methods and materials and experimentation with them. It is much easier to be critical of classroom teaching than it is to provide the means of overcoming these criticisms. Yet recurring observations of the type which follow suggest that the quality of instruction in general education must receive attention.

1. Students are typically given little opportunity for participation in planning or even in discussion. Teachers talk most of the time.

2. Audio-visual aids do not appear to be extensively used. Three map references, two cases of passing pictures, three cases of use of recordings, three uses of projection techniques, and one use of newspapers constituted the complete listing of such aids, other than use of the blackboard, as observed in sixty-four classes.

3. As much as ten minutes was used in some classes for checking attendance, distribution of papers, and similar clerical details.

4. Out of sixty-four classes visited only two had an informal and flexible seating arrangement. Others used the traditional chairs with writing arms, arranged in rows, or laboratory tables and stools.

5. Students commonly do not respond to questions in complete sentences. Teachers use an incomplete sentence and individuals or groups answer with a word or phrase. Students who begin a sentence which apparently will convey the correct answer are often cut off by the teacher—presumably to save time. Even communications teachers are not immune from use of this practice.

6. A common reply to a student question was that time simply would not permit going into that phase of the subject. This response reflects the heavy load of material to be covered in most general education courses. General education courses are surveys in fact even if the name has fallen into disrepute.

The preceding six observations may be regarded as minutiae; yet they do mean that general education classes are not well planned to make the most economical use of time, of teaching aids, or of student motivation and interest. This is not to say that general education instruction is bad but rather that it has not, in the large, met the challenge involved in general education objectives.

Student Reactions to General Education

Interviews with student groups on seven campuses supplemented our classroom observations. The technique for selection of the students varied, but since we wanted those who had completed some work in general education, most were sophomores or above. In a few cases our interest in visiting with some students was simply announced and they came in of their own accord.

In most cases after we made a few brief remarks about general education and mentioned the courses involved in the local general education program, students indicated by their responsiveness an awareness of the nature of general education and gave some evidence that it was a topic of interest in student bull sessions. On only one of seven campuses was there evidence that students were unaware of the existence of a general education program which, in that case, they saw as only a group of required courses, about which, however, they could vocalize readily. In fact, it was only necessary to raise an occasional question with most groups in order to direct a lively discussion into the particular channels in which we were interested. Essentially three questions were raised with the students:

1. What values do you see in general education courses? (Are they good or bad, and why?)
2. What differences seem to you to exist between general education courses and specialized courses?
3. If you were to advise someone on setting up a general education program, what three major suggestions would you make?

All but one of fourteen student groups, varying in size from three to twelve students, unanimously endorsed the idea of a limited general education requirement. Even in the remaining group only a minority held out against the idea. The principal values noted for general education readily summarize into three major points: (1) the general informational and cultural value; (2) the practical value in that general education courses tend to be more closely related to life problems; and (3) the orientational value including (a) the opening up of new areas of interests (b) aid in choice of major and vocation, (c) provision of a perspective on society and on one's chosen vocation.

All groups made these points and all agreed unanimously to

these values. Culture apparently is a genuine concern of students. Many indicated that their general education courses provided a basis which they had previously lacked for entering into serious conversations with adults.

In every group there were one or more students who claimed to have made a complete change of vocational plans as a result of one or more general education courses. All were able to name other students who had had this experience. Several students had sufficient insight to suggest that the general education courses were excellent for students who took only a year or two of college. Scattered but reasonably frequent references to such values as learning how to think, more effective communication, and the like, indicated that a few students had been exposed to general education objectives.

Despite their general approbation of general education, students identified some differences between general education and other courses which are not entirely complimentary to the former. Among these were remarks that:

1. General education courses are oversimplified and do not challenge the better students.
2. Required general education courses are resented by freshmen, who typically see no reason for them.
3. General education classes are usually larger than other classes and provide less opportunity for individualization.
4. General education courses have less flexibility because there is so much to cover.
5. General education courses are more apt to have poor teachers or ones who are not interested in the course.
6. Tests in general education classes are heavily factual.
7. General education courses overlap many other courses.

Comments 1, 2, 3, 4, and 7 were made in all groups and usually received strong support from a large majority of the students. Comments 5 and 6 were heavily emphasized on four of the seven campuses.

Despite the critical remarks, all groups—as we have already noted —approved in principle and in fact of the general education courses which they had taken. We found absolutely nothing to back up the contention that students are so oriented to a particular major that they bitterly resent general education requirements. The most that our interviewees would admit to is that there is such a tendency at first, but that it can be overcome by careful explanation. There was further agreement that any required course has to bear some resentment and that exceptionally good teaching is necessary to justify the requirement.

A questionnaire study stimulated by a desire to investigate further these favorable student reactions was based on a listing of over twenty objectives, some typically general education in nature and others typical of specialized courses. Students were asked to select the objectives of primary importance for attainment in the first two years of college. In the case of every student group thus far surveyed and tabulated, the general education objectives have been ranked ahead of the specialized objectives. This investigation, although growing out of the Study, has been carried on independently and will be reported in detail elsewhere. The evidence added to our summaries above demonstrates conclusively to us that student opinion can be cultivated into one of the strongest and most constructive forces for the development of general education.

The Role of Evaluation

In chapter 2 the various attitudes of faculty members to evaluation were described, but some additional reactions are worth noting. Even if they accept evaluation as important, it detracts from other matters equally or possibly more important. Reactions of teachers—particularly in evidence among those not on the working committees, but even to some extent with that group—to certain of the instruments developed in the Study exemplify the attitude in another way. Any instrument such as the Critical Analysis and Judgment Test which requires considerable time to master and to use may be regarded as a curiosity rather than as a practical instructional or evaluatory tool. Aside from the complications and the time element, another objection to such instruments is to be found in the uniformity of judgment required for effective use of such devices.

Although objective tests are heavily criticized by teachers, an objective test is more likely to be used than novel, complicated essay or rating techniques. However, the tests are often used without sufficient study or understanding or acceptance of the definitions and objectives involved, so that unfavorable results are used as a basis for discarding the test rather than as a basis for re-examination of educational practices.

Effective use of a completed test requires either construction by the instructors using it or sufficient study of it by the users so that the purpose of the test is fully understood. Successful introduction of evaluative activity into a general education program involves both the development of interest in such practices and of some proficiency in making and criticizing evaluation instruments. The types of activities in which committee members of the Cooperative Evaluation Study engaged are precisely the sort to be encouraged among all general education staff members. Almost inevitably both evaluation and instruction will thereby be improved.

THE NEED FOR EXPERIMENTATION

The need for encouragement of experimentation was the major reason for this Study. The type of experimentation originally envisaged involved comparisons of courses using different methods and materials. Ultimately some such experimentation was done but only after teachers became more fully aware of the meaning of certain objectives and were therefore made conscious of a disparity between existing practices and accepted outcomes. One cannot simply demand that a general education faculty embark on a program of experimentation. The demand has no meaning until a need is seen for it. Evaluative activity on the part of the faculty which leads to clarification of objectives and the development of means of measuring student attainment suggests deficiencies in instruction and also points to possible variations in instruction which can become the object of experimentation.

Even at this point, much of the experimentation done is apt to be without significance. General education courses commonly cover so much material that new materials or techniques are simply superimposed on an already crowded course or, at best, insufficient attention is given to them to make possible significant comparisons. Only as courses and total programs are completely revised and compared with former ones can sufficient impact be generated even to give hope for major differences in the development of abilities such as critical thinking or of attitudinal traits. The use of the discussion method at the College of the University of Chicago, or of the case method at Colgate and Harvard demonstrates that fundamental revisions of instruction are possible, but they are not common. Even the variations in teacher proficiency and enthusiasm raise problems of experimental design which make careful experimentation so difficult that few faculties are apt to engage in it. The planning and carrying-out of significant research on the learning process require the cooperation of psychologists, evaluators, teachers, and students. It requires time for program replanning, for the development of additional evaluatory techniques, for extensive testing, observation, and follow-up of students. In a period of increasing enrollments it is improbable that much experimentation will be done. Nevertheless, the final chapter of this report will be devoted to the presentation of a rationale and a rough indication of one direction which such experimentation might take.

Lacking such experimentation, there is still much that can be done to improve general education. First of all, the experiences of colleges which have already embarked upon novel approaches can be studied and drawn upon by others. The case method certainly has possibilities for use in many courses. Few teachers will want to adopt it to the exclusion of all other methods, but moderate usage and even a subjective appraisal of the results will be beneficial. Second, the introduction of the principle of relevance as a basis for classroom planning can be used. If an objective of critical thinking is accepted and if it is interpreted to mean that this ability is to carry over to problems faced outside the classroom, it is not unreasonable to expect that sheer coverage and learning of content might be somewhat reduced to provide in the course opportunities for critical thinking on the part of each student. Moreover, it is reasonable that the opportunities provided bear some relation to the situations in which this ability is usable outside the classroom. This is simply an application of the principle of relevance. From one point of view, this is the justification for the use of the case method. Relevance can best be determined when objectives are operationally defined in terms of student behavior. Once again, evaluation-centered thinking must be mentioned as a significant approach to the problem.

The Need for Cooperative Effort

Teachers are busy people and general education teachers are busier than the average. The production of syllabi embracing broad areas, not all of which are familiar to the teacher, has commonly been an assignment added to a full teaching load. Release of time for planning, for evaluation, or experimentation is rare if not unheard of. Even if some slight time release is given, manifold routine duties have a way of infringing upon it so that little is accomplished.

Another difficulty in general education planning is that even a new course rather quickly crystallizes. New ideas proposed by an individual to his own associates may be greeted with indifference if not derision. Even administrators hesitate to suggest that rethinking of a course is necessary.

Faculty workshops prior to the opening of college have been successfully used in some colleges to provide a time free of interruption during which curricular revisions and other matters can be studied. Cooperative activity among a group of colleges also offers many possibilities. Association with individuals from other colleges and a study of common problems result in a wider range of ideas than would be found on one campus. A division of responsibilities among colleges may make for more progress and it provides an incentive to each person to fulfill his assignment. Meetings of intercollege groups ensure a period free for concentrated effort on the problem. Selection for the assignment and the investment of some funds in such activity confer a prestige on those selected and assure the faculty that such activity is considered important by the administration.

In brief, smaller and geographically limited versions of the Cooperative Study of Evaluation in General Education could well be organized as a means of assuring continuing attention to and progress on the problems attacked by the Study. An article by the authors has presented the arguments for such regional cooperative projects in greater detail.[2]

---

[2] Paul L. Dressel and Lewis B. Mayhew, "Cooperation among Colleges in Educational Planning and Research," *Educational Record*, April 1953, pp. 121–31.

A RE-EXAMINATION OF THE ROLE OF OBJECTIVES
IN GENERAL EDUCATION

General education has been characterized by concern about objectives; yet months and even years of effort by faculty committees and by total faculties have been expended on objectives with little overt effect in the program. There are many reasons why this is true:

1. The effort of harmonizing philosophical differences and overcoming semantic blocks commonly makes for sufficient difficulty that the achievement of agreement on objectives may be seen as a task complete in itself rather than as an initial and even incomplete step in the development of a curriculum. The maximum effect in such cases is that each teacher reinterprets or justifies what he is doing—and continues to do—in the light of these objectives.

2. The tendency of administrators or faculty committees is to write objectives primarily for catalogues without involving faculty and with little attention to whether faculty know, care, or do anything about the objectives. The remark of a general education department head when asked about his course objectives illustrates the point. His reply was to the effect that he believed that the dean had a set in his file but no one paid any attention to it.

3. The tendency to relate objectives to courses—noted in the organization of the Study committees—defeats the directing and integrating force supposedly inherent in objectives by making them appear to be descriptions of the *status quo*. The more integrative type of objective applicable to all courses may be largely ignored by all. General education courses have made some strides in overcoming the fragmentation of knowledge but have done little about overcoming the fragmentation of objectives.

4. The number of objectives commonly stated and their generality encourage teachers to take the view that no single teacher or course can contribute to all objectives. The result is reflected in the remark of a communications teacher in regard to the introduction of some group dynamics techniques in the classroom. It was to the effect that this could be justified only if it resulted in greater improvement in speaking and writing than was achieved by his current methods.

5. The tendency to separate the statement of objectives from the delineation of the educational experiences necessary to evoke and give practice in the behaviors implied by these objectives makes statements of objectives an academic exercise.

With the completion of a statement of objectives, the process of course construction proceeds in the time-honored manner by deciding on a group of courses and by selection of appropriate materials. Indeed, the complexity and the number of the objectives make that solution seem the only practicable one, particularly when no one knows quite what has to be done to further the development of students with regard to many of the objectives stated. The result is that the development of a list of general education objectives is commonly a semantic and logical task helpful in developing some common vocabulary and a superficial unity in verbally expressed viewpoints but just as commonly having little effect on instruction. We wish to propose one solution to this problem in our final chapter, but before doing so, a review of the experience of the Study with regard to objectives will aid in grasping the point of view developed out of this experience and basic to the proposal.

Although the Study made no attempt to deal with all general education objectives, let us for the moment ignore this and assume that it is subject to criticism for ignoring objectives pertaining to home and family living, to health, and to selection of a vocation. The validity of such a criticism cannot be ascertained by reference solely to the objectives actually studied, but rather must be judged only after a careful study of the interpretations placed upon these objectives.

Even a study of the interpretations must not stop with a consideration of the list of specific behaviors developed but must also take into consideration the variety of situations in which these behaviors are regarded as operative. Next the supposedly ignored objectives must be similarly analyzed into behaviors and the variety of situations in which these behaviors are operative likewise delineated. Comparisons of these sets of behaviors and situations become the basis for reaching a decision as to whether the objectives have been ignored.

For example, the concern of the Science Committee with the reading of current scientific articles and the associated abilities involving scientific method and attitude may obviously be applied to materials dealing with health, selection of a mate, child care, and the like. Such materials were represented in the original collection from which the test selections were drawn, and their absence or near absence from the final product simply reflects lack of emphasis on such matter in current science courses. Again, the "content" axis of the Critical Thinking Committee includes problems involving self, others, society, values, and ethical standards. Marriage and vocational choice problems, among others, were considered as entirely appropriate situations for the application of critical thinking. Certainly the problems and statements employed by the Attitudes Committee impinged upon all areas of living. Thus, the behaviors and the range of situations of the objectives actually investigated, included or might readily have included much of what is involved in objectives dealing with home and family living and choice of a vocation.

One reason for this inclusiveness is that some general education objectives like critical thinking involve a type of behavior while others define a class of situations wherein this behavior is applicable. A more important reason is that the objectives of general education are not discrete even though they appear so in a list. The evaluator or teacher who seeks earnestly to find the full significance of any objective as it assumes meaning in the living of an individual will find all other objectives inextricably interwoven with it. In a sense, our concern with many discrete objectives betrays either an unwillingness to view education as, and for, living or an inability to do so.

The antidote for this, we believe, is to be found in the following steps:

1. Select a limited number—four or five at most—of objectives without concern as to whether these cover every item of knowledge, every ability, or every area of living.

2. Ask each instructor to describe the contributions made to each of these objectives in relation to materials covered, techniques used, and experiences available to or required of students.

3. Consider the relevancy and the scope of these learning experiences in reference to the applicability of the behaviors implied by the objectives in nonacademic situations.

4. Suggest ways of relating the educational experience of the student more directly to the type of situation in which it is expected that he apply the abilities.

5. Seek for ways to evaluate the effect of these experiences in promoting changes in students.

Certainly objectives and classroom practice must bear some relationship to each other, and it is more likely that these can be worked out for a limited than for a large number of objectives. Only as objectives become explicitly interpreted in terms of instructional practice will they have any vital effect on the development of a general education program.

SUMMARY

This chapter has included a variety of implications, hypotheses, and conclusions. Re-examination of evidence reported upon in earlier chapters suggests that: (1) there are institutional, course, and teacher variations in the amount of gain made by groups of students and that these variations may be associated with identifiable characteristics of the total educational experience; (2) the concept of integration may be associated with intertest correlations and that these intercorrelations may increase or decrease depending on the nature of the educational program.

Observations in classrooms, student interviews, and the opinions of Study committee members and other general education faculty members led to the conclusions that:

1. General education objectives frequently do not play a significant role in planning a course, with the result that much of teaching is highly traditional.

2. The multiplicity of general education objectives frequently results in association of one or two objectives with a specific course; thus, independent courses are encouraged and broader general education thinking and planning are discouraged.

3. Students are generally favorable to general education but complain that it is inadequately explained to them and that they

have little opportunity to contribute to the development of the general education program.

4. Because general education objectives are interdependent and because some specify behavior while others specify only classes of problems or situations to which those behaviors are applicable, broad interpretation of one or two objectives may actually include all those usually stated.

5. The objective of critical thinking is one of major concern to a majority of instructors of general education courses.

The importance and general acceptability of critical thinking and the conviction that concentration on one or two pervasive objectives by entire general education faculties is necessary if anything approaching an integrated program is to be achieved, lead us to devote the last chapter to an examination of the possibilities inherent in such an approach. The nature and the generality of critical thinking, the development of appropriate materials and methods of instruction, the evaluation of instructional effectiveness in terms of student achievement, and the active involvement and consequent motivation of students form a complex but inseparable set of problems central to the further development of general education which appear to be amenable to attack through concentration on this one objective.

10

WHAT NEXT IN GENERAL EDUCATION?

THE GENERAL education movement at its inception derived its energy from the fact that it was a protest movement against many practices in American education. It was a protest against the compartmentalization of knowledge and the proliferation of courses, and the associated evil of the free elective system. It developed in refutation of the Germanic conception of a university as essentially a research-oriented institution. It decried the tendency of American scholars to be more concerned with the content and logic of their subject than with undergraduate students as individuals. Polemical writings on the subject during the past decade have fairly well exploited these protest possibilities. Dynamism of protest, however, is quickly expended; and unless it be replaced by a less nihilistic source of energy, a movement dependent on a dynamic growth is bound to falter and to cease being a significant factor. Particularly is this true for the general education teacher who, trained as a specialist himself, has not always been as impressed with the validity of the protests as have administrators and other writers and speakers on educational problems. The general education movement is presently in need of a more positive dynamic, a positive integrating principle to replace the principle of protest.

Other systems of education have been more fortunately placed with respect to this matter of integration. Catholic colleges and universities have generally not accepted general education as it has here been conceived because of the feeling that their education was already well integrated around a theological point of view. This is succinctly expressed by Rattigan. "However much the non-Catholic educator must disagree with this viewpoint, he must agree at least that the authority of the approach is capable of effecting a remarkable degree of unanimity amongst those who do accept it. The contrast between the confusion that prevails in secular institutions and the unanimity of thought in Catholic colleges has often been noted."[1]

Items for inclusion in or exclusion from the curriculum of the Catholic college or university can be judged by the single criterion of relevance to the major goal of such institutions. "The core of the Catholic system is theology; theology in turn conditions Catholic ethics and Catholic philosophy; and the Catholic point of view in the interpretations of history and literature is unmistakable."[2] For Catholic institutions no further integration is needed.

Some technical and professional education has been similarly well placed with respect to integration, at least in the minds of some administrative officials of certain institutions. Curricular materials, teaching practices, and even administrative procedures of engineering, medical, law, and dental schools are determined by the goal of producing successful professional practitioners—and American society has fairly well-defined criteria of success in those fields. This is not to suggest that the professional schools have an easy task of curriculum construction. As a matter of fact, the medical and law schools are currently reappraising themselves with the thought that their programs have not resulted in the best possible doctors or lawyers for American needs. Medical schools in particular have, with the assistance of foundation subsidies, been investigating the possibilities of providing a broader, more general kind of medical education.[3] However, the point still remains that as compared with most programs of general education, the various forms of specialized education are remarkably well integrated toward some clearly discernible objective. Unfortunately, society has not provided a complete job description of the generally educated person in the sense that it has prescribed the roles of professional persons. This does not mean that there have not been attempts to make explicit the characteristics of such generally edu-

[1] B. T. Rattigan, *A Critical Study of the General Education Movement* (Washington: Catholic University of America Press, 1952), p. 167.

[2] Howard M. Jones, "The Relation of the Humanities to General Education," *General Education: Its Nature, Scope and Essential Elements* (Chicago: University of Chicago Press, 1934), pp. 33–34.

[3] *Annual Report of the Commonwealth Fund,* 1952.

cated persons. Many views are argued with great vehemence, but none has satisfied all or even a majority of people concerned with general education.

THE INADEQUACIES OF VARIOUS INTEGRATING CONCEPTS

Common Knowledge

One view originates in a concern that general education provide a background of common knowledge. Certainly general education courses heavily emphasize knowledge. Teachers do commonly admit that it is not possible to determine just what knowledge the student should possess, but having selected certain materials and specified certain knowledge, there is the tendency to emphasize these elements to the exclusion of all else. One might accept that one institution finds it imperative to require a course in physical science, while another requires biological science, and still another requires both, if the materials were primarily or even partly means to the mastery of certain abilities and understandings transcending the particular materials. However, there is little evidence that such transcendental objectives are prominently in mind, the whole orientation implying the importance of knowing the particular ideas covered in class. Because so many ideas are covered and their essential importance is not accepted by everyone, such courses are faced with the troublesome charge of superficiality. As the amount of knowledge increases, attempts to cover it adequately, even by sampling, must become more and more sketchy. The solution to this difficulty has frequently been some adaptation of a block-and-gap system whereby certain segments of information are taught quite thoroughly with large gaps of knowledge left untouched. Once again the particular blocks taught and the gaps excluded have been decided upon by whatever group of teachers holds the balance of power in a particular general education course. That such decisions are difficult to defend is obvious. That they preclude the possibility of making general education truly general should be equally so. Worse, whatever the gaps left, the size of the blocks included still results in most courses being survey courses. Emphasis on and selection of a body of common knowledge is not an adequate basis for further progress in general education.

Good Citizenship

Some individuals have argued that general education courses ought to be oriented toward some more pragmatic value than knowledge. One fairly popular principle has been that the integating factor should be the goal of effective citizenship in American democracy. If this goal be construed broadly, there can be no quarrel with it. Unfortunately, when attempts have been made to define this objective operationally, they have either failed completely because of the disagreement or dissatisfaction aroused, or else they tend to resemble the indoctrination found in totalitarian states. In addition, teaching for citizenship in American democracy is too frequently a provincial concept resting upon the assumption of the superiority of the cultural heritage of Western civilization.

Adult Life

A closely related integrating principle suggested by some is that of preparation for adult life. This conception is based on an assumption that teachers can identify the present and future needs of each student and can select courses relevant to these needs. Again the principle is a good one, but general education so conceived often includes such a variety of course offerings as to be guilty of the weaknesses of that which it seeks to replace. This conception may also lead to the altering of the essential quality of general education to the extent that it threatens to become mere vocational and avocational education. The complexity and vagueness of citizenship and of preparation for adult life, coupled with the reluctance of many believers in general education to accept them as other than ultimate goals with little direct implication for curriculum building, make these objectives unacceptable as integrating principles.

Values

There are others who would insist that religious or humanitarian values should be the basis for planning the general education curriculum. This would bring to general education something of the unity of the Catholic position earlier noted. Observation of the difficulties of the Cooperative Study Committee on the

Evaluation of Objectives in the Area of Attitudes, Values, and Personal Adjustment, and of a committee composed of representatives from the several general education courses at one college (which gave up entirely—after two years—on the task of defining value outcomes) suggests that any acceptance of common values by college faculties is a rather remote possibility and even if achieved would be at such a level of generality as to have little significance in planning the day-to-day activity of a general education course. If the commonly accepted objectives of general education have had as little effect on the general education classroom as our experience suggests, it seems unlikely that emphasis on the most intangible of all those objectives will change that situation.

Summary

The above is not intended to imply a lack of validity to the contributions these orientations have made and can make to American education. There is need for education for citizenship. The colleges must continue to produce technical skill for individuals' vocations and avocations, and there must be logical relationships established among hierarchies of course offerings. There is certainly a crucial need for colleges to provide some basis for developing of values. These orientations, however, do not appear practicable as the central principles of organization for general education courses which are to be taken by all or most students enrolling in a particular institution. None possesses a logic which can be accepted as valid by all teachers and by all students. Some other principle appears necessary, and the experience of this Study suggests the possibility of critical thinking.

CRITICAL THINKING AS A POSSIBLE PRINCIPLE OF INTEGRATION

Importance in General Education

As the Cooperative Study began, it was agreed that critical thinking was considered as one of the important outcomes of general education with which the project would be concerned. As each of the six committees defined its sphere of interest, the objective of critical thinking began to assume greater proportions. Regardless of whether a committee labeled the trait "critical analysis and judgment" or "critical thinking" or "the ability to read current science materials," the skills which seemed to be involved were all quite similar. Whether the similarity in conception of thought is attributable to some basic quality or whether it is merely attributable to the influence of Aristotle, Bacon, and Dewey in American schools remains a question. This common concern, however, served to emphasize the importance of critical thinking and suggested that critical thinking, viewed broadly, might provide the emphasis whereby general education courses, individually, could be better planned and taught, and whereby general education programs might achieve among the courses some larger degree of integration. We would suggest, therefore, that critical thinking might serve where other principles have failed, and we shall try to demonstrate the validity of this position.

First we need to clarify something of the meaning attached to critical thinking. By critical thinking in this connection we do not mean the limited conception implicit in some of the tests of critical thinking previously described in this report. Nor do we mean some pat formula to be taught at the beginning of a course followed by material presented in the same old content-oriented way. Rather, by critical thinking we mean a point of view toward problems and their solutions and a way of thinking about basic problems faced by mankind. Such a conception of critical thinking, of course, implies that it be given the central position in curriculum planning and not regarded as something peripheral to a more traditional approach.

One reaction to this is that such a conception of critical thinking is no more pertinent to general education than to education generally. Perhaps not. It is entirely possible for courses not usually considered as general education to have as a major objective the development of thinking in the context of a particular subject. Even courses in technical or professional fields may contribute to the development of the higher mental processes. However, more frequently than not, such courses or programs attempt to present students with certain knowledge and to teach certain technical skills. Any increase in ability to think critically is apt to be limited to specific types of problems or to be regarded as merely a concomitant of the other aspects of the course. General education courses specify critical thinking as an important educational goal, and thereby assume a special obligation in regard to the objective. Other courses which do make overt attempts to develop critical thinking skills can and should make a definite contribution to the general education of a student. Their impact is likely to be enhanced if many teachers are attempting to develop the same skills at the same time and with the same rationale.

Appropriateness in Various Courses

In the field of communications all aspects—reading, writing, listening, speaking—involve or should involve thinking and may be approached in this way rather than as discrete elements. The act of writing, consisting of formulating a problem, exploring it, and reaching a conclusion would thus be viewed as having much in common with giving a speech. Although the medium is different, the problems of choice of words, adapting to the audience, and ordering the presentation, are similar.

In the humanities, regardless of the subject matter, the goal might be the development of critical facility with respect to humanistic materials. If courses in general education in the humanities are to have lasting value, they ought to provide students with the means for enjoying artistic work as adults. To do so demands criteria for discrimination between the valid and invalid, the sentimental and the genuine feeling. These criteria may well involve the same method of thought involved in the communications processes. They consist of determining what ideas the artist is trying to communicate, deciding how he has used his medium, and judging the validity of his conclusions. Certainly, from a rich work of art such as Beethoven's *Ninth Symphony* varied interpretations are possible, even by the same person on different occasions. The steps or the process by which one arrives at these, however, seem not to be greatly different. Even in the more controversial areas of religion and philosophy the critical processes by which meaning is obtained from basic documents are in essence the same as in painting, music, or literature—and this does not imply any diminution of religious feeling. The processes involved when students were required to compare Jesus' point of view with the hedonistic one of Omar and the social-criticism orientation of *Walden* are desirable ones to teach.

With the scientific knowledge increasing beyond the bounds of ordinary human comprehension, a significant factual knowledge of science from one course is rather hopeless. Such courses can develop, by constant attention, some grasp of the methods of science and of the limitations of scientific inquiry. Instead of organizing a social science course according to logical subject-matter divisions, sustained efforts to teach problem-solving might achieve greater rewards. Similarly counseling—whether academic, vocational, or personal—can facilitate work in classrooms as well as the personal adjustment of the students if counselors attempt to develop on the part of counselees a rational method for solving problems which is at the same time being stressed in academic courses.

The issue arises as to whether, even if the term critical thinking be accepted as useful in all fields, the same phenomenon is meant thereby. The nature and generality of critical thinking is still a matter for research. Tentatively, however, we hypothesize that although some differences exist from one field to another, there are many common aspects of critical thinking which apply equally well in all areas. Once the semantic barriers are overcome, the methods of science may not be appreciably different from the methods involved in viewing a work of art or in making one. Some analysis of the problem and a marshaling of evidence about it are necessary. Although the conclusions may differ—on the one hand an estimate of approximate truth, and on the other an esthetic judgment of beauty—the processes by which one arrives at these conclusions may be similar. Even if they are more distinctive than they appear, real value would be attached to assisting students to see the differences. If teachers of humanities and teachers of science would each teach for the development of the same skills applied to different materials, the interdependence of knowledge might be demonstrated and a richer meaning for each subject implanted in the student's mind.

Critical and Creative Thinking

Emphasis on critical thinking might appear to neglect or even be antithetical to creative thinking. Knowledge about creative thought, like knowledge about critical thought, is actually quite scarce, but we can venture some hypotheses about creative thinking which would indicate that it is not entirely distinct from critical thinking. First, we suspect that creativity as exemplified by a Pascal, a Leonardo, a Marx, or a Picasso, is probably of such a high and rare order as to be of little practical concern to general education teachers. Certainly, it would be unrealistic and uneconomical to build a program for persons who occur so infrequently. The creative thinking which general education teachers must seriously consider might be roughly equated with originality in thinking and might well be developed on the part of all students coming under the influence of general education courses. Viewed as originality of thinking, creative thought becomes nothing more than the achieving of more spontaneous and less stereotyped solutions to a variety of problems. Whether or not other individuals at other times have solved the same problems in the same way is relatively unimportant. What is important is that students be given every opportunity to exercise and develop some individuality and originality in their thinking.

In courses in which the instructor organizes the material and presents it to a largely passive audience of students, individuals other than the teacher have virtually no opportunity to demonstrate any originality or creativity in thinking. Problems are presented to the student in the form of periodic quizzes which require as solutions repetition of organization presented by teachers in the context of their lectures. The only creativity demanded is that of creating a smaller facsimile of a larger body of content presented by the professor's lecture. On the other hand, in a thought-oriented course demanding student practice and demonstration of a variety of the higher mental processes, students might develop into highly original thinkers. In place of the professor defining an area of subject matter and presenting his exegetical remarks, the teacher would present problems frequently for which even he himself had no ready solution. Students would be required to solve either orally or in writing these problems, with the premium being placed on accurate intellectual processes and spontaneous, imaginative solutions resting firmly on a rational set of premises.

An approach to teaching used by a noted botanist illustrates what we mean by creativity. He presented his students each with a leaf and told them to observe it, study it, and then describe their findings to him. Their first reports were rather prosaic statements of the very obvious leaf structure. He then sent the students back to look again. Gradually the students came to observe the structural beauty, the organic efficiency, and the inherent possibilities for further study in that single leaf. At this point and only at this point would the teacher be satisfied with the student performance. Very obviously the professor had observed all of these things before, but he was forcing students to see the same things for the first time, and was demanding of them creativity of thought.

Or, again, creativity might well be encouraged by asking students to consider a view of the *Notre Dame de Paris,* the *Summa Theologica,* and descriptions of medieval manor and town life. Students in arriving at generalizations regarding the medieval period might demonstrate considerable creativity or originality, even though other people have arrived at similar syntheses. In the context of a social science class students might be led from a theoretical consideration of the dynamics of personality to introspection about themselves. Resulting insights are original with the student and may exemplify creative thinking. Creative thought viewed this way, whether or not it embraces all of creativity, fits quite readily into a rationale of critical thinking.

Relation to Other Integrating Concepts

In addition to providing a rational basis for organizing general education courses and programs and to allowing for the development of creativity, critical thinking as an integrating principle may prove to be the one most acceptable to many educational points of view.

Whether one believes that the fundamental purpose of a college or university is the inculcation of moral and spiritual values, the transmission of knowledge, the development of traits of citizenship, the preparation of individuals for adult life, or the development of intellectual keenness, critical thinking must play a major role. To all save the most doctrinaire of religious sectarians there is a willingness, even a demand, that rational methods of inquiry be used in all fields of human activity, including religion. In American democracy there exists the hope that its values and traditions be subjected to constant scrutiny so that those who accept them do so reasonably and not by blind faith. Knowledge acquired without reason becomes a mere jumble of facts and not the essential instruments of an educated man. The techniques by which knowledge can be effectively utilized are those involved in critical thinking. Individuals sympathetic to a student-centered or to a needs point of view may decry major emphasis on critical thinking as a move which accepts a dualistic concept of the nature of man and places emphasis on intellectual outcomes. This is not our position. Those who accept responsibility only for cultivation of the mind will view critical thinking as an intellectual process, but others will see critical thinking as involving the total person. Although critical thinking may be interpreted somewhat differently according to the preconceptions of the individual teacher, it is these preconceptions that limit critical thinking rather than any limitation intrinsic to critical thinking itself. Even so, adherents of these different viewpoints should find a large area of common ground upon which they can work. Critical thinking must be based on knowledge; and the effectiveness of materials in providing experience in critical thinking can actually become a criterion of relevance in choosing materials from the various broad general education areas. Likewise it can become the integrating factor for developing comparisons and contrasts among the various areas. The importance of critical thinking in citizenship and in adult life suggests that problems drawn from life situations can be used extensively. Critical thinking cannot ignore values. Rather, attempts at critical thinking should cause each student to examine and define his own value position since it is irretrievably interwoven into the thinking he does and the solutions that he reaches. Critical thinking can take place in the context of quite differing value systems but thinking is not truly critical unless it recognizes the existence of several value systems and the acceptance—too often unconscious—of one of them. In fact, our proposal regarding critical thinking is not at all a revolutionary one, for the increased freedom of choice central to many discussions of the liberal arts implicitly requires ability to propose and analyze alternative ideas prior to making a choice.

The Status of Knowledge about Critical Thinking

We have hypothesized that critical thinking involves mental processes and a point of view which are much the same from one field to another. The extent to which this is so and even whether it is so needs to be explored by research. Further, the kind of research which is necessary before critical thinking can be definitely assigned such a prominent place needs to be of a different order than that heretofore reported. Prior research has been carried on for the most part by psychologists, educators, and logicians operating quite independently. While the insights these individuals have gained are valuable and must provide the basis for future work, their various conceptions of critical thinking and the assumptions from which they operate have been more limited than is necessary if critical thinking is to become the central and integrating objective of general education.

Psychologists have attempted to infer mental process from the observed products of thought, and much of the experimental work has been done with respect to lower animals or quite young children. The descriptions of trial-and-error behavior in animals, studies of insight in anthropoids, facing children with puzzle-type problems, and the examining of language of children in spontaneous talk, are illustrative of what has been done. Considerable work has also been carried on by using a variety of tests allowing the experimenter to consider not only the test results but the behavior of subjects while taking the tests. All such approaches are subject to considerable error, for they all rest on the assumption that the nature of a complex, internalized process can be inferred from observation of relatively few overt behaviors. Experimenters are always faced with the dilemma of acquiring more and more information about their subjects to such an extent that the resultant resembles a psychoanalytic protocol for advancing inferences which are extremely questionable.

Educators rely to a considerable extent on the methodology of psychologists and also assume a correspondence between mental products and processes. They generally assume that individuals having the largest number of correct responses on an examination are the individuals best endowed with desirable mental traits. It is obvious that such a conception is limited in usefulness, for until the educator can know and understand the relationship between student solutions to problems and the thought processes leading to those solutions, they are unable to determine effective from ineffective instructional procedures.

The logicians, with perhaps the longest history of disciplinary concern for thought processes, attempt to postulate thinking as a series of logical, rational steps. The logicians have tended to talk in terms of ideal methodology by which the final goal or solution to a problem is reached with a minimum of effort by means of precise steps. It is quite likely, however, that the majority of people do not solve problems in such a methodical way, and that most of the problems faced by individuals and by society cannot be solved in quite so straightforward a fashion. While the logicians may provide for use of idealized schemes of thought and tools with which thinking processes may be taught, their insights may not be too relevant in investigating internalized thought processes.

Some insight into the thinking process has been achieved by various investigators through introspection or from narrative accounts from individuals as to how they arrived at a particular conclusion after they had completed a process or experience. Thus, Dewey reports on the ways in which he attacked certain problems and the conditions which led him to select one solution in place of another. Einstein's reported thinking which led to his enunciation of the theory of relativity has also been described. Certain autobiographical materials such as *The Education of Henry Adams* have been studied for ideas concerning thought processes. This use of introspection and retrospection, however, in spite of being highly interesting and provocative, has many major difficulties. Persons find it hard, if not impossible, to report all of the major steps in their thinking and to report them in a way in which they originally occurred. The reporter frequently is inclined to edit and, if he has been exposed to the Western tradition of logical thinking, is inclined to portray his thinking as paralleling the logician's steps in thought. Once a solution has been arrived at, the reporter frequently forgets the many dead ends he might have explored prior to making his decision. Since so much of this editing is done unconsciously, a bias is introduced in the data so accumulated which is almost impossible to ferret out.

In addition to the weaknesses already mentioned, research to date in the area of critical thinking has been characterized by several other limitations. The fact that this research can be described under several disciplinary rubrics itself suggests that research has been too compartmentalized. The logicians have followed their bent, the psychologists have frequently been exclusively concerned with animal psychology, and the educators have moved in still another direction. It appears to us that the insights from all of these disciplines need to be brought together to supplement each other in providing an integrating base of research evidence from which other attacks on the problem may be launched.

Much of the research accomplished to date has been divorced from teaching practice. In the case of retrospective inquiries, recourse has been made to the autobiographical writings of outstanding individuals. In the case of psychological investigation, much has been done with animal experiments and with highly artificial experiments far removed from conditions as they would be in a classroom. Much, for example, has been written about retention, but such experiments deal with the retention of nonsense material or discrete factual information, neither of which is ideally the major outcome of general education college classes.

In this same connection there is a noticeable lack of suggestions and evidence as to how critical thinking can be taught or, for that matter, how any mental trait of adult humans can be developed through planned experiences. A survey of psychological literature for the past eight years reveals not more than a score of articles which truly provide evidence on learning and the development of the higher mental characteristics. Almost any printed review of psychological research suggests strongly that this is an area in which research should be undertaken, but to date almost nothing has been done.

What research has been carried out and described in either psychological, philosophical, or educational literature has frequently been so couched as to repel rather than attract teachers of other kinds of courses. For example, some studies regarding learning have been carried out by educational psychologists in classes of educational psychology. Teachers of other subjects are quite likely to regard such findings as being applicable, at most, only to educational psychology. Further, when teachers outside of the fields of psychology, logic, and educational psychology refer to these research findings, they find a technical jargon which defies interpretation by the uninitiated.

Still one further weakness in critical thinking research lies in the fact that the way it is presented too often suggests that emphasizing critical thinking can be a mechanical sort of operation tacked onto some particular college course. Such an implication leaves teachers free either to reject attempts to teach for critical thinking as an improper and unbearable extra burden, or to regard it as an extra frill requiring little time and no real modification of their heavy factual orientation.

Some Suggestions

Having pointed out the lack of adequate research data to date, we are constrained to advance some ideas which we believe might be fruitful in the area of critical thinking. Perhaps the first step in the development of major research in this area is for teachers to become concerned about the development of thinking on the part of their students. We have repeatedly stressed in the preceding chapters how cooperative consideration of evaluation problems in connection with the Cooperative Study made numbers of teachers suddenly aware that their classroom practices bore little relationship to their stated objectives. So long as teachers are unaware or unconcerned about the apparent fact that imparting information by means of class lectures or reading textbooks is relatively ineffective in the development of the higher mental processes, the importance of research in connection with critical thinking is likely to be overlooked. Means, then, must be discovered by which the need for research can be brought before teachers in all fields of general education.

Merely becoming aware of a lack in research about teaching techniques, however, does not bridge important philosophic differences separating teachers. We have suggested that critical thinking might serve as the common ground on which various viewpoints of general education can meet. Before this meeting of minds can take place the validity of critical thinking for each position must be made explicit and be accepted by all teachers.

Teachers who insist on a particular value orientation for general education might be shown that teaching for critical thinking does not demand questioning basic religious assumptions. It implies only that these assumptions be recognized and that their role in the solution to life problems be made explicit. Those who hold that man's intellect can be sharpened by close contact with the great minds from all ages, might be led to question to what extent this is true and whether or not some "great books" might not be better than others as devices for this disciplinary function. Those who emphasize the primacy of knowledge may be reassured that making critical thinking central need in no way minimize the importance of knowledge, and that one possible outcome of concentration on critical thinking might be acquisition of more knowledge in more meaningful form on the part of students. Teachers who hold that general education should be directed toward more utilitarian ends should recognize that a problem-solving approach can be most effective in bringing education to the level of student needs.

If a fairly large number of teachers became concerned enough to give serious consideration to research in critical thinking and to reconcile their differences, they are well on the way toward meeting still a third need, which is to combine competence in their own fields of specialization with some awareness of and concern about research findings and with the study and development of appropriate instructional materials and methodology. For the most part, college teachers have been skilled in the field of their major specialization. They have assumed that knowledge about history made a good history teacher. Their consideration of research has been for the most part a consideration of research in history. Teachers are needed who are willing to grant that their knowledge of their own subject does not automatically induce proficiency in developing skills and abilities on the part of students. Teachers are needed who are sufficiently concerned about their teaching function that they will gladly undertake any kind of research or experimentation in connection with their own classes which will yield increased insight into teaching. This need, incidentally, is not restricted to general education courses but characterizes all education as well. It is, however, particularly appropriate to speak of it in connection with general education courses, for one can at least hope that teachers working with such course offerings for a period of years will come to view knowledge from a somewhat broader base than that provided by their own specialty. In addition, we can at least hope that general education will gradually attract persons trained along broader lines than customary graduate programs in some one or other of the college curricula.

These three needs seem to converge to underscore the major need of research in connection with critical thinking. It is essential for such research to be basically oriented toward and integrally related to classroom practice. By this we do not mean to suggest that certain kinds of philosophic and psychological research should not be encouraged. It should be, but it should be undertaken to the end goal of providing insights for teachers. It should be regarded as applied research having very definite practical goals in view. Research findings when discovered need to be written in such a way that their implications for classroom teaching stand clear. They need to be described in terminology equally clear to teachers of all fields.

It must be apparent that the improvement of teaching and the evaluating of teaching effectiveness, which are subjects of extensive study and discussion, are enmeshed with the problem of teaching critical thinking. Despite the extensive research on evaluation of teaching, few conclusions of any significance have resulted, although the teacher variable is probably the most important one in any educational process. Without minimizing the contributions or the role of the teacher in his school and community, it is reasonable that the major criterion of his teaching effectiveness is to be found in the extent to which his students achieve the objectives set for the courses which he teaches. Unless one believes either that scholarship and good teaching are synonymous or that "good teachers are born and not made," there is some basis for believing that more adequate instruction with regard to specified objectives can result from more precise understanding of objectives and from the development of educational experiences selected in relation to stated objectives.

There is evidence in this Study that teachers do vary greatly in their success as determined by the gains made by students on tests of critical thinking, but this project was not designed to isolate the differences in the teachers, in the classroom experience afforded by them, or in the means of motivation which resulted in these differential improvements. Only careful observation of classes over a period of time could yield reliable evidence on these matters.

Coincidentally, it was found that in the case of teachers trying to modify their techniques for the avowed purpose of achieving better results in critical thinking, the differentials between gains made by the experimental groups and those taught by the customary approach were commonly small. Moreover, these experimentally obtained individual gains were often smaller than those made by students of other teachers in classes where no avowed special effort was made with respect to the objectives. The implication is that minor changes in technique imposed upon a course wherein the major emphasis remains on coverage of content are inadequate as a solution to the problem. The alternative conclusion that small gains are characteristic of such objectives and that variations in instruction are of little importance seems less tenable because of the fact that students of some teachers apparently do achieve fairly sizable gains. Whether the differences in student achievement are a result of what teachers do or what they motivate or require students to do is in itself an issue for research.

The implication, to us, at least, of all the preceding discussion in this chapter is that the identification of one major objective such as critical thinking, the review of all research done upon this mental process, the observation and distillation of instructional practice most conducive to effective learning, the development of one or more integrated instructional programs aimed at the objective, and the evaluation of the results, constitute a major research task. The attack should simultaneously involve teachers, psychologists, evaluators, administrators, and students. It should provide information on the nature of the objective and its teachability, on the qualities of good instruction, and the extent to which teachers can acquire them, and on the learning processes of students and the characteristics of individuals which facilitate or impede the development of critical thinking. Comprehensive and complicated as such a research project would be, it is realistic in the same sense that the objectives, instruction, materials, and techniques are all facets of the learning experience which must finally be evaluated by its effect on students.

This, we believe, is the task that general education must undertake if it is to bring classroom practice and student achievement into a reasonable correspondence with its objectives.

LIST AND AVAILABILITY OF MATERIALS DEVELOPED BY THE COOPERATIVE STUDY OF EVALUATION IN GENERAL EDUCATION

I. TESTS AND INVENTORIES

A stock of the following tests and inventories has been deposited with the Educational Testing Service, 20 Nassau Street, Princeton, New Jersey, and copies of them may be purchased from the Service so long as the supply lasts:

Inventory of Beliefs, Form I, and Instructor's Manual

Problems in Human Relations, Form I, and Instructor's Manual

A Test of Critical Thinking, Form G, and Instructor's Manual

A Test of Critical Thinking in Social Science, and Instructor's Manual

A Vocabulary Test for Use with A Test of Critical Thinking in Social Science

Test of Science Reasoning and Understanding, Natural Sciences, Forms C and D, and Instructor's Manual

Test of Science Reasoning and Understanding, Biological Sciences, Form A

Test of Science Reasoning and Understanding, Physical Sciences, Form A

(There is no instructor's manual for the Biological Sciences and Physical Sciences tests, but the manual for Forms C and D provides appropriate explanatory background.)

Test of Critical Analysis in Reading and Writing and Instructor's Manual

A Guide to Critical Analysis and Judgment in the Humanities, and Instructor's Manual. Four separate forms for:

Music

Art

Literature

Philosophy

A List of Abilities in Critical Judgment in the Humanities (for use in scoring the student responses to the Guide)

Humanities Participation Inventory, and Instructor's Manual
Humanities Vocabulary Test (no manual available because of lack
   of data)

II. RATING SCALES

These scales may be reproduced and utilized by interested teachers.

Scale for Evaluating Speaking and Writing (see Figure 2, facing
   page 79)
Scale for Evaluating Speaking (see Fig. 3, pages 80–81)

III. INSTRUCTIONAL HANDBOOKS

The following three items are published by the Wm. C. Brown Company, Dubuque, Iowa.

Critical Thinking in Social Science: A Handbook for Evaluation and
   Teaching
Science Reasoning and Understanding: A Handbook for College
   Teachers
Handbook for Theme Analysis

IV. OTHER MATERIALS

Requests for information about other materials referred to in this volume but not included in the preceding lists should be directed to the authors.

OBJECTIVE TESTS IN THE
AREA OF COMMUNICATIONS

THE DRAKE UNIVERSITY TEST OF READING AND WRITING

This test attempts to evoke from the student as many as possible of the mental processes he should go through in close reading and careful writing and to evaluate their results. The questions on reading and writing are interspersed to utilize a single passage to evaluate both types of activity in the order that they occur in reading. The first assumption behind the test is that an author's use of symbols and their arrangement is the means whereby he communicates his meaning and intention, and that the perception of this use and arrangement is the best index to that meaning and intention. The second assumption is that a high correlation exists between the ability to analyze and describe fully a piece of writing and the ability to write. The materials employed as passages for analysis are intended to sample a wide range of the student's daily experience in written communication. The test is untimed because it is believed that tests for comprehension are more valid if the time factor is omitted.

The test items fall roughly into six large categories with from eight to twenty-four items in each, depending upon the importance of the respective mental processes. Some items probably test more than one category. The categories are:

1. The ability to organize material and to recognize relational clues, patterns of development, and structures.
2. The ability to recognize the semantic function of words and sentences: whether the reference is to objective facts, or judgments, or the language is figurative, etc.
3. The interpretation of words in context, meaning in sentences, nuances of feeling, and shades of thought.
4. The recognition of soundness of argument.
5. The recognition of grammatical form and functioning, including punctuation.
6. The esthetic judgment of word choice, rhythm, metaphor, structure, and the whole passage.

MICHIGAN STATE COLLEGE READING TEST

The Michigan State College Reading Test is composed of 150 multiple-choice test items. Sixty-five of these are vocabulary and the remainder are of a largely self-contained type based upon reading passages; that is, no information outside the paragraph is needed to answer them. The administration time is two hours, and it is anticipated that nearly all students will be able to finish within the allotted time. In other words, it is not a time test.

The vocabulary items deal with words selected from the outlines of study of the basic courses at Michigan State College. These items are of two types: (1) those in which the words are given in the stems and the student is asked to select from the responses the word or phrase which is most appropriate, and (2) those in which definitions are given in the stems and the student is asked to select the appropriate word from the responses. Examples are:

Provincial
1. significant
2. prejudiced
3. narrow
4. insignificant

Anything that an organism does
1. attitude
2. behavior
3. motive
4. personality

Generally speaking, the items in the reading portion seek to determine the student's ability to derive meaning from passages selected from the literature of the Basic College areas. "Derive meaning" would include th eskills of synthesizing, drawing conclusions, making inferences, translating figurative phrases, etc. A typical paragraph contains about three hundred and fifty words and is followed by approximately eight to ten items.

STEPHENS COLLEGE TEST OF READING COMPREHENSION

The Stephens College Test of Reading Comprehension is an untimed test of the student's ability to read for comprehension of precise meanings. This test is based on the assumptions that tests of reading for comprehension are more valid if the speed factor is omitted; that textual material composed of one complete passage for analysis presents a more realistic and functional situation than textual material composed of a series of paragraphs on unrelated subjects; and, finally, that a close analysis of the material for recognition of precise meanings and relationships adequately tests the level of comprehension ability.

The major factors of comprehension measured in this test are:

Recognition of them and purpose
Author's background, experience, point of view
Comprehension of main ideas
Comprehension of details, the drawing of inferences
Tone and attitude of author

Vocabulary meaning in context
Comprehension of details, vocabulary relationship
Vocabulary and allusions
Association and inference

STEPHENS COLLEGE TEST OF WRITING ABILITY, FORM A1

The Stephens College Test of Writing Ability is an untimed test of the student's ability to recognize and evaluate important elements in writing and its revision. This test is based on the assumptions that the use of textual material which is interesting to the student creates a functional testing situation; that extensive passages of student and professional writing analyzed for improvement of communication or recognition of skill in communication will measure a student's functional knowledge of important elements in writing; and finally that such a test will correlate more favorably with grades independently assigned on actual writing than will grades on an English usage test.

The sections of the test include items which measure such common elements of writing as structure, organization, level of usage, relevance, reference, repetition, emphasis, style, punctuation, point of view, development, transition, and word choice.

THE BROWN-CARLSEN LISTENING COMPREHENSION TEST

The Brown-Carlsen Listening Comprehension Test (available through World Book Company) is a test of a student's ability to comprehend material presented orally. It is administered orally, student responses being recorded on IBM-type answer sheets, for machine or hand scoring. Administration time is under 50 minutes.

The following aspects of listening are explored:

	Number of Test Items
Test 1. Immediate Recall	20
Test 2. Following Directions	20
Test 3. Word Clues	20
Part A: Recognizing Transitions Part B: Recognizing Word Meanings	
Test 4. Lecture Comprehension (10-minute lecture)	30

Part A: Getting the Details
    Part B: Getting the Central Ideas
    Part C: Depth of Understanding	

In general, the 90 items making up the test are of two kinds: items requiring an accurate *reception* of details, and items requiring *reflection* on the details—a synthesizing, an interrelating, or an evaluating. Tests 1, 2, and Part A of Test 4 contain items that measure accuracy of reception. Test 3 and Parts B and C of Test 4 contain items which measure reflective aspects of the listening process.

STEPHENS COLLEGE TEST OF LISTENING COMPREHENSION

The Stephens College Test of Listening Comprehension is an untimed test of the student's ability to listen for comprehension of a speaker's meanings in expository oral communication. This test is based on the assumptions that textual materials composed of extensive excerpts from talks present a realistic functional situation common in the student's daily experience; that two passages, one primarily explanatory, the other primarily argumentative, represent two very common listening situations; that testing a student's recognition of main ideas and details, logical inferences, and relationships of ideas will give a valid measure of a student's general listening ability; and, finally, that pre-testing and post-testing of such general ability, with intervening instruction in listening, will yield a measure of growth in this ability. Since the above processes occur more or less simultaneously in the listening situation, items testing them are interspersed throughout the test.

INDEX

AMERICAN COUNCIL ON EDUCATION

Arthur S. Adams, *President*

The American Council on Education is a *council* of national educational associations; organizations having related interests; approved universities, colleges, teachers colleges, junior colleges, technological schools and selected private secondary schools; state departments of education; city school systems and private school systems; selected educational departments of business and industrial companies; voluntary associations of higher education in the states; and large public libraries. It is a center of cooperation and coordination whose influence has been apparent in the shaping of American educational policies as well as in the formulation of American educational practices during the past thirty-six years. Many leaders in American education and public life serve on the commissions and committees through which the Council operates.

25478